VIRGINIA WOOLF
The Echoes Enslaved

ALLEN McLAURIN

CAMBRIDGE

AT THE UNIVERSITY PRESS

1973

Published by the Syndics of the Cambridge University Press
Bentley House, 200 Euston Road, London NW1 2DB
American Branch: 32 East 57th Street, New York, N.Y. 10022

© Cambridge University Press 1973

Library of Congress Catalogue Card Number: 72–83589

ISBN: 0 521 08704 X

Printed in Great Britain
by W & J Mackay Limited, Chatham

Contents

Preface vii

INTRODUCTION

1 Samuel Butler on convention and repetition   3

PART ONE: ROGER FRY AND VIRGINIA WOOLF

2 Roger Fry and the problem of representation   17
3 Verisimilitude and illusion: *The Voyage Out* and *Night and Day* 26
4 Sensation in language and art: *Mrs Dalloway* and *Flush*   38
5 Autonomy: *Between the Acts*   49
6 Craftsmanship   60
7 Colour   70
8 Space: 'hollowing out a canvas'   85

PART TWO: REPETITION AND RHYTHM

9 An introduction to the problem   97
10 The double nature of repetition: *The Waves*   128
11 The symbolic keyboard: *Mrs Dalloway*   149
12 Plot, history and memory: *The Years*   158
13 Character   166

CONCLUSION

14 *To the Lighthouse*   177

Appendix A 207
Appendix B 210
Notes 212
Bibliography 223
Index 229

FOR MY PARENTS

Preface

Virginia Woolf believed that new books could surprise the secrets of the old, and it is true that certain aspects of recent writing bring into relief an underlying pattern in her own novels. J. Sturrock, for example, in *The French New Novel* indicates the importance of repetition in the work of Robbe-Grillet. Another striking instance is Max Frisch's novel, *A Wilderness of Mirrors*, which contains in a very schematic form many of the aspects of repetition which will be discussed here in relation to Virginia Woolf's work (I am thinking here of the sense of *déjà vu*, the 'doubling' of character, and so on). From this modern perspective we might obtain an insight into the 'sense of repetition' which one of Virginia Woolf's artists, Lily Briscoe, sees as the unchanging element in experience. A growing sense of the importance of repetition and rhythm in aesthetics deepened my own interest in Virginia Woolf's work, where repetition is half-submerged, not quite so plainly set forth or systematically exploited and investigated as in some more recent writers. This interest led me back to the theories of Samuel Butler, one of Virginia Woolf's 'influences', but more importantly, one of the 'moderns' in his awareness of the significance of convention. The introductory chapter relates his theories to Virginia Woolf's work and Chapters 9–13 take further the investigation into rhythm and repetition begun there.

'Rhythm' is an important element in Roger Fry's criticism, and Virginia Woolf's association with him enabled her to enclose her repetitions in a form which parallels his description of visual art, especially that of the Post-Impressionists. This, together with Fry's important literary activities, is the theme of Chapters 2–8. A phrase from Fry's translation of a poem by Mallarmé supplies the subtitle of this book, which is an investigation into the repetitive and visual aspects of Virginia Woolf's work.

The book is a modified version of a PhD. thesis. I would like to thank my supervisor, Mr G. D. Klingopulos, for the help and encouragement he gave me while I was a student at University College, Cardiff.

September 1972 A.McL.

Introduction

1

Samuel Butler on convention and repetition

Jean Guiguet in his Preface to a collection of Virginia Woolf's essays called *Contemporary Writers* indicates that Butler is an important figure in considering the 'background' to her work. He says that Butler 'looms too large in Virginia Woolf's background to be omitted' and speaks of 'His general importance, as well as the admiration and sympathy Virginia Woolf felt for his books and personality...'[1] Certainly, there was what amounted to a Butler 'school' at the beginning of the twentieth century, for his influence can also be seen in the works of Shaw, Wells, and E. M. Forster.[2] It is the aesthetic rather than the scientific or ethical ideas which are particularly interesting in relation to Virginia Woolf (although it is especially difficult in Butler's work to make any strict separation between these aspects). Virginia Woolf did read and review a number of Butler's books, but it would perhaps be more useful to look at his work for interesting parallels rather than a narrowly defined 'influence'. In his writings he deals with certain aesthetic problems which Virginia Woolf also tried to solve, and the solutions embodied in her novels often have interesting features in common with his discussions.

Virginia Woolf herself testified that Butler was so deeply implanted in her thought that his ideas seemed to be her own. She expressed this indebtedness in a review:

We should not like to say how often in the course of reading *The Way of All Flesh* we found ourselves thus pulled up. Sometimes we had committed the sin of taking things, like genius, on trust. Then, again, we had fancied that some idea or other was of our own breeding. But here, on the next page, was Butler's original version, from which our seed had blown. If you want to come up afresh in thousands of minds and books long after you are dead, no doubt the way to do it is to start thinking for yourself. The novels that have been fertilized by *The Way*

3

of All Flesh must by this time constitute a large library, with well-known names upon their backs.[3]

With that sensitivity and perceptiveness which she so often shows in her literary criticism, Virginia Woolf employs a botanical metaphor which Butler himself would have enjoyed and used. Her criticism is typically impressionist here, for she allows the writer's images to be carried over into her own writing.[4] The image of the seed perhaps had its origin in this passage by Butler:

It almost seemed as if the seeds and germs were always going about in the air and grew wherever they found a suitable environment. I said it was the same with our thoughts; the germs of all manner of thoughts and ideas are always floating about unperceived in our minds and it was astonishing sometimes in what strange places they found the soil which enabled them to take root and grow into perceived thought and action.[5]

This is from Butler's *Note-Books*, which contain many of his significant ideas, and, what is perhaps as important, give us the essential flavour of his thought. A member of the Bloomsbury Group, Desmond MacCarthy, had a hand in their first publication, and the volume was singled out for special praise by Virginia Woolf in a review entitled 'A Man With a View'. When she first read the *Note-Books* in 1912 she wrote down her impressions in a letter to Lytton Strachey. She found them 'full of amusement' and thought Butler 'very intelligent' but 'oddly limited'.[6] Her later reviews indicate that she came to think of him as more important.

Butler argues that life itself is irrational and, indeed, based on contradictions. These antitheses, especially the interpenetration of life and death, are the 'granite and rainbow' of Virginia Woolf's work. The door which keeps swinging open and shut in *The Waves* is a recurrent image of these opposites and possibly had its germination in these notes by Butler:

Antitheses

Memory and forgetfulness are as life and death to one another. To live is to remember and to remember is to live. To die is to forget and to forget is to die. Everything is so much involved in and is so much a process of its opposite that, as it is almost fair to call death a process of life and life a process of death, so it is to call memory a process of forgetting and forgetting a process of remembering. There is never either absolute memory or absolute forgetfulness, absolute life or absolute death. So with light and darkness, heat and cold, you never can get either all the light, or all the heat, out of anything. So with God and the devil; so with everything. Everything is like a door swinging backwards and forwards. Everything has a little of that from which it is most remote and to which it is most opposed and these antitheses serve to explain one another.[7]

One of these antitheses is that of 'connection' and 'separation'. For Virginia Woolf this is the fine spider's thread spun by Clarissa Dalloway in order to bring people together, as opposed to Peter Walsh's egotistic knife. Once again both image and point of view are similar to Butler's, as we can see in this note:

Joining and disjoining

These are the essence of change.

One of the earliest notes I made, when I began to make notes at all, I found not long ago in an old book, since destroyed, which I had in New Zealand. It was to the effect that all things are either of the nature of a piece of string or a knife. That is, they are either for bringing and keeping things together, or for sending and keeping them apart. Nevertheless each kind contains a little of its opposite... [8]

E. M. Forster often takes the general idea of contraries from Butler (prose and passion, Sawston and Italy and so on), whereas Virginia Woolf, with her impressionist approach takes the *images* of these antitheses. In this way, her novel *The Waves* might be seen as a kind of expansion of Butler's image of life as 'the gathering of waves to a head, at death they break into a million fragments each one of which, however, is absorbed at once into the sea of life and helps to form a later generation which comes rolling on till it too breaks.'[9]

The moral narrowness which Butler disliked in the Victorians is related by Virginia Woolf to the artistic problem of 'professionalism'. In this way, she finds *The Way of All Flesh* refreshing because 'it bears in every part of it the mark of being a home-made hobby, rather than the product of high professional skill'.[10] She feels that it is his anti-professionalism which distinguishes Butler from his age quite as much as his particular 'views'. This is an aspect of his work which has a direct bearing on her own concern with the art of writing. Her mock biographies, *Flush* and *Orlando*, are a reaction against the solid pudding of Victorian biographical writing. She describes this anti-professional feeling in a review of a biography of Butler:

These words seem to us to indicate the most vital distinction that there was between Butler and his contemporaries. The Victorian age, to hazard another generalization, was the age of the professional man. The biographies of the time have a depressing similarity; very much overworked, very serious, very joyless, the eminent men appear to us to be, and already strangely formal and remote from us in their likes and dislikes. Butler, of course, hated nothing more than the professional spirit; and this may account for the startling freshness of his books, as if they had been laid up all these years in sweet-scented roots and pungent spices.[11]

An attack on 'craftsmanship' in literature is a constant theme throughout her criticism, and the anti-professional feeling she finds congenial in Butler is strongly reinforced by the anti-Academicism of Roger Fry, as we shall see later.

Alongside Butler's questioning of moral convention went an awareness of the immense importance of convention in art. This was the inevitable outcome of an apprehension of the problem of arbitrary (or natural) moral law and luck (or cunning) in evolution. Butler's investigation of the conventional basis not only of art, but of language itself is of some value in trying to understand the art of Virginia Woolf. One of Butler's 'connections' is that between nerves and postmen. The problem of communication between people is related to the connection between different parts of ourselves:

Nerves and postmen

A letter, so long as it is connected with one set of nerves, is one thing; loose it from connection with those nerves – open your fingers and drop it in the opening of a pillar box – and it becomes part and parcel of another nervous system. Letters in transitu contain all manner of varied stimuli and shocks, yet to the postman, who is the nerve that conveys them, they are all alike, except as regards mere size and weight. I should think, therefore, that our nerves and ganglia really see no difference in the stimuli that they convey.[12]

This kind of fusion of image and idea, or mind and matter, appealed strongly to Virginia Woolf, who often expresses mental connection in images of impalpable strands or webs. Her characters are often linked together by such threads as they think of each other when physically apart. The connection between art and life she expresses in a similar way. 'A new book', she writes, 'is attached to life by a thousand minute filaments. Life goes on and the filaments break and disappear.'[13] As we saw earlier, it is the image which appeals to her (though, of course, image and idea cannot be separated in any simple way). Butler goes on in the same note to carry the analogy further until he reaches the limits of language:

And yet the postman does see some difference: he knows a business letter from a valentine at a glance and practice teaches him to know much else which escapes ourselves. Who, then, shall say what the nerves and ganglia know and what they do not know? True, to us, as we think of a piece of brain inside our own heads, it seems as absurd to consider that it knows anything at all as it seems to consider that a hen's egg knows anything; but then if the brain could see us, perhaps the brain might say it was absurd to suppose that that thing could know this or that. Besides what is the self of which we say that we are self-conscious? No one can say what it is that we are conscious of. This is one of the things which lie altogether outside the sphere of words.[14]

In *Jacob's Room* Virginia Woolf sees letters in these terms of the connection between body and mind:

Let us consider letters – how they come at breakfast, and at night, with their yellow stamps and their green stamps, immortalized by the postmark – for to see one's own envelope on another's table is to realize how soon deeds sever and become alien. Then at last the power of the mind to quit the body is manifest, and perhaps we fear or hate or wish annihilated this phantom of ourselves, lying on the table.[15]

An aesthetic twist is then given to this Butlerian meditation, for Virginia Woolf is concerned with the artistic problem of letters: that they are personal, like speech, yet have an existence apart from us, like art. Unlike art, they are usually trivial and ephemeral, but they do have the power of connecting us to each other, and of lacing our days together. The idea of the letter contains all the problems of body and mind, of ephemerality and endurance, and so of life and death. Great writers 'have turned from the sheet that endures to the sheet that perishes' and this leads Virginia Woolf to express that dissatisfaction with language which haunts her works: 'But words have been used too often; touched and turned, and left exposed to the dust of the street. The words we seek hang close to the tree. We come at dawn and find them sweet beneath the leaf.'[16] The letter can also illustrate an aspect of artistic convention. Throughout

7

Jacob's Room we meet the repeated assertion that 'the eighteenth century has its distinction',[17] and this address to the reader on the subject of letters reminds us of the formal informality of the eighteenth century epistle. (Which is a letter by virtue of the fact, not that it is informal and personal, but that it is the least formal in a scale which begins with the epic.) This in turn was not distinct from the decorum of social life. But if the arbitrary nature of the code is brought to our conscious attention, then our investigation leads inevitably to the paradox which, according to Butler, we meet at the end of every inquiry:

The highest thought is ineffable; it must be felt from one person to another but cannot be articulated. All the most essential and thinking part of thought is done without words or consciousness. It is not till doubt and consciousness enter that words become possible.

The moment a thing is written, or even can be written, and reasoned about, it has changed its nature by becoming tangible, and hence finite, and hence it will have an end in disintegration. It has entered into death. And yet till it can be thought about and realised more or less definitely it has not entered into life. Both life and death are necessary factors of each other. But our profoundest and most important convictions are unspeakable.

So it is with unwritten and indefinable codes of honour, conventions, art-rules – things that can be felt but not explained – these are the most important, and the less we try to understand them, or even to think about them, the better.[18]

Virginia Woolf tries to explore precisely this forbidden area. The awareness of the conventional basis of social behaviour leads inevitably to self-consciousness in art-rules and conventions. Butler himself was an agent of this increasing awareness, in spite of his claim that it is better not to try to understand or even think about convention. He is trying to point out that convention cannot 'look at itself', which is true; but although conventions cannot be explained, they do, by some mysterious process, change. Butler seems to be pointing towards the intuitive aspect of convention, and what is beyond definition for him is not any particular convention or code, it is the life and death of convention; what is inexplicable is *change*.

Virginia Woolf in that rightly admired essay 'Mr Bennett and Mrs Brown' points out the boundaries of 'explanations' by showing the way in which composition and explanation are one:

You may well complain of the vagueness of my language. What is a convention, a tool, you may ask, and what do you mean by saying that Mr Bennett's and Mr Wells's and Mr Galsworthy's conventions are the wrong conventions for the Georgians? The question is difficult: I will attempt a short-cut. A convention in writing is not much different from a convention in manners. Both in life and in literature it is necessary to have some means of bridging the gulf between the hostess and her unknown guest on the one hand, the writer and his unknown reader on the other. The hostess bethinks her of the weather, for generations of hostesses have established the fact that this is a subject of universal interest in which we all believe. She begins by saying that we are having a wretched May, and, having thus got into touch with her unknown guest, proceeds to matters of greater interest. So it is in literature.[19]

We can see the reason for Bloomsbury's attachment to the eighteenth century, and this passage also helps to explain why Virginia Woolf places such emphasis on the apparently trivial parties of Mrs Dalloway and Mrs Ramsay. A convention, like a party, is a meeting place and the intimacy between host and guest, or writer and reader 'should be reached easily, almost instinctively, in the dark, with one's eyes shut'.[20] Virginia Woolf is in agreement with Butler in seeing the convention as something 'instinctive', a current which, in his words, 'must be felt from one person to another but cannot be articulated'.[21] Virginia Woolf points out in her essay that the Edwardian conventions were acceptable to that age and generation, but that new tools are needed now, for the Georgians. Simply to use old conventions is lazy, and indeed, completely futile. We are beginning to see here the underlying reasons for Virginia Woolf's formal experiments:

But if I had done that I should have escaped the appalling effort of saying what I meant. And to have got at what I meant I should have had to go back and back; to experiment with one thing and another; to try this sentence and that, referring each word to my vision, matching it as exactly as possible, and knowing that somehow I had to find a common ground between us, a convention which would not seem to you too odd, unreal, and far-fetched to believe in.[22]

The aspect of life which the Edwardian conventions tended to leave out is described at the beginning of the *Note-Books*. Butler prefigures much stream-of-consciousness writing with his sense of how 'loosely our thoughts must hang together when the whiff of a smell, a band playing in the street, a face seen in the fire, or on the gnarled stem of a tree, will lead them into such vagaries at a moment's warning'.[23] Virginia Woolf's experiments are in part an attempt to capture these 'vagaries'. Although one convention can be replaced only by another, the novelist often feels that he is trying to discover something more fundamental than previous writers; he is searching for a more basic 'reality'. One of the forms this might take is an attempt to recapture the richness of physical sensation. Here we might find the very essence of what is involved in our dealings with the world outside ourselves, with external or objective reality. Butler therefore proposes a study of 'The Sense of Touch: An essay showing that all the senses resolve themselves ultimately into a sense of touch, and that eating is touch carried to the bitter end . . .'[24] We can see from the rest of the *Note-Books* that Butler believed mind to be a function of matter, and so one cannot speak of a *physical* sensation simply. There is, he believes, only one universal substance, which changes its form according to the different vibrations within it.[25] This is a more general statement of the conclusion which he had reached in trying to connect memory with our physical constitution:

Memory is a kind of way (or weight – whichever it should be) that the mind has got upon it, in virtue of which the sensation excited endures a little longer than the cause which excited it. There is thus induced a state of things in which mental images, and even physical sensations (if there can be such a thing as a physical sensation) exist by virtue of association, though the conditions which originally called them into existence no longer continue.

This is as the echo continuing to reverberate after the sound has ceased.[26]

This is clearly helpful in trying to understand Virginia Woolf's attempt to 'record the atoms as they fall upon the mind',[27] or, in Lily Briscoe's phrase, to give the 'jar on the nerves'.[28]

Mrs Dalloway owes something, perhaps, to Butler's theory of vibrations and shock. There are images of scraping and grazing throughout, in an attempt to convey the vibrations which even a seismograph could not measure.[29] By using the image of the cobweb, which was to be one of Virginia Woolf's favourite images, Butler tries to illustrate the strange nature of shock: 'If you walk at night and your face comes up against a spider's web woven across the road, what a shock that thin line gives you! You fristle through every nerve of your body.'[30] In *Mrs Dalloway* Virginia Woolf tries to give us the sense of being shocked out of internal thoughts and memories into consciousness of the outside world:

And as she began to go with Miss Pym from jar to jar, choosing, nonsense, nonsense, she said to herself, more and more gently, as if this beauty, this scent, this colour, and Miss Pym liking her, trusting her, were a wave which she let flow over her and surmount that hatred, that monster, surmount it all; and it lifted her up and up when – oh! a pistol shot in the street outside![31]

The wave-like continuous movement of the prose is brought to an abrupt halt, as in this passage, where a shock from outside interrupts Clarissa's reverie:

So on a summer's day waves collect, overbalance, and fall; collect and fall; and the whole world seems to be saying 'that is all' more and more ponderously, until even the heart in the body which lies in the sun on the beach says too, that is all. Fear no more, says the heart. Fear no more, says the heart, committing its burden to some sea, which sighs collectively for all sorrows, and renews, begins, collects, lets fall. And the body alone listens to the passing bee; the wave breaking; the dog barking, far away barking and barking.

'Heavens, the front-door bell!' exclaimed Clarissa, staying her needle. Roused, she listened.[32]

In these passages lulling repetitions lead up to the shock of the outside world interrupting a reverie. In both there is the image of a wave (another form of 'vibration'); there is the same sense of movement; and they culminate in a shock and exclamation.

Here begins to sound a note which will be heard throughout the following chapters, that is, the idea of repetition. Repetition and change are much discussed in Butler's *Note-Books* and have great significance in the work of Virginia Woolf. Butler sees 'sameness and difference' as the basis of all art:

The arts of the musician, the painter and the writer are essentially the same. In composing a fugue, after you have exposed your subject, which must not be too unwieldy, you introduce an episode or episodes which must arise out of your subject. The great thing is that all shall be new, and yet nothing new, at the same time; the details must minister to the main effect and not obscure it; in other words, you must have a subject, develop it and not wander from it very far. This holds just as true for literature and painting and for art of all kinds. [33]

Butler delights in embodying his perception of antithesis in the vocabulary of widely different areas of thought, and in this way can cut across traditional boundaries between 'art', 'philosophy', 'science' and so on. The idea of repetition and variation which he sees as the basis of art is itself a variation on his constant theme of evolutionary development:

The ova, spermatozoa and embryos not only of all human races but of all things that live, whether animal or vegetable, think little, but that little almost identically on every subject. That 'almost' is the little rift within the lute which by and by will give such different character to the music. [34]

This little rift is the mutation by which creatures differentiate and become species, and parallels the transformation from one convention into another in art. We might remember here Leslie Stephen's comparison between changes in convention and in species:

In every form of artistic production, in painting and architecture, for example, schools arise; each of which seems to embody some kind of principle, and develops and afterwards decays, according to some mysterious law. It may resemble the animal species which is, somehow or other, developed and then stamped out in the struggle of existence by the growth of a form more appropriate to the new order. The epic poem, shall we say? is like the 'monstrous efts', as Tennyson unkindly calls them, which were no doubt very estimable creatures in their day, but have somehow been unable to adapt themselves to recent geological epochs. [35]

This change is the paradox of something apparently coming from nothing, of the mysterious changes which result in the differentiation of the species. Butler again uses evolutionary theory to illustrate the problem of how we acquire any new knowledge:

Kant says that all our knowledge is founded on experience. But each new small increment of knowledge is not so founded, and our whole knowledge is made up of the accumulation of these small new increments not one of which is founded upon experience. Our knowledge, then, is founded not on experience but on inexperience; for where there is no novelty, that is to say no inexperience, there is no increment in experience. Our knowledge is really founded upon something which we do not know, but it is converted into experience by memory.

It is like species – we do not know the cause of the variations whose accumulation results in species and any explanation which leaves this out of sight ignores the whole difficulty. We want to know the cause of the effect that inexperience produces on us. [36]

It is this sameness and difference which we find in metaphor and which we feel in the disjunction between the clumsiness of language and the rich diversity and intricacy of our sensations. In that gap between repetition and change Clarissa Dalloway sees the 'emptiness at the heart of life' out of which she creates something, a convention – her party. But transmutation involves a loss of some kind and Samuel Butler has a sense of the very definite limits to what can be expressed in words:

We want words to do more than they can. We try to do with them what comes to very much like trying to mend a watch with a pickaxe or to paint a miniature with a mop; we expect them to help us to grip and dissect that which in ultimate essence is as ungrippable as shadow. [37]

Virginia Woolf's writing is an attempt to grasp this shadow.

Part One: Roger Fry and Virginia Woolf

2

Roger Fry and the problem of representation

Previous critics[1] have commented upon the close co-operation between Roger Fry and Virginia Woolf and have indicated the importance of this friendship for Virginia Woolf's creative and critical work. These comparisons with Fry's work often concentrate on the similarity of certain opinions of Fry and certain techniques of Virginia Woolf. Another method, and one which I will now attempt, is to concentrate less on shared or contrasted *opinions* and more on common *problems*. This method will enable us to make a comparison which is not distorting and which will allow comparison with other writers and aestheticians. To do this we must look at what is involved in the idea of representation in general, seen as a continuing problem for all artists and critics. Previous studies have rather neglected the large number of essays and reviews by Fry which have not been collected in book form, yet these, as I hope to show, give us a much fuller picture of his work.

All aesthetic inquiries must eventually deal with the problem of representation in art. The connection between art and 'life' is a continuing problem for all artists even if they do not consciously agonise over it in a theoretical way. It is characteristic of self-conscious artists, however, that they face the problem explicitly, and this is certainly the case with Virginia Woolf and Roger Fry, who were both critics as well as practitioners of their arts. They were both constantly preoccupied with the problems involved in representation, and it is in this area that discussion of their views often centres. If we look at it as an ever-new problem for the artist and critic we avoid the danger of the mere statement of opinions or the opposite danger of taking a partisan position for or against the representational element in art, which would bring the discussion too quickly to some false conclusion.

One thing which strikes us on reading Fry's criticism is that he did

17

not hold consistent views about the value of representation in art. The overall development of his critical standpoint is often seen as an acceptance in his early criticism of a certain amount of representation (the 'dramatic' element which he describes in his early essay on Giotto is often cited here), followed by a progressively more formalistic approach culminating in the footnote to that same essay when it was reprinted in *Vision and Design*, in which he repudiates his earlier talk of a dramatic element.[2] Then, towards the end of his career, many critics have seen a return to his earlier position, noting that Fry found that Rembrandt, for example, could not be adequately appreciated without allowing him a 'psychological element' as well as a purely formal one.[3] Desmond MacCarthy, Fry's close friend and associate, expresses this idea of his development in his obituary note:

That there was such a thing as a purely aesthetic response, and the reward of discovering it and of fixing attention on it, inestimable, was the fundamental postulate of his criticism. He firmly believed this. But he was too much of a philosopher, too much of an intellectual, not to know that it was in part an act of faith. What he kept trying to do was to make us analyse our experiences, in order to discard from them what was irrelevant to this peculiar thrill, this separate joy in contemplation, though the irrelevant might be in itself delightful. About the degree to which the content of a picture for the imagination, the meanings of a poem or a statue or a drawing, might enter into this peculiar experience, or heighten it in an ancillary way, he seems to have held different views at different times. It would be most interesting to trace the curve of his opinion on this vital matter in his works. My own impression is that latterly he was inclined to attribute more importance to imaginative content. But at whatever stage one happens to read him the great benefit one derives is the same: we are forced to inquire into the sources of our pleasure, the nature of our interest in a particular work of art. Does it spring from what is visible or from what is suggested, from the eye or from the imagination? If from what is presented to the eye alone, can we trace the means by which the miracle of pleasure is effected? Or if there is a hitch in the communication of that delight, to what part of the work then is that hitch due?[4]

Certainly, wherever we dip into Fry's criticism, 'representation' is seen as a problem. He may for the moment stress the formal aspect of art, but he never 'solves' the problem by entirely dismissing the representational element. This approach has the immense value of being close to that of the artist, who never 'solves' the problem of composition by the discovery of one formula which can be applied to work after work.

The critic has the task of comparing different works of art, different artists, and different cultures. He must therefore find some general formal basis if he is going to have a recognisable 'point of view', rather than a host of separate criteria and conflicting opinions. Quentin Bell believes that it was the catholicity of Fry's taste which forced him, during the years 1910–25 into an exclusive concern with plastic form. There is the danger in this situation, which Bell hints at, but which I think Fry avoids, of using formal analysis in a kind of despair in the face of such variety. But what is so valuable about Fry's criticism is that he does not see the critical problem as separate from that of creation. His classical stance was precisely a belief that artists as well as critics should imaginatively absorb as much as possible of the tradition of art. Bell correctly points out that we now see with Fry's eyes in this matter of tradition and pass from Raphael to Poussin to Cézanne with no sense of incongruity.[5] But we see things from his point of view in a deeper sense than this, for it is Fry who raises the problem of eclecticism and tradition, which is still relevant, and he supplies the critical ideas by which Professor Bell himself attacks the problem. In speaking of the conjunction between catholicity and formalism in Fry's criticism, Bell is using an insight which Fry himself described. The following passage was written in 1926, but even during his earlier 'formal' period, he was aware of the difficulties of extreme formalism and never completely dismissed the value of the 'instinctive response':

The outside rim of one of these dishes has those bracket-shaped reversed curves, like that of a 'swept' frame, which suggest irresistibly to the European mind the rococo period, so vividly indeed that one cannot help attributing to the owners of such objects just such a complex, sophisticated refinement of civilization as the eighteenth century spells for us, an assumption which the poetry of the time bears out well enough. I suspect, indeed, that eclecticism such as the T'ang artists displayed always implies that careful savouring of style which distinguishes a self-conscious culture. But T'ang art is only an extreme case, for however far we go back in Chinese art we never seem able to get behind the self-consciousness of the artist to a purely instinctive response.[6]

Earlier in the article he exempts from his strictures the depiction of animals in Chinese art. We might compare this with the way in which, in our time, Lawrence and Ted Hughes try to escape from the solipsism of a self-conscious culture in their animal poems, which have the kind of vitality which Fry saw in Chinese animals.

Howard Hannay points out that there are many examples in the history of taste of insistence on the superiority of one kind of art. He believes that Fry's ideas are of this kind and they have, there-fore, only a 'contemporary truth'. Fry was aware of these distortions and of the fact that he was biased in favour of a certain kind of art, which he called, for the sake of convenience, 'classic'. It is Fry's *awareness* of his bias which critics often misrepresent, and it is this which makes him our contemporary. His co-operation with Virginia Woolf is more exciting than the mere sharing of certain opinions – they were both self-aware in their engagement with the problem of representation. Various opinions abstracted from Fry's work may have only a 'contemporary truth', but his approach to the problems, indeed the nature of the problems which he raises, and his develop-ment as he struggled with them, have a continuing interest for us, because they are still our problems. To see him merely as a figure in the 'history of taste' is too patronising.

As such a 'historical' figure, he had an impact on the intellectual life of his day and on the imagination of subsequent writers which is distinct from the significance which we might find in his writings. There is a mythical Roger Fry who is distinct from the man who knew and impressed Virginia Woolf. This ghostly figure has a peculiar relationship to reality which is itself a problem of represen-tation – here, the representation involved in the creation of a myth. This Roger Fry is a puritan. William Gaunt gives a picture which is widely accepted to-day:

Colouring his outlook was a combination of factors – the native Puritan-ism of his family which did in fact lead him to seek something pure, some principle uncorrupted and untarnished by worldly contacts... [7]

And Gaunt's final evaluation is the damning statement that 'Roger Fry placed round the visual arts the barriers of a rigid system.'[8]

But Fry always put criticism before systematic aesthetics and was prepared to change his mind in so many ways that it is difficult to see any rigid system in his work. His attitude can be seen in the following:

The miscellaneous collection of pictures now on view at the French Gallery is labelled 'Ingres to Picasso'. It is none the worse for being miscellaneous. Indeed, it is from the accidental confrontations of such collections as these that one learns most. Here new lights on the relative position of the great names surprise one into revising afresh for the hundredth time one's theories and assumptions.[9]

His reviews and books, written over the many years of his critical career, round out our picture of Fry, showing him to be less one-sided than Gaunt and others suggest, less of the dogmatic formalist. We gain from his work as a whole a sense which those who knew him best testify to; a great receptiveness, at times bordering on gullibility, the very opposite fault to rigid dogmatism. The over-simplified view of Fry has been revived recently by Angus Wilson:

There is in this 'pure' objection not a little of that moral puritanism which in various ways easily bedevils even the most purely aesthetic English criticism. If, for example, for Roger Fry any non-formal ele-ment in painting was impermissible in criticism, he surely gave to this view a moral flavour in itself inconsistent with the idea of the purely aesthetic; to consider the religious impulse of El Greco or the didactic-ism of Hogarth was made to seem almost morally disreputable. To suspect all sources outside the text in literary criticism suggests a similar confusion. Allied with this confused puritanism is the under-lying suggestion that such aids are suspect simply because they may often be easy short-cuts to textual analysis; they make the critical game too simple.[10]

Angus Wilson is right in seeing the moral flavour of Fry's criticism, but it is moral in the widest sense, better described as 'serious' rather than 'puritan'. He saw the non-formal element as a problem in art rather than something to be dogmatically excluded. To call his seriousness 'puritanism' is misleading, as this has overtones of that repressive morality which Fry specifically opposes, for example in his article 'The Garden of Eden'.[11] Solomon Fishman expresses his idea of Fry's seriousness more fairly than Wilson, calling it 'austerity':

The search for plastic form is endowed by Fry with a quasi-ethical value, corresponding to the scientist's search for truth. Insights such as these served to reinforce the native austerity of Fry's temperament. He became increasingly suspicious of technical virtuosity, of surface

charm particularly exemplified in the marvellous texture of Impressionist painting, of emotive expression.[12]

This is a fair summary of Fry's dislikes, although rejection of
virtuosity, of mere charm, and of painting which has a palpable
design upon us does not indicate to me an excessive austerity. Instead of the usual 'puritan' label we are given the slightly less
pejorative 'quasi-ethical'. But it can be argued that if art is a serious
study, then a mistaken interpretation of a work of art is a serious
mistake. Ultimately this seriousness involves saying that good art is
morally superior to poor art (not quasi-ethically superior). How
can we distinguish, other than by moral or spiritual values between
a work which is excellent, or even perfect in its way, and one which
is great art?[13] Fry does not reject 'the marvellous texture of
Impressionist painting' as Fishman suggests, he finds it less great
than the plastic form of the Post-Impressionists. The alternative to
this scale of spiritual value is the philistinism of *de gustibus* against
which Fry constantly argues.[14]

The narrator in *Brideshead Revisited* again uses the unfortunate
'puritan' smear, but he does indicate a valid difference in taste
which Fry would have found tenable even if he did not accept it himself:

but, though in opinion I had made that easy leap, characteristic of my
generation, from the puritanism of Ruskin to the puritanism of Roger
Fry, my sentiments at heart were insular and medieval.
This was my conversion to the Baroque.[15]

As McCarthy points out, Fry was well aware of his own perspective:
'No critic was ever more aware of the angle from which he was
judging what was before him, or more candid in communicating that
attitude to his readers.'[16] The distinction between opinion and
sentiment in the passage from Waugh is an interesting one when we
consider the connection between Virginia Woolf and Roger Fry, for
she found the bias of his mind congenial and more helpful than any
of his particular opinions or ideas.

Another common misunderstanding about Fry, implied in
Waugh's novel, is that 'modern aesthetics' is of a piece, with Fry
and Bell mounting a joint attack on representation. The following
passage contains the essence of the debate about the relation of art to
nature, and the representation of 'space' and of 'sentiment':

Collins had exposed the fallacy of modern aesthetics to me: '...the whole argument from Significant Form stands or falls by *volume*. If you allow Cézanne to represent a third dimension on his two-dimensional canvas, then you must allow Landseer his gleam of loyalty in the spaniel's eye'...but it was not until Sebastian, idly turning the page of Clive Bell's *Art*, read: '"Does anyone feel the same kind of emotion for a butterfly or a flower that he feels for a cathedral or a picture?" Yes. *I* do,' that my eyes were opened.[17]

But we must remember that Fry sharply dissociated himself from Bell on the question of representation:

Whatever Mr Clive Bell may have said, I personally have never denied the existence of some amount of representation in all pictorial art. I have always admitted the purely representative nature of the present-ment of the third dimension on the flat surface of a picture. What I have suggested is that the purer the artist the more his representation will be of universals and the less of particulars.

I may sometimes have used the word representation in opposition to design to denote more or less particularised representation, but I think in its context this use or misuse of the word is sufficiently clear.[18]

This was written during Fry's most formalist period, and so, even at his most plastic, he is still a little bit representational (like Butler's universal matter, which is still a little bit dead when it is most alive, and vice versa). Fishman points out Fry's fondness for dualist formulations, such as linear and plastic, order and variety, vision and design and so on. Fry shares with Butler this love of antitheses. Fishman, who gives a fine short account of Fry's work, realises that Fry never completely abandoned representation in art, and explains his formal bias by saying that for a large part of his career he was combating the prevailing attitude towards painting, which stressed the illustrative and literary aspects. He tended, says Fishman, to go to the opposite extreme and isolate art from human experience. He failed to establish the idea of autonomy, but did establish the primacy of form in the investigation of visual art. Perhaps the following extract from Fry's review of a book on Botticelli, written in 1926, illustrates the way in which he held the balance between representa-tion and autonomy. He had no intention of 'establishing the idea of autonomy of form' as Fishman suggests; he was simply aware of his own needs and preferences, and so able to see the opposite view as well:

Now this change is of great importance in the history of contemporary taste. One may almost say that taste is always pendulous between Raphaelitism and Pre-Raphaelitism. Pre-Raphaelitism conceives of a content rich in ideas, interesting in the forms chosen for delineation – interesting both by their *recherché* nature and by their evocations of sentiment – and finally, rich in the decorative display of these forms. But Raphaelitism envisages no such interesting or curious content – is, in fact, satisfied with the most commonplace and banal content that comes to hand, and searches in the delineation of that content the utmost richness and intensity of plastic stimulus to the imagination; and in order to give this its full effect it eschews the disturbing influence which the rich decoration of the picture surface implies.

What appears to happen is that we get now tired of the dullness of content and the sentimental poverty, or even vulgarity of Raphaelite art, and now tired of the too elaborate conceits, the complexity, and want of unity of Pre-Raphaelite. Now, Botticelli symbolizes for us better than any other artist the essentials of Pre-Raphaelitism, and his reputation is likely to rise and fall with that.

It may be that Mr Yashiro's book announces for us a new return to Pre-Raphaelitism. In England, with our curious lack of the pure plastic sense, the pendulum almost always swings more vigorously towards the Pre-Raphaelite pole.[19]

This ability of Fry to see his own bias and admit differences of taste can be illustrated by a further passage which also shows that his stress on the formal was not so much an attack on representation, as on illusionism. Here, the counterparts of Raphaelitism and Pre-Raphaelitism are Classic and Baroque:

Now this tendency of the Baroque to tumble into 'illusionism' must have always disgusted the finer natures among painters. And already in the seventeenth century we find two striking examples of this revolt. One is Poussin, who deliberately based himself on the 'Classical' tradition...

The other great instance is Rembrandt himself. It may seem strange to cite Rembrandt as a witness on this side, seeing that he is himself not only the greatest but in some ways the most Baroque of all Baroque artists. Indeed it is perhaps due to him, more than to anyone else, that the weapon of illusionism was forged. No one denied the flatness of the picture plane more violently than he, none created depth into the picture space more convincingly. None designed more 'open' composition, and yet precisely because he was so great he was also the first to see the

24

dangers of what he had set in motion, and so at the end of his life we find signs of a return to 'Classical' principles. I do not want to exaggerate this. Even the latest of Rembrandt's pictures are infinitely removed from Raphael's, they still remain essentially Baroque, but they are far less illusionist than his early ones...Rembrandt had learned how to throw away the methods by which he had previously aroused the idea of relief. Actually the impression of mass and volume is increased, but these notions are communicated more directly to the imagination and no longer through the dangerous and roundabout path of illusion.

In spite of Dr Wölfflin's admirably detached attitude I seem to trace in him a slight bias in favour of the Baroque idea. This may be due to the fact that I certainly have a personal bias in favour of the 'Classical'. None the less it would be absurd not to recognise how immensely important the Baroque innovation has been, how it has vivified and enriched European art, given it a power and weight which is lacking in some purer traditions. But in proportion to this new power it has run more disastrous risks and tends to fall into deeper abysses. Still, though it may have given us the Royal Academy, it gave us Rembrandt; we are not forced to see the Royal Academy, and we should be infinitely poorer without Rembrandt.[20]

These two extracts are surely enough to refute Gaunt's assertion that Fry 'placed round the visual arts the barriers of a rigid system'. They indicate a more balanced attitude toward representation than many critics suggest, and one which is more helpful in relation to literature than dogmatic formalism. Few people would now argue against his attack on illusionism; but at that time, even among serious art lovers, Alma Tadema's marble was the touchstone of artistic excellence. Here, on the question of verisimilitude and illusion, we might bring Virginia Woolf into the discussion.

3

Verisimilitude and illusion:
'The Voyage Out' and 'Night and Day'

Fry states the case against a simple-minded mimetic theory in 'An Essay in Aesthetics':

A certain painter, not without some reputation at the present day, once wrote a little book on the art he practises, in which he gave a definition of that art so succinct that I take it as a point of departure for this essay.

'The art of painting,' says that eminent authority, 'is the art of imitating solid objects upon a flat surface by means of pigments.' It is delightfully simple, but prompts the question – Is that all? And, if so, what a deal of unnecessary fuss has been made about it. Now, it is useless to deny that our modern writer has some very respectable authorities behind him. Plato, indeed, gave a very similar account of the affair, and himself put the question – is it then worthwhile? And, being scrupulously and relentlessly logical, he decided that it was not worthwhile, and proceeded to turn the artists out of his ideal republic. For all that, the world has continued obstinately to consider that painting was worthwhile, and though, indeed, it has never quite made up its mind as to what, exactly, the graphic arts did for it, it has persisted in honouring and admiring its painters.

Can we arrive at any conclusions as to the nature of the graphic arts, which will at all explain our feelings about them, which will at least put them into some kind of relation with the other arts, and not leave us in the extreme perplexity, engendered by any theory of mere imitation? For, I suppose, it must be admitted that if imitation is the sole purpose of the graphic arts, it is surprising that the works of such arts are ever looked upon as more than curiosities, or ingenious toys, are ever taken seriously by grown-up people. Moreover, it will be surprising that they have no recognisable affinity with other arts, such as music or architecture, in which the imitation of actual objects is a negligible quantity.[1]

This questioning of attempted verisimilitude in art is one of the main themes of Virginia Woolf's biography of Roger Fry. The

Royal Academy was a major target in his attack on the 'literary' aspects of painting, and Virginia Woolf quotes as evidence of this Fry's remark that the Hon. John Collier 'is really outstripping the camera in his relentless exposition of the obvious and the insignificant'.[2] He criticises Sargent on similar grounds, calling him a 'précis writer of appearances'.[3] Virginia Woolf shares this dislike of Royal Academy art, and the work of Sargent in particular. She uses her own image of mindless repetition, the parrot, to describe his art. The parrot is a recurrent image in Virginia Woolf's writings and represents the inhuman aspect of repetition. It is the linguistic counterpart of the time-honoured image of pictorial mimesis, the mirror, and Virginia Woolf uses it to show that illusionism in language and visual art are equally abhorrent:

But Mr Sargent was the last straw. Suddenly the great rooms rang like a parrot-house with the intolerable vociferations of gaudy and brainless birds. How they shrieked and gibbered! How they danced and sidled! Honour, patriotism, chastity, wealth, success, importance, position, patronage, power – their cries rang and echoed from all quarters. 'Anywhere, anywhere, out of this world!' was the only exclamation with which one could stave off the brazen din as one fled downstairs, out of doors, round the motor-cars, beneath the disdain of the horse and its rider, and so out into the comparative sobriety of Picadilly. No doubt the reaction was excessive; and I must leave it to Roger Fry to decide whether the emotions here recorded are the proper result of one thousand six hundred and seventy-four works of art.[4]

Both E. M. Forster and Virginia Woolf objected specifically to a picture of Sargent's called *Gassed*. Forster says that the painting gives an unreal picture of war and is therefore immoral. The battlefield is tidy and 'no one looked lousy or over-tired'. The correct response should not be 'how touching', but rather 'how obscene'.[5] Virginia Woolf objected to the expressionism, the over-emphasis of the picture; her criticism, like that of Forster, is concerned with the subject matter of the painting:

A large picture by Mr Sargent called *Gassed* at last pricked some nerve of protest, or perhaps of humanity. In order to emphasise his point that the soldiers wearing bandages round their eyes cannot see, and therefore claim our compassion, he makes one of them raise his leg to the level of his elbow in order to mount a step an inch or two above the ground.

This little piece of over-emphasis was the final scratch of the surgeon's knife which is said to hurt more than the whole operation. [6]

They dislike the picture because they believe it to be unreal. By concentrating on the literary or anecdotal aspect of painting it is easy to be led into an irrelevant discussion. We can understand from these comments why Fry concentrates on formal aspects in his criticism, for discussion of the subject-matter leads to largely irrelevant questions about what 'really happened'. A letter from a field ambulance man appeared in *The Athenaeum* a fortnight after Virginia Woolf's article, and it shows the way in which the discussion can drift away from the work of art into all sorts of peculiar considerations such as, in this case, the way in which blind men walk:

On three occasions in France – once in a front-line trench, and twice between 'bearer-relays' and 'first-aid posts' – I saw Mr Sargent collecting his details. I have seen the picture in question, also, and it is the man at the end of the file that Mr Sargent has portrayed in this action. It *is* 'over-emphasis', but on the part of the man – not that of the artist. Whether it be good art to depict this peculiarity I am not competent to say, but it is a depiction of the truth. [7]

The final sentence leaves the problem unsolved. It is Fry's contention that such illusionism is a distortion of the truth, for his truth is the fusion of vision and design and the creation of formal significance rather than the copying of something given. This kind of perception he carried over into his literary ideas. Virginia Woolf describes his attitude in her biography:

Literature was suffering from a plethora of old clothes. Cézanne and Picasso had shown the way; writers should fling representation to the winds and follow suit. But he never found time to work out his theory of the influence of Post-Impressionism upon literature... [8]

J. K. Johnstone rightly points out that Fry's attack on photographic representation in visual art is closely paralleled by Virginia Woolf's rejection of the 'materialism' of Galsworthy, Bennett and Wells. But Johnstone does not come to grips with the problems involved in the idea of representation in art. He states that Fry 'reiterated the half-forgotten truth that art is autonomous. He showed where art touches life and where it is separate from it'. [9] This is too simplified, for autonomy in art is a problem for Fry, not simply a truth which can be asserted. It is true that Virginia Woolf was influenced by Roger Fry's point of view, but she always took it as that of an art critic and painter, and certainly did not simply accept his opinions about literature. We can see in the following passage that she could appreciate his perspective without being hampered by his particular opinions, and this is true of all the writers who influenced her, as her essays, with their emphasis on perspective and point of view, clearly show:

As a critic of literature, then, he was not what is called a safe guide. He looked at the carpet from the wrong side; but he made it for that very reason display unexpected patterns. And many of his theories held good for both arts. Design, rhythm, texture – there they were again – in Flaubert as in Cézanne. And he would hold up a book to the light as if it were a picture and show where in his view – it was a painter's of course – it fell short.[10]

In spite of her association with Fry and her attacks on illusionism and materialism, most critics have nevertheless seen her first two novels as traditional. It is true that they are manifestly less experimental than her later works, but it would be astonishing if they were completely in the Bennett or Galsworthy tradition. Perhaps we will gain something if we hold these novels up to the light, as Virginia Woolf claims was Fry's method. We will concentrate on what is experimental in them, what is fruitful and points the way to her later work.

The main theme of *The Voyage Out* is traditional enough: the journey of a young girl from a sheltered childhood to adult awareness. It is a psychological voyage, into dreams and the 'subconscious', but also an exploration of the world outside European culture, stimulated by a dissatisfaction with 'the enormous accumulations of carved stone, stained glass, and rich brown painting which they offered to the tourist'.[11] There was an increasing interest in primitive art and culture which Fry had a part in fostering – 'new forms of beauty' such as 'primitive carvings coloured bright greens and blues'.[12] The theme is not developed; like many of the ideas in the novel it is loosely thrown in. This is more or less true of the novel as a whole, which contains many ideas and hints which point the way to Virginia Woolf's future development, but which here remain unconnected. Her own criticism of this novel, written five years after its publication, is clear-sighted in this matter:

The mornings from 12 to 1 I spend reading *The Voyage Out*. I've not read it since July 1913. And if you ask me what I think I must reply that I don't know – such a harlequinade as it is – such an assortment of patches – here simple and severe – here frivolous and shallow – here like God's truth – here strong and free flowing as I could wish. What to make of it, Heaven knows. The failures are ghastly enough to make my cheeks burn – and then a turn of the sentence, a direct look ahead of me, makes them burn in a different way. On the whole I like the young woman's mind considerably. How gallantly she takes her fences – and my word, what a gift for pen and ink! I can do little to amend, and must go down to posterity the author of cheap witticisms, smart satires and even, I find, vulgarisms – crudities rather – that will never cease to rankle in the grave. Yet I see how people prefer it to *N. and D.* I don't say admire it more, but find it a more gallant and inspiring spectacle.[13]

I would like to look at those elements in the novel which Virginia Woolf describes as 'a direct look ahead of me'.

First, there is an intermittent concern with the conventions which she is using, and with language itself; a self-consciousness not found in the wholly traditional 'well-made' novel. One does not want to claim too much for the novel, for the interesting elements are given in the form of ideas or opinions held by the characters rather than embodied dramatically or structurally, and so the novel is something of a 'fluid pudding'. However, in view of her future development these elements are interesting and worth examining. It is an important part of Virginia Woolf's development, for she was interested at this time in a 'hold-all' form in which she could put anything. She admired Byron's *Don Juan* for this reason, and found her diary useful in practising this type of writing.[14] She was later to use Fry's formal perspective as a counterweight to this fluidity.[15] One of the themes of the novel is a portrayal of the non-rational part of mental activity seen especially in dreams, or in the mind fevered by emotion or disease. In this passage we see the Butlerian image of the drifting seed which shows 'how loosely our thoughts are held together':

Inextricably mixed in dreamy confusion, her mind seemed to enter into communion, to be delightfully expanded and combined with the spirit of the whitish boards on deck, with the spirit of the sea, with the spirit of Beethoven Op. 112, even with the spirit of poor William Cowper there at Olney. Like a ball of thistledown it kissed the sea, rose, kissed it again, and thus rising and kissing passed finally out of sight. The rising and falling of the ball of thistledown was represented by the sudden droop forward of her own head, and when it passed out of sight she was asleep.[16]

The rhythmical repetition and rise and fall of the mind point forward to *The Waves*, as does the later image of '...the breaking of the waves on the shore sounded like the repeated sigh of some exhausted creature...'[17] In that later novel Virginia Woolf tries to carry out Hewet's idea 'to write a novel about Silence...the things people don't say'.[18] This is connected with the disjunction between the sounds of words and their meanings:

The silence was then broken by their voices which joined in tones of strange unfamiliar sound which formed no words....Sounds stood out from the background making a bridge across their silence; they heard the swish of the trees and some beast croaking in a remote world.[19]

There is a disjunction between words and things[20] and between the sounds of words and their significance, clearly the beginning of an investigation into the representation involved in language. We can also see in this novel the beginning of Virginia Woolf's concern with repetition, which was to be of great importance in her later works. So, we are told that 'The repetition of Hewet's name in short, dissevered syllables was to them the crack of a dry branch or the laughter of a bird...'[21] There is also a hint of that underlying sense of repetition, which is here connected with the pulsing of the mind:

The morning was hot, and the exercise of reading left her mind contracting and expanding like the mainspring of a clock. The sounds in the garden outside joined with the clock, and the small noises of midday, which one can ascribe to no definite cause, in a regular rhythm...[22]

Even in this first novel, then, there is a questioning of the power of ordinary language to represent 'reality', and also a move towards questioning other conventions, such as the traditional portrayal of character. Again, this is on the level of ideas and opinions, as when Hewet asks '...can you imagine anything more ludicrous than one person's opinion of another person?'[23] Rachel thinks of life as simply the movement of light,[24] an idea which points forward to *Jacob's Room* in particular, but more generally to the rejection of 'character' in the traditional sense in all her later works. Here this is simply an idea:

'Does it ever seem to you, Terence, that the world is composed entirely of vast blocks of matter, and that we're nothing but patches of light' – she looked at the soft spots of sun wavering over the carpet and up the wall – 'like that?'[25]

It is the use of these visual effects to destroy conventional representation which Fry noted and admired in her early work. It is here that we can directly locate his importance in helping her to develop in a certain direction. Although many critics have seen only the traditional aspect of her early novels, Fry at the time held up her work to the light and perceived a new pattern. We can see in his verbal translation of a picture by Survage[26] how he realises the colour, shape, and the shadowy human figures of Virginia Woolf's writing. The kind of comparison he makes in this article could not fail to affect her subsequent development, and we must remember that it was written as early as 1919. He is probably referring to her sketches 'The Mark on the Wall' and 'Kew Gardens' rather than to *The Voyage Out*, but that earlier work does have hints of these visual elements. The description of London at the beginning of the novel, with its emphasis on the shapes of the buildings, is close to Fry's little parody. Here, for example: 'London having shrunk to two lines of buildings on either side of them, square buildings and oblong buildings placed in rows like a child's avenue of bricks.'[27] Later, music is seen in terms of spaces and columns. In *The Waves* these architectural and musical elements come together in Rhoda's squares and oblongs, which she sees as the basis of all human conventions in art and life. One of the more important visual elements in *The Voyage Out*, that of space, will be examined in a later chapter.

Night and Day is important partly becaue it is in some ways a first version of her much later novel, *The Years*. One of the corollaries of seeing the earlier novel as traditional is the view that *The Years* is a relapse into 'realism' after the innovations of *To the Lighthouse* and *The Waves*. I hope to show that *Night and Day* is not conventional and that *The Years*, although perhaps inferior to the preceding two novels is not straightforwardly traditional and is directly related to her last novel, the extremely experimental work *Between the Acts. Jacob's Room* is often regarded as Virginia Woolf's first experimental novel, but much of its technique develops directly from *Night and Day*. But these questions of Virginia Woolf's overall development will perhaps become clearer in later chapters.

The questioning of the traditional idea of character hinted at in *The Voyage Out* is here continued and can be related to Fry's attack on the psychological interpretation of visual art. Katherine does have a moment of disinterested contemplation such as Fry described as conducive to the true aesthetic vision:

All this talk about Shakespeare had acted as a soporific, or rather as an incantation upon Katherine. She leant back in her chair at the head of the tea-table, perfectly silent, looking vaguely past them all, receiving the most generalised ideas of human heads against pictures, against yellow-tinted walls, against curtains of deep crimson velvet. [28]

Virginia Woolf was not yet turning to the visual effects or the formal structure which would in a sense compensate for the loss of traditional character creation which she renounces. Her remarks in her diary about an unwritten novel indicate that she was still in search of a completely open form some months before the publication of *Night and Day*:

Suppose one thing should open out of another – as in an unwritten novel – only not for 10 pages but 200 or so – doesn't that give the looseness and lightness I want; doesn't that get closer and yet keep form and speed, and enclose everything, everything? My doubt is how far it will enclose the human heart – Am I sufficiently mistress of my dialogue to net it there? For I figure that the approach will be entirely indifferent this time: no scaffolding; scarcely a brick to be seen; all crepuscular, but the heart, the passion, humour, everything as bright as fire in the mist. [29]

We can see the way in which she brings to the surface in her new works elements which had been latent in her previous writings, for *Night and Day* is full of mist and dream and disembodiment when we look at it with a knowledge of Virginia Woolf's subsequent development. The solidity of the chronicle structure and setting are really an illusion, and illusion itself is the hidden theme of the novel. This is brought out more starkly in *The Years*, yet even this later work, which became a best-seller, many people have read as a traditional family saga.

Roger Fry and Virginia Woolf were engaged, in their different ways, in an investigation into representation, and their work overlapped in many respects. But one must not forget that other novelists were experimenting in this matter of representation, and of special importance in this instance is Conrad. Virginia Woolf had written three reviews of Conrad in 1917 and 1918, and in his work there are interesting parallels with certain aspects of *Night and Day*. We saw earlier that 'moment of vision' which was near to Fry's aesthetic contemplation, but it is also close to the heightened 'moments' which she praises in Conrad's novels.[30] In that same essay, she uses terms which Fry might have employed to describe a painting: 'After the middle period Conrad never again was able to bring his figures into perfect relation with their background.'[31] This is exactly the kind of perfect relation which Fry ascribes to Cézanne's painting. Virginia Woolf admires, precisely, Conrad's painterly qualities:

Picture after picture he painted thus upon the dark background; ships first and foremost, ships at anchor, ships flying before the storm, ships in harbour; he painted sunsets and dawns; he painted the night; he painted the sea in every aspect; he painted the gaudy brilliance of Eastern ports, and men and women, their houses and their attitudes. He was an accurate and unflinching observer...[32]

Her dualistic way of dealing with Conrad's work reminds us of Fry's method and her criticism in turn affected her creative works. She sees Conrad as a double personality; the sea captain who dominates the early tales, and Marlow, whose subtle intelligence is most in evidence later. The moments of vision in Conrad's work she relates especially to his creation of character, and it is this aspect of his work that is most closely paralleled in *Night and Day*:

But I almost prefer his sudden direct pounce right across the room like a cat on a mouse. There's Mrs Schomberg, for instance, 'a scraggy little woman with long ringlets and a blue tooth', or a dying man's voice 'like the rustle of a single dry leaf driven along the smooth sand of a beach'. He sees once and he sees forever. His books are full of moments of vision. They light up a whole character in a flash.[33]

Her reference is to the Mrs Schomberg of the short story 'Falk', but of more direct importance here is the other tale in which she appears, *Victory*. Here she is without that blue tooth which Virginia Woolf admired so much, but she is still the mechanical doll-like figure of the earlier tale:

While he was staring at the poster, a door somewhere at his back opened, and a woman came in who was looked upon as Schomberg's wife, no doubt with truth. As somebody remarked cynically once, she was too unattractive to be anything else. The opinion that he treated her abominably was based on her frightened expression. Davidson lifted his hat to her. Mrs Schomberg gave him an inclination of her sallow head and incontinently sat down behind a sort of raised counter, facing the door, with a mirror and rows of bottles at her back. Her hair was very elaborately done with two ringlets on the left side of her scraggy neck; her dress was of silk, and she had come on duty for the afternoon. For some reason or other Schomberg exacted this from her, though she added nothing to the fascinations of the place. She sat there in the smoke and noise, like an enthroned idol, smiling stupidly over the billiards from time to time, speaking to no one, and no one speaking to her. Schomberg himself took no more interest in her than may be implied in a sudden and totally unmotivated scowl. Otherwise the very Chinamen ignored her existence.[34]

All the characters in the novel are either puppets like Mrs Schomberg, or animals like Pedro and Ricardo, or shades like Heyst and Lena. In this way, Wang appears and disappears like a phantom, his face like a cardboard mask.[35] The life of the natives is a 'mere play of shadows'[36] and 'enchanted Heyst' casts an insubstantial feeling over the whole tale. It is strongly visual, an impressionist fantasy, something like the Whistler whom Conrad speaks of in 'The Partner'. We can see this visual impressionism in the following passage: 'The black spokes of darkness over the floor and the walls, joining up on the ceiling in a path of shadow, were like the bars of a cage about them.'[37] One of the main themes of *Night and Day* is precisely this of dream and illusion. Katherine Hilbery has a Conradian moment of vision in this way:

The view she had had of the inside of an office was of the nature of a dream to her. Shut off up there, she compared Mrs Seal, and Mary Datchet, and Mr Clacton to enchanted people in a bewitched tower, with the spider's webs looping across the corners of the room, and all the tools of the necromancer's craft at hand; for so aloof and unreal and apart from the normal world did they seem to her, in the house of innumerable typewriters, murmuring their incantations and concocting their drugs, and flinging their frail spiders' webs over the torrent of life which rushed down the streets outside.[38]

Ralph, like Heyst, looks past character and ideals to see the nothingness, the emptiness at the heart of life which is Virginia Woolf's most consistent vision:

'In what can one trust, then?' he thought, as he leant there. So feeble and insubstantial did he feel himself that he repeated the world aloud.

'In what can one trust? Not in men and women. Not in one's dreams about them. There's nothing – nothing, nothing left at all.'[39]

We see here a hint of the repeated 'nothing' which was to haunt the rest of Virginia Woolf's work. There follows a passage which comes very close to Heyst's point of view:

Now Denham had reason to know that he could bring to birth and keep alive a fine anger when he chose. Rodney provided a good target for that emotion. And yet at the moment, Rodney and Katherine herself seemed disembodied ghosts. He could scarcely remember the look of them. His mind plunged lower and lower. Their marriage seemed of no importance to him. All things had turned to ghosts; the whole mass of the world was insubstantial vapour, surrounding the solitary spark in his mind, whose burning point he could remember, for it burnt no more. He had once cherished a belief, and Katherine had embodied this belief, and she did so no longer. He did not blame her; he blamed nothing, nobody; he saw the truth. He saw the dun-coloured race of waters and the blank shore. But life is vigorous; the body lives, and the body, no doubt, dictated the reflection, which now urged him to movement, that one may cast away the forms of human beings, and yet retain the passion which seemed inseparable from their existence in the flesh. Now this passion burnt on his horizon, as the winter sun makes a greenish pane in the west through thinning clouds. His eyes were set on something infinitely far and remote; by that light he felt he could walk, and would, in future, have to find his way. But that was all there was left to him of a populous and teeming world.[40]

This is similar in idea and image to our introduction to Heyst in the first chapter of *Victory*:

Everyone in that part of the world knew of him, dwelling on his little island. An island is but the top of a mountain. Axel Heyst, perched on it immovably, was surrounded, instead of the imponderable stormy and transparent ocean of air merging into infinity, by a tepid, shallow sea; a passionless offshoot of the great waters which embrace the continents of this globe. His most frequent visitors were shadows, the shadows of clouds, relieving the monotony of the inanimate, brooding sunshine of the tropics. His nearest neighbour – I am speaking now of things showing some sort of animation – was an indolent volcano which smoked faintly all day with its head just above the northern horizon, and at night levelled at him, from amongst the clear stars, a dull red glow, expanding and collapsing spasmodically like the end of a gigantic cigar puffed at intermittently in the dark. Axel Heyst was also a smoker; and when he lounged out on his veranda with his cheroot, the last thing before going to bed, he made in the night the same sort of glow and of the same size as that other one so many miles away. [41]

In *Victory* the characters are shades and animals, and in *Night and Day* they are ghosts and birds. Cousin Caroline is like a cockatoo[42] and the chairman of the committee is a bald-headed sparrow. Aunt Eleanor looks like a parrot[43] and Katherine becomes a snowy owl.[44] There is a misty, vaporous indistinctness throughout the novel. A vision of the insubstantial nature of our world and life is reinforced and symbolised, as in Conrad, by a visual impressionism, where there are no hard outlines, and where the nature of reality depends on the point of view, or the quality of the light. But there is the beginning of an attempt in *Night and Day* to give a more solid 'geometrical' structure, an attempt to move from impressionism to post-impressionism by the use of the recurring image of the web. This is an attempt to give a net, a grid, on to which the impressions can fall at random, and yet retain some symmetry or design. But there is only this slight hint of an underlying structure here, and we must turn to her later novels, especially *To the Lighthouse* and *The Waves*, to see this kind of design fully developed.

4

Sensation in language and art:
'Mrs Dalloway' and 'Flush'

Language and art do not copy our physical sensations. Cassirer asks simply 'What would be accomplished by a mere copy of something already present?'[1] and he goes on to point out that the value of language lies precisely in its difference from sensation:

If, for example, we regarded it as the true and essential function of language to express once again, but merely in a different medium, the very same reality that lies ready-made before us in particular sensations and intuitions – we should be struck at once by the vast inadequacy of all languages. Measured by the limitless richness and diversity of intuitive reality, all linguistic symbols would inevitably seem empty; measured by its individual concretion, they would inevitably seem abstract and vague.[2]

This difference is the 'little rift' which Butler speaks of, the fact that 'association does not stick to the letter of its bond'.[3] Art, however, often claims to be more concrete than ordinary language, to be connected in some particularly close way to sensation. It is often felt to be in some way nearer to the sensational world than, say, science or mathematics. Wimsatt, following Cassirer, says that the fully concrete use of language, in poetry, can only draw attention to the difference between itself and the reality which it symbolises:

What may seem stranger is that the verbal symbol in calling attention to itself must also call attention to the difference between itself and reality which it resembles and symbolises. As one of the fathers of 'symbolic form' has expressed it: 'Even the most primitive verbal utterance requires a transmutation of a certain cognitive or emotive experience into sound, i.e., a medium that is foreign to the experience, and even quite disparate.' In most discourse we look right through this disparity. There is a one-way transparent intellectual reference. But poetry by thickening the medium increases the disparity between itself and its referents.[4]

In Butler's terms, the relationship between sensation and language is a juncture which always has within it an element of dissociation, a characteristic which he ascribes to all 'connections'. In the discussion of Butler's *Note-Books* we saw how his idea of 'shock' was transmuted into fiction in *Mrs Dalloway*. The novel is, in one of its aspects, an expansion of Butler's idea for an essay on 'The Sense of Touch'.[5] Also relevant here is an interesting discussion by Roger Fry in *A Sampler of Castile*, which Leonard and Virginia Woolf published in 1923, two years before *Mrs Dalloway*. Fry asks 'How can I suppose that I can hand over to you, through language, the faintest image of a single moment's physical sensation?'[6] Clearly, this is not possible, but there remains the desire to make language and art come as close as possible to sensation, or at least not to lose sight of the physical world altogether. Fry goes on to praise the Spanish words 'echar' and 'sacar' (that which you let go from you, and that which you pull towards you). He feels that they are better than their English equivalents 'let' and 'get' because they retain a 'kinesthetic quality'. He feels that the muscular effort in pronouncing the Spanish words somehow keeps them in touch with the physical actions out of which the more abstract ideas 'let' and 'get' have developed.

An attempt to convey Butler's sense of shock and Fry's kinaesthesia is an important element in *Mrs Dalloway*. In Virginia Woolf's circle there was a considerable interest in linguistics and she would probably have come across some of these ideas in her reading of Butler.[7] Leonard Woolf reviewed Jespersen's *The Philosophy of Grammar* along with *Four Words* by Logan Pearsall Smith, who was, indeed, a friend of the Woolfs.[8] Leonard Woolf entitles his review *Words* and points out that it is '...a curious thing with regard to writers that most of them seem to take no interest in the material in which they have to work. I call that material words...'[9] (Virginia Woolf was later to castigate Forster for exactly this fault of not saying enough about his medium in *Aspects of the Novel*.)[10] This background interest in language should be emphasised, I think, in opposition to a view generally held, that *Mrs Dalloway* is a Bloomsbury version of *Ulysses*. The value of stressing this more general linguistic background can be seen, perhaps, if we look at Owen Barfield's interesting study *Poetic Diction*. (There is no question of it being an 'influence', for it was published three years after *Mrs*

Dalloway.) Barfield traces the growth of linguistic research over the previous few years, and his remarks on the word 'cut' are helpful in analysing Virginia Woolf's novel. He criticises Jespersen by saying that although Jespersen finds language becoming more figurative as we look into the past, he sees it as *beginning* from monosyllables with *general* meanings. Barfield goes on to say:

a meaning may be 'perceptual' (that is to say, the word's whole reference may be to some sensible object or process) and at the same time 'general' or 'abstract'. . . It is just those meanings which attempt to be most exclusively material ('sensuel'), which are also the most generalised and abstract – i.e. remote from reality. Let us take the simple English word *cut*. Its reference is perfectly material; yet its meaning is at the same time more general and less particular, more abstract and less concrete, than some single word which should comprise in itself – let us say – all that we have to express to-day by the sentence: 'I cut this flesh with joy at this moment'. If it is impossible to cut a pound of flesh without spilling blood, it is even more impossible 'to cut'.[11]

Barfield draws on anthropology to illustrate the difference between concrete and abstract meanings: 'in some crude tongues, although you can express twenty different kinds of cutting, you cannot say 'cut'. . .[12] This insight, together with Butler's antithesis of cutting and joining (the knife and string which we saw in the earlier discussion), is a good introduction to one of the themes of *Mrs Dalloway*.

There are a great variety of divisive activities covered by the word 'cut', and many of these appear in the novel. Clarissa at the beginning of the novel goes to buy cut flowers for her party. Like her party, and for that matter, Clarissa herself, they will last only a short while, but they will be fresh and colourful during their brief life, not grey and 'cut and dried' like Holmes and Bradshaw (for whose sake Lady Bradshaw has 'pared and pruned' herself).[13] Clarissa goes herself for the flowers because Lucy has her work 'cut out' for her.[14] She feels that her portion of life has been 'sliced' when Lady Bruton cuts her (does not invite her to the luncheon party); Clarissa is 'cut' (hurt).[15] She is poised between exclusion and inclusion in life and hesitates to have any clear-cut opinion of her 'character' or that of her friends:

She would not say of any one in the world now that they were this or were that. She felt very young; at the same time unspeakably aged.

She sliced like a knife through everything; at the same time was out-side, looking on. She had a perpetual sense, as she watched the taxicabs, of being out, out, far out to sea and alone...and yet to her it was absolutely absorbing; all this; the cabs passing; and she would not say of Peter, she would not say of herself, I am this, I am that.[16]

She feels inclined to criticise Peter because he constantly plays with his pocket knife; she is glad she did not marry him, for his egoism would have cut her off from her private life, her own separate exist-ence, which her marriage to Richard allows. She does not spare his lady friend from the knife: 'She flattered him; she fooled him, thought Clarissa; shaping the woman, the wife of the Major in the Indian Army, with three strokes of a knife.'[17] Septimus, her double, believes that the world will cut him (deal him a blow with a whip), for he has become alienated from his fellow creatures by his madness:

Septimus Warren Smith, aged about thirty, pale-faced, beak-nosed, wearing brown shoes and a shabby overcoat, with hazel eyes which had that look of apprehension in them which makes complete strangers apprehensive too. The world has raised its whip; where will it descend?[18]

These different meanings of 'cut' are its objective, abstract aspect. They are related in the novel to its concrete, subjective significance – to the *sensation* of cutting or being cut. We saw in the discussion of Butler how Clarissa's stream-of-consciousness is suddenly inter-rupted by the explosion outside the florist's[19] and by the sudden ringing of the door bell.[20] In an attempt to give the immediate perception of life, to give that feeling which precedes the division into the 'cut' and the 'uncut', Virginia Woolf uses words and images of touch and movement. It is an attempt to give the very process of the world impinging upon our senses. Roger Fry's Spanish words are less neutral than the images of Virginia Woolf, for there is a self which pulls and pushes in his examples, whereas the combination of sensation and movement which I am speaking of here is much less sharply differentiated. The 'scraping' and 'grazing' which con-tinues throughout the novel is an attempt to capture that interaction between the self and world before the two have been separated. These images also move in that area between absolute connection and absolute separation, between inclusion and exclusion, which lie at the centre of the novel. In this way, images of scraping establish the affinity between the 'doubles' Clarissa and Septimus, who are themselves connected yet separate. Clarissa is convalescing and puts her irritation at her own ungenerosity quite naturally in terms of that physical pain which is its cause:

It rasped her, though, to have stirring about in her this brutal monster! to hear twigs cracking and feel hooves planted down in the depths of that leaf-encumbered forest, the soul; never to be content quite, or quite secure, for at any moment the brute would be stirring, this hatred, which, especially since her illness, had power to make her feel scraped, hurt in her spine; gave her physical pain, and made all pleasure in beauty, in friendship, in being well, in being loved and making her home delightful, rock, quiver, and bend as if indeed there were a monster grubbing at the roots, as if the whole panoply of content were nothing but self love! this hatred! [21]

Septimus, too, is ill, but as Clarissa moves towards the life of her party, he plunges deeper into mental illness, and the news of his death makes her return only a muted climax. These images of scraping are linked with the vibrations which we looked at briefly in the chapter on Butler. This is also true in the case of Septimus:

and Septimus heard her say 'Kay Arr' close to his ear, deeply, softly, like a mellow organ, but with a roughness in her voice like a grass-hopper's, which rasped his spine deliciously and sent running up into his brain waves of sound which, concussing, broke. [22]

These scraping images do convey the slightly oblique view of the world which Clarissa and Septimus share, but the physical sensation which is evoked does not simply 'mean' this point of view. There is a network of interconnected images which cannot, without a disturb-ing 'cutting' be abstracted from the context of the novel. The images graze against an obscure layer of existence where intuition and sensation and meaning are not quite separate. In this way, Clarissa and Septimus are linked in some obscure way to the official car: 'For the surface agitation of the passing car as it sunk grazed some-thing very profound.' [23] Later, the shock of Lady Bruton 'cutting' her causes similar vibrations in Clarissa: 'for the shock of Lady Bruton asking Richard to lunch without her made the moment in which she had stood shiver, as a plant on the river-bed feels the shock of a passing car and shivers: so she rocked: so she shivered'. [24] But the scraping does not mean simply a sense of exclusion, it is a feeling, a sensation which the reader is meant to share by means of this related imagery. In this passage the scraping is connected not with apartness from life, but inclusion and social interchange:

For this is the truth about our soul, he thought, our self, who fish-like inhabits deep seas and plies among obscurities threading her way between the boles of giant weeds, over sun-flickered spaces and on and on into gloom, cold, deep, inscrutable; suddenly she shoots to the surface and sports on the wind-wrinkled waves; that is, has a positive need to brush, scrape, kindle herself, gossiping. [25]

This wealth of cuttings and scrapings in the novel is an attempt to capture in language the richness and diversity of our intuitive and sensational life. Virginia Woolf constructs a keyboard on which there is a scale running from smooth cutting to rough scraping, from inclusion to exclusion, from sensation to abstract symbolism. This musical analogy, so important in the aesthetics of Charles Mauron, involves the whole question of autonomy in art which will be discussed in subsequent chapters.

That 'one way transparent intellectual reference' which Wimsatt sees in most discourse is similar to what Fry calls 'the practical vision of our instinctive life' in which 'we have no more concern after we have read the label on the object; vision ceases the moment it has served its biological function'.[26] When we react to sensations, persons and events, it is this kind of vision which we use. Refuting I. A. Richards' claim that our response to art is the same as our response to other situations, Fry posits an 'esthetic experience'. Art, like language, gains its value from arousing a different feeling from that which we experience in everyday life:

Now the crucial fact which appears to me to arise from the comparison of a number of these experiences which are the subject of our inquiry is that in all cases our reaction to works of art is a reaction to a relation and not to sensations or objects or persons or events. This, if I am right, affords a distinguishing mark of what I call esthetic experiences, esthetic reactions, or esthetic states of mind. [27]

And yet there is a problem here, for art clearly deals in some way with sensations, with the way in which the 'outer' world interacts with the 'inner' world of our consciousness. The artist cannot copy a pre-existing reality, and yet there is a constant struggle, which we can see in *Mrs Dalloway* to look behind the mirror of art and grasp the inmost form of the world. But the madness of Septimus Smith, and by association, of Clarissa, indicates that Virginia Woolf was well aware that, in Cassirer's words 'the thoroughly individual, singular perception which sensationalism and with it the skeptical critique of language sets up as a supreme norm, an ideal of know-ledge, is essentially nothing more than a pathological pheno-menon...'[28] Indeed, Virginia Woolf faced this difficulty in her own life.[29] Complete subjectivity is insanity, but objectivity gives too little of the 'truth' as seen by the individual. Cassirer states the problem in this way:

Always there remains an evident and distressing opposition: 'outer' and 'inner' never completely correspond. But these restrictions, which the artist must acknowledge, do not stop his efforts. He continues to create for he knows that it is only by doing so that he can discover and gain possession of his own self. His world and his true self can be had only in the shape which he gives to them.[30]

This belief that the artist does not describe a given, objective reality lies behind Fry's attack on the 'illusionists' and Virginia Woolf's on the 'materialists'. The art of Sargent and Bennett is untruthful be-cause it claims to be what it cannot possibly be, namely, a faithful copy of the 'real world'. According to Fry, what the artist can give us, and what we respond to, is a relation:

Our emotional reactions are not, I say, about sensations. This may at first sight appear paradoxical, because the arts seem to be peculiarly preoccupied with agreeable sensations, with relatively pure colours and pure sounds. But it is not difficult to see that, however valuable a pre-disposing and accompanying condition of esthetic apprehension such agreeably pure sensations may be, they are not essential, nor have we any difficulty in distinguishing between our response to sensations and our response to works of art. Those responses to sensation may be very rich and complex and tinged with emotion, but they are distinct.[31]

In responding to the images of *Mrs Dalloway* we certainly find this to be true, for our reaction is to the *relation* between different images of 'cutting' and 'scraping' and so on. Anything else would be merely a trick, such as providing sandpaper in the margin on which the reader could really scrape himself. And even this, in the context of a book, takes on a rhetorical meaning, as Sterne's amusing devices clearly show. We have a hint here as to why Virginia Woolf admired Sterne's work and why she saw him as a forerunner of the moderns.[32]

Fry continues his discussion by arguing that there can be no art which employs the sense of smell:

Thus a smell may, as Proust has admirably shown, produce a very profound response. By its associations in memory it may even excite a more poignant state of mind than many works of art, but we easily distinguish it from our feeling about a work of art. The evocations of smell are indeed so powerful that they would doubtless form the basis for an art similar to music in its deep emotional evocations, if only different perfumes could be perceived in relation one to another. It is this impossibility alone that deprives us of yet another art.[33]

This gives us a cue to examine *Flush*, which, being the biography of a dog, naturally confronts this very problem. Flush understands the world almost entirely through his sensations, particularly through smells. For the dog, the evocations of smell are powerful indeed:

The cool globes of dew or rain broke in showers of iridescent spray about his nose; the earth, here hard, here soft, here hot, here cold, stung, teased and tickled the soft pads of his feet. Then what a variety of smells interwoven in subtlest combination thrilled his nostrils; strong smells of earth, sweet smells of flowers; nameless smells of leaf and bramble; sour smells as they crossed the road; pungent smells as they entered bean-fields. But suddenly down the wind came tearing a smell sharper, stronger, more lacerating than any–a smell that ripped across his brain stirring a thousand instincts, releasing a million memories – the smell of hare, the smell of fox. Off he flashed like a fish drawn in a rush through water further and further. He forgot his mistress; he forgot all human kind.[34]

For the dog, smell takes precedence over vision – he is bored by the Apennines. As Fry points out, there is no relation established between the smells themselves; we can be given only a list of things associated with smells:

But as Flush trotted up behind Miss Mitford, who was behind the butler, he was more astonished by what he smelt than by what he saw. Up the funnel of the staircase came warm whiffs of joints roasting, of fowls basting, of soups simmering – ravishing almost as food itself to nostrils used to the meagre savour of Kerenhappock's penurious fries and hashes. Mixing with the smell of food were further smells – smells of cedarwood and sandalwood and mahogany; scents of male bodies and female bodies; of men servants and maid servants... [35]

How else, except by such a list, could Virginia Woolf convey the range of smells, which the dog perceives? One of the writer's difficulties is the deficiency in our vocabulary of smell, for although there are many words for what we see, there are only 'two words and one-half for what we smell'. [36] As the infinite gradation between roses at one end of the scale and dung at the other cannot be given directly, Virginia Woolf employs repetition in order to represent the bewildering diversity of the sensational world. A list of smells and repetition of the word 'smell' stands in place of the impossible direct evocation:

Love was chiefly smell; form and colour were smell; music and architecture, law, politics and science were smell. To him religion itself was smell. To describe his simplest experience with the daily chop or biscuit is beyond our power. Not even Mr Swinburne could have said what the smell of Wimpole Street meant to Flush on a hot afternoon in June. As for describing the smell of a spaniel mixed with the smell of torches, laurels, incense, banners, wax candles and a garland of rose leaves crushed by a satin heel... [37]

The repetition of the word 'smell' illustrates the difference between sensation and language, for as Cassirer points out, '... on the plane of sensory experience itself there is no " recurrence of the same"'. [38] And so Flush 'noses his way from smell to smell' for two more pages until we are told that 'Not a single one of his myriad sensations ever submitted itself to the deformity of words.' [39] It is true in a sense that language 'deforms' sensation, for the dog's sense of smell is much richer and more concrete than the words 'smell' and 'aroma'. The sensuous aspects of art and language are not significant. His portrait is simply a smudge to Flush, and speech and writing are merely simple sounds and black marks on paper:

When he heard her low voice syllabling innumerable sounds, he longed for the day when his own rough roar would issue like hers in the little simple sounds that had such mysterious meaning. And when he watched the same fingers for ever crossing a white page with a straight stick, he longed for the time when he too should blacken paper as she did. [40]

The Browning infant learns language and therefore its sensations become more and more distant. This might be seen as the knowledge which banishes us from Paradise, but Flush, living between the animal and the human worlds, feels the sword of flame:

But though it would be pleasant for the biographer to infer that Flush's life in late middle age was an orgy of pleasure transcending all description; to maintain that while the baby day by day picked up a new word and thus removed sensation a little further beyond reach, Flush was fated to remain for ever in a Paradise where essences exist in their utmost purity, and the naked soul of things presses on the naked nerve – it would not be true. Flush lived in no such Paradise. The spirit, ranging from star to star, the bird whose furthest flight over polar snows or tropical forests never brings it within sight of human houses and their curling wood-smoke, may, for anything we know, enjoy such immunity, such integrity of bliss. But Flush had lain upon human knees and heard men's voices. His flesh was veined with human passions; he knew all grades of jealousy, anger and despair. Now in summer he was scourged by fleas. [41]

With language, we move away from the 'naked soul of things'. In our perception of things we learn to read appearances and so are not bewildered, as Flush is, by changes of light or by mirrors and paintings:

Nothing in the room was itself; everything was something else. Even the window-blind was not a simple muslin blind; it was a painted fabric with a design of castles and gateways and groves of trees, and there were several peasants taking a walk. Looking-glasses further distorted these already distorted objects so that there seemed to be ten busts of ten poets instead of five; four tables instead of two. And suddenly there was a more terrifying confusion still. Suddenly Flush saw staring back at him from a hole in the wall another dog with bright eyes flashing, and tongue lolling! [42]

Although a book may be printed on fine paper and covered with an artistic wrapper, its value as literature is not enhanced in any way, as Roger Fry points out:

In literature there is no immediate sensual pleasure whatever, though it may be a favourable predisposing condition for poetry to be spoken by a beautiful voice. There is, of course, the pleasure of rhythmic utterance, but this is already concerned with relations, and even this is, I believe, accessory to the emotion aroused by rhythmic changes of states of mind due to the meanings of the words. [43]

The rhythmic changes in *Flush* come from the oscillation of the mind as it ponders the connection between sensation and meaning. It is the rhythm of ambiguity and paradox set up by imagining a 'human' animal which explores the middle ground where sensation is 'de-formed' into meaning. One of these ambiguities is synaesthesia. Things which are lighter in tone seem to move more quickly than darker material: 'Swiftly over the counters flashed yards of gleaming silk; more darkly, more slowly rolled the ponderous bombazine'.[44] The rhythm of the phrases accentuates this relation, the sound of the first part of the sentence giving an impression of speed compared with the pause and the heavy 'o' sounds of the latter part. Colour-smell and smell-sound synaesthesia eke out our miserable vocabulary of smell:

He devoured whole bunches of ripe grapes largely because of their purple smell; he chewed and spat out whatever tough relic of goat or macaroni the Italian housewife had thrown from her balcony – goat and macaroni were raucous smells, crimson smells.[45]

Here we reach the boundary of the relatively inarticulate senses of touch, taste and smell; in later chapters we will consider the highly complex visual sense.

in proportion as poetry becomes more intense the content is entirely remade by the form and has no separate value at all. You see the sense of poetry is analogous to the things represented in painting. I admit that there is also a queer hybrid art of sense and illustration, but it can only arouse particular and definitely conditioned emotions, whereas the emotions of music and pure painting and poetry when it approaches purity are really free abstract and universal. Do you see at all and do you hate it? The odd thing is that apparently it is dangerous for the artist to know about this. [4]

This final sentence is of crucial importance in trying to understand much modern art. Like many of Fry's hints, it points forward to a great deal of modern aesthetic speculation. Anton Ehrenzweig in *The Hidden Order of Art* [5] tries to examine this problem of the modern artist's awareness of his own processes. He points out that modern art has brought surface and depth sensibilities into open conflict, which results in fragmentation and a vicious circle of creative destruction too quickly becoming a mere device or mannerism. Here again is the tension between the outer and inner worlds which we saw in the previous discussion of 'representation'. Ehrenzweig believes that it is time for the outer world to be emphasised now – alienation rather than self-expression. The artist should now concern himself with events outside himself rather than his private mental experiences. We return inevitably to the age-old yet continuing problem of the way in which art holds a mirror up to nature. For Fry, the alternatives were not self-expression or alienation, but self-expression, which he also rejects, and tradition. He sees a pendulum movement in tradition between Raphaelite and Pre-Raphaelite art, or, to put it another way, between Classic and Baroque. If completely separated from each other, these two kinds of art fall into their respective faults: on the one hand an insipid 'ideal type', and on the other, a trivial illusionism. Holding the mirror up to nature involves, according to Fry, an avoidance of both these dangers:

And with that aloofness on the artist's part from any one emotional *parti pris*, there comes a wider range of sympathetic observation and the power of conceiving and visualising a number of distinct types with varying ranges of emotions. It is by such an art that the mirror is held up to nature; not by the construction of a single abstract type of ideal beauty, nor by the careful imitation of individuals, but by the construction of a world of perfectly realized and concrete types, more complete than any one individual, by which we apprehend, and to which we refer a number of individuals. [6]

This is the middle position between the merely typical and the entirely individual which Wimsatt calls the 'concrete universal'. Virginia Woolf wonders if this balance might not be possible in prose fiction: 'But also we desire synthesis. The novel, it is agreed, can follow life; it can amass details. But can it also select? Can it symbolise? Can it give us an epitome as well as an inventory?'[7] If we look closely at the way in which Fry uses the mirror image in this early work on Bellini we can see that his classical bias always makes itself felt. The looking-glass itself is not simply a copy of our ordinary experience; it can remove a scene from the sphere of practical activity, a requirement which Fry sees as the minimum for a work of art. We see things in a new and unfamiliar way: 'For here the landscape...has, by virtue of the carved marble frame which encloses it, something of the unfamiliarity and impressiveness of a landscape seen unexpectedly in a mirror.'[8] We can see from this that it is the *framing* which is all-important. A frame takes the scene out of the sphere of possible action, and therefore removes us from the everyday instinctive vision which is dominated by practical purpose. The mirror is important not because it reflects the world, but because it frames it. In normal vision we see things, in artistic vision we look at them. Looking into a mirror, argues Fry, is an imaginative act:

A somewhat similar effect to that of the cinematograph can be obtained by watching a mirror in which a street scene is reflected. If we look at the street itself we are almost sure to adjust ourselves in some way to its actual existence. We recognise an acquaintance, and wonder why he looks so dejected this morning, or become interested in a new fashion in hats – the moment we do that the spell is broken, we are reacting to life itself in however slight a degree, but, in the mirror, it is easier to abstract ourselves completely, and look upon the changing scene as a whole. It then, at once, takes on the visionary quality, and we become true spectators, not selecting what we will see, but seeing everything equally, and thereby we come to notice a number of appearances and relations of appearances, which would have escaped our notice before, owing to that perpetual economising by selection of what impressions we will assimilate, which in life we perform by unconscious processes. The frame of the mirror, then, does to some extent turn the reflected scene from one that belongs to our actual life into one that belongs rather to the imaginative life. The frame of the mirror makes its surface into a very rudimentary work of art, since it helps us to attain to the artistic vision.[9]

In *Between the Acts*, an understanding of the importance of the mirror and frame is essential for a full appreciation. Before looking closely at that novel, perhaps it would be as well to look at an area in which we can come face to face with the problem of autonomy, in Fry's introduction to and translations of the poems of Mallarmé.

Although not published until after Fry's death, these translations were begun before 1920. Virginia Woolf in her biography points out that 'Almost any guest invited to dine with him about 1920 would find him, manuscript in hand, seeking the right words with which to fill in a gap in his translation of Mallarmé.'[10] Seeking Mallarmé's 'miroitement en dessous' he would ask his guest to share what Virginia Woolf calls the 'dangerous delight' of trans-lating the poems. This atmosphere would clearly have an effect on her work, even though she has strong reservations about Fry's sweep-ing condemnation of much English literature which he felt did not achieve Mallarmé's 'purity'. A poet who is concerned with absence would obviously interest a writer who wishes to write a novel about silence, and whose characters so often see an emptiness at the heart of life. *The Waves* is in many ways a symbolist novel, and in the figure of Rhoda, Virginia Woolf embodies that area of ambiguity between 'purity' and 'sterility' which is one of Mallarmé's principal concerns. Fry believes that artistic purity stems from the self-awareness of the artist:

I wish to leave aside for the present the question of whether purity is desirable or not in a work of art, and will merely constate that in proportion as he becomes more conscious of his purpose the artist tends towards purity – tends to concentrate his attention and his powers on the detached esthetic emotions.[11]

The danger implicit in the idea of purity is indicated in *The Waves* by Rhoda's suicide. Purity in art is an extremely difficult problem. Martin Turnell in his review of Fry's translations sees Mallarmé's interest in language as an unhealthy means of evading experience. Fry's ideas of purity, he believes, are not merely a mistaken art theory, but a symptom of a deep perversion in our civilisation.[12]

Yet Fry was aware, as we have seen, of the danger of the artist being too aware of his own processes, and for Virginia Woolf, who also never accepted any simple idea of purity in literature, the problem was an intense and continuing one which she related to the illnesses in society as a whole. But this relationship between art and society is precisely the problem of the way in which we represent 'reality', a problem which is ever new for the artist and which Virginia Woolf tries to solve in aesthetic terms.

The problem of self-consciousness and autonomy is one which Fry, Virginia Woolf and Lawrence[13] have in common. Virginia Woolf's intense concern with this at the time of working on *Between the Acts* is evident when we look at two articles she was writing at that time, 'The Man at the Gate' and 'The Leaning Tower'. She describes the genesis of the latter article in her diary:

All books now seem to me surrounded by a circle of invisible censors. Hence their selfconsciousness, their restlessness. It would be worth while trying to discover what they are at the moment. Did Wordsworth have them? I doubt it. I read 'Ruth' before breakfast. Its stillness, its unconsciousness, its lack of distraction, its concentration and the resulting 'beauty' struck me. As if the mind must be allowed to settle undisturbed over the object in order to secrete the pearl.

That's an idea for an article.[14]

The writers of the thirties, she says, have developed 'auto-analysis' in reaction to the suppression of the Victorians.[15] Future writers, as she makes clear in the article itself, must develop the unconscious:

The leaning-tower writer has had the courage, at any rate, to throw that little box of toys out of the window. He has had the courage to tell the truth, the unpleasant truth, about himself. That is the first step towards telling the truth about other people. By analysing themselves honestly, with help from Dr Freud, these writers have done a great deal to free us from nineteenth-century suppressions. The writers of the next generation may inherit from them a whole state of mind, a mind no longer crippled, evasive, divided. They may inherit the unconsciousness which, as we guessed – it is only a guess – at the beginning of this paper, is necessary if writers are to get beneath the surface, and to write something that people remember when they are alone. For that great gift of unconsciousness the next generation will have to thank the creative and honest egotism of the leaning-tower group.[16]

This is close to Fry's notion that an artist must absorb tradition on a conscious level, then let it sink below the surface and finally come to fruition in his work in a transformed and unconscious way. It is dangerous for him to know too much about this process. John Middleton Murry describes this very well in his article 'The Future of English Fiction': 'Complete artistic self-consciousness is an exciting but a dangerous condition; it stimulates, but it also inhibits. It enables a writer to discern the quality necessary to the thing he desires to create; it also weakens his creative energy'.[17]

Fry's influence pervades *Between the Acts*. Bartholomew, like Fry, comments on the fact that the English are unresponsive to visual art.[18] There is a discussion about two contrasting portraits, each representing a different kind of art. One is the portrait of an ancestor, and represents all the elements which Fry was careful to distinguish from the truly aesthetic. It is a historical record and has only an antiquarian interest. Painted for a philistine, more interested in hunting than in art, it is not a genuine aesthetic object but what Fry would have called an 'opifact'. This Royal Academy anecdotal painting is contrasted with a genuine work, the formal excellence of which leads to silence:

He was a talk producer, that ancestor. But the lady was a picture. In her yellow robe, leaning, with a pillar to support her, a silver arrow in her hand, and a feather in her hair, she led the eye up, down, from the curve to the straight, through glades of greenery and shades of silver, dun and rose into silence. The room was empty.[19]

There follows a passage which, with its threefold repetition, mirrors the form of the novel as a whole. The image of the vase, a form which encloses nothing and which has no 'content', illustrates the central theme of Virginia Woolf's art – the emptiness at the heart of life which must be given shape and form: 'Empty, empty, empty; silent, silent, silent. The room was a shell, singing of what was before time was; a vase stood in the heart of the house, alabaster, smooth, cold, holding the still, distilled essence of emptiness, silence.'[20] If we want dates and likenesses and names, Buster the horse and Colin the hound, then we must look, not to art, but to 'opifact', to the portrait of the ancestor.

Virginia Woolf's concern with self-consciousness at the time of writing *Between the Acts* was reinforced by her reading of Coleridge.

In an essay written in 1940 she describes him as 'this Micawber' who 'knows that he is Micawber. He holds a looking-glass in his hand. He is a man of exaggerated self-consciousness, endowed with an astonishing power of self-analysis'.[21] In order to get to the truth, she continues, we must 'have it broken into many splinters by many mirrors and so select'.[22] In her pageant, Miss La Trobe tries to approach the truth in precisely this way. The disjointed language mirrors the meaning; it is a style, like that of Coleridge's letters 'pocketed with parentheses, expanded with dash after dash':[23]

Look! Out they come, from the bushes – the riff-raff. Children? Imps – elves – demons. Holding what? Tin cans? Bedroom candlesticks? Old jars? My dear, that's the cheval glass from the Rectory! And the mirror – that I lent her. My mother's. Cracked. What's the notion? Anything that's bright enough to reflect, presumably, ourselves?
Ourselves! Ourselves![24]

In order to articulate reality it must be broken up in this way – it gains its value by being different from inarticulate intuition and sensation. Miss La Trobe's idea of holding up a broken mirror and other reflecting fragments is an attempt, perhaps, to capture the effect of Matisse's art as described by Fry:

By the magic of an intensely coherent style our familiar every day world, the world where a model sat on a carpet, in front of Matisse's easel, has been broken to pieces as though reflected in a broken mirror and then put together again into a far more coherent unity in which all the visual values are mysteriously changed – in which plastic forms can be read as pattern and apparently flat patterns read as diversely inclined planes.[25]

We saw earlier Fry's idea of the importance of the frame. In *Between the Acts* Old Oliver achieves a framing effect by looking over the edge of his paper: 'But the breeze blew the great sheet out; and over the edge he surveyed the landscape – flowing fields, heath and woods. Framed, they became a picture.'[26] Later, Miss La Trobe tries to 'douche' her audience at the pageant with 'present-time reality'. However, a frame, that minimum requirement for art, is lacking. We can see quite clearly here that the simple presentation of 'reality' is meaningless. She tries to employ the most extreme kind of 'copy' theory in her play, but she finds that some exclusion is necessary:

But something was going wrong with the experiment. 'Reality too strong,' she muttered. 'Curse 'em!' She felt everything they felt. Audiences were the devil. O to write a play without an audience – *the* play. But here she was fronting her audience. Every second they were slipping the noose. Her little game had gone wrong. If only she'd a back-cloth to hang between the trees – to shut out cows, swallows, present time! But she had nothing. [27]

And so she hits on the idea of reflecting fragments, the form which Virginia Woolf chose for *Between the Acts* itself, with its mixture of poetry, narrative and drama. In its setting and mood, and in its consciousness of its own processes, the novel comes close to Chekhov's *The Seagull*, where Trepliov has much the same idea as Miss La Trobe in his play within a play:

There's a theatre for you! Just the curtain and the two wings and beyond it – open space. No scenery. You have an unimpeded view of the lake and the horizon. We'll raise the curtain at half past nine when the moon comes up. [28]

Books may be the 'mirrors of the soul', but they are tarnished, reflecting the soul bored. [29] In a splintered age, what could literature reflect apart from the mere jostling of accumulation and diversity:

'The library's always the nicest room in the house,' she quoted and ran her eyes along the books. 'The mirror of the soul' books were. *The Faerie Queene* and Kinglake's *Crimea*; Keats and the *Kreutzer Sonata*. There they were, reflecting. What? What remedy was there for her at her age – the age of the century, thirty-nine – in books? Book-shy she was, like the rest of her generation; and gun-shy too. Yet as a person with a raging tooth runs her eye in a chemist shop over green bottles with gilt scrolls on them lest one of them may contain a cure, she considered: Keats and Shelley; Yeats and Donne. Or perhaps not a poem; a life. [30]

All mirrors are tarnished, that is the penalty of living in an old civilisation with a notebook. The very complex nature of the 'framing' of reality in the novel can be illustrated by the following passage. Here, her eyes in the mirror hold Olwen's imaginary love life, which contrasts with the mundane reality of the dressing table and of her life with her husband. Then she looks above the mirror and through the window, where she sees her son, for whom she feels an undefined emotion, and this again is framed by the window:

She lifted it and stood in front of the three-folded mirror, so that she could see three separate versions of her rather heavy, yet handsome, face; and also, outside the glass, a slip of terrace, lawn and tree tops.

Inside the glass, in her eyes, she saw what she had felt overnight for the ravaged, the silent, the romantic gentleman farmer. 'In love', was in her eyes. But outside, on the washstand, on the dressing-table, among the silver boxes and tooth-brushes, was the other love; love for her husband, the stockbroker – 'The father of my children', she added, slipping into the cliché conveniently provided by fiction. Inner love was in the eyes; outer love on the dressing table. But what feeling was it that stirred in her now when above the looking-glass, out of doors, she saw coming across the lawn the perambulator; two nurses; and her little boy George, lagging behind?

She tapped the window. . . [31]

We see that ordinary fiction provides only conventional cliché and cannot describe the complexities of experience or the possibilities of life. Olwen's eyes form mirrors, and so we have the mirror-on-mirror effect which is so important in trying to understand the problem of autonomy in art. The mirror itself is a three-folded one, in keeping with the rest of the novel, which has a 'three-fold ply'. This 'triple melody' is the very form of the novel, its 'frame', and the whole is repeated in the parts down to the three-fold repetition of words throughout.

Blake might help us here to understand the very difficult connection between art and 'reality'. Roger Fry quotes approvingly his attack on 'facsimiles': Blake felt that painting needed to be rescued from the 'copy' theory:

'Poetry' says Blake, 'consists in bold, daring, and masterly conceptions; and shall painting be confined to the sordid drudgery of facsimile representations of merely mortal and perishing substances, and not be, as poetry and music are, elevated into its own proper sphere of invention and visionary conception?' [32]

'Elevated to its own proper sphere' certainly sounds like a plea for the autonomy of painting. Yet Blake was well aware of the problem involved here and his poem 'The Crystal Cabinet' is especially helpful in elucidating the passage from *Between the Acts* discussed above. Lytton Strachey quotes the poem as an example of Blake's attitude towards 'reason', which involves the poet, according to Strachey, in an inevitable dilemma: 'To be able to lay hands upon "the inmost form", one must achieve the impossible; one must be inside and outside the crystal cabinet at the same time.'[33] Strachey objects to the 'unreasonableness' of this position, but as I have been suggesting, it is this very tension between the inner and the outer worlds which is the basis of art; without these contraries there is no progression. The three worlds of the poem are the imaginary (innocence), the real (experience), and the world of the imagination which combines these two. These correspond to Olwen's inner love, outer love, and the undefined feeling which she has for her child. Blake's poem contains many of the ambiguities and problems raised by the idea of 'reproduction' in life and art:

> O, what a smile! a threefold Smile
> Fill'd me, that like a flame I burn'd;
> I bent to Kiss the lovely Maid,
> And found a Threefold Kiss return'd.

> I strove to sieze the inmost Form
> With ardor fierce & hands of flame,
> But burst the Crystal Cabinet,
> And like a Weeping Babe became –

> A weeping Babe upon the wild,
> And Weeping Woman pale reclin'd,
> And in the outward air again
> I fill'd with woes the passing Wind.[34]

Virginia Woolf has a similar triple way of looking at things in *Between the Acts*. An artist can try to break out of the crystal cabinet only by being extremely self-conscious, and this involves holding up yet another mirror, giving an infinite number of reflections, which confirm his prison all the more. An attempt to break out into the 'outward air' reinforces our sense of the enclosing medium, as in the passage from *Between the Acts*, where Olwen speaks of 'the cliché conveniently provided by fiction'. This kind of self-consciousness means that art begins to 'mirror the form of its own activity' (Cassirer's definition of the highest objective truth). It begins to turn inward in search of that greatest freedom which Kierkegaard describes as 'freedom defined in relation to itself'. When we seek this kind of freedom, repetition is welcomed, for it testifies to the eternal nature of freedom. But repetition has a double aspect and this introspection might lead us to a barren 'wilderness of mirrors'. It is for this reason that Virginia Woolf repeats, in a sketch which itself is subtitled 'a reflection', the warning: 'People should not leave looking-glasses hanging in their rooms.'[35]

6

Craftsmanship

As Virginia Woolf points out in her biography of Fry, his early training was in science, and he retained his interest throughout his life. He was concerned with trying to differentiate our responses to art and to science, which had, he felt, certain points in common. Abstract aesthetics, being analytical, will tend to stress those aspects of art which are most immediately available for analysis – the logical, geometrical and formal. Fry moved naturally in this direction, but was always aware of the danger of simply reducing art to these 'scientific' elements. Science and art do have certain ideas in common, such as 'unity' and 'balance', but there is something else in art which can only be hinted at:

Aesthetics hint at numberless analytical explanations which all leave the last essence uncaptured. Still, the general lines of approach are clear enough. What is common to most Florentine design, and what is hardly found out of Florence, is here raised to its highest efficiency – perfect plastic synthesis of the design, its extraordinary compression and its intellectual lucidity. It is through the compression of these ample forms within the picture-space, through the apprehended effect of momentum in their large and simple gestures that the mysterious significance of the whole appears.

And yet these explanations carry us but a step; they serve to classify rather than to explain. . . [1]

There is throughout Fry's work a tension between the scientific bent of his mind, which constructed analytical explanations, and his direct response to works of art which constantly modified his theories. It is a fruitful tension, which makes his work so valuable to us, and also one which does not make a false and sharp division between the artist and the critic, for he believed that the tension between 'science' and 'sensibility' was of fundamental importance to both. And so

throughout his criticism he is always drawing together the geo-
metric and the organic, vision and design, and so on, in order that
they might be more clearly distinguished. This dualistic method
reminds us immediately of Samuel Butler. In Fry's study of Matisse
these dualities are quite sharply focused.

In this work he says that painting has a dual nature, for it is
simply a diversely coloured surface, and yet it claims a relationship
with the three-dimensional world. As with language, painting gains
its value from its difference from the 'reality' which it symbolises.
This is its inspiration, yet the painter is tormented by the desire
to tell as much as possible about that reality. Because of this, Fry
claims that the artist 'has a double nature and double allegiance'.
He is pulled in different directions by the demands of vision and of
craft. The word 'craft' here indicates a change of emphasis from his
earlier idea of 'vision and design'. The new formulation is much
broader and more useful in its application to literature. Indeed he
speaks of Matisse in terms which could be applied almost directly
to Samuel Butler: Matisse's deformations are 'epigrammatic', and
by his use of 'paradox' and compression he achieves an equivocal
and evocative effect. He gives us 'exhilarating variations on the
theme of the dual nature of painting'. There is obviously a change
of emphasis in Fry's new duality, for whereas 'design' was honorific,
'craft' holds all sorts of dangers. It is not that he simply contradicts
himself; his criticism honestly reflects that same double nature which
he sees in Matisse's art. The pendulum swings from organisation
to sensibility and back again. He explains this in *Transformations*:

There are, roughly speaking, two avenues of approach to a complete
work of art. The artist may work through his sensibility towards the
perfect organisation of form, or he may attack the organisation of form
deliberately, and, when once he has mastered that, allow his sensibility
to give body and substance to what began as an abstraction. By either
route the way to a perfect fusion of the two elements, which is essential
to a complete work of art, is generally a long one – that is why so many
artists only achieve their real expression late in life – and what is done
by the way, will always be rather a work of promise than of fulfilment.
The influence of Cubism on modern art has caused many, perhaps the
majority, of the younger generation to adopt this second route – to
begin, that is, by a conscious study of organisation. [2]

Fry is increasingly insistent in pointing out the dangers of 'craft'.

In 1905, in his edition of Reynolds[3] he felt that he had to combat the notion of the romantic untutored genius by pointing out the importance of a rational research into the tradition of art. Increasingly, the power of technology was making itself felt and the danger was then seen to lie not in emotional romanticism so much as in over-exact geometrical exactitude. Speaking of a Chinese mirror in an article written in 1923, he says:

Whatever we may think of it from an aesthetic point of view, it becomes a fascinating object as a historical document. It throws a light on that varied and complex civilisation of the Han period, and reminds us that the spiritual forces which have in our own day accomplished so widespread a degradation of taste have always been latent in humanity, and have wanted opportunity rather than power to manifest themselves. That power the incredible mechanical ingenuity and inventiveness of Chinese producers seems to have occasionally supplied even in remote ages. Nothing, I think, is more paradoxical in Chinese art than the tendency to replace sensibility by mechanism in the art of a people whose sensitiveness to *matière* was so great as theirs. And yet, already in the exquisite bronze bowl of Chou times, now in the British Museum, the pattern round the rim is clearly impressed on the wax by a die, the impression being repeated successively round the border.

And the makers of our mirror have gone a step further; they have made the unnecessary and fatal step to which mechanism always invites. The Chou craftsman, though he stamped his pattern, allowed the artist who cut the die to exercise all his sensibility to form, but the Han manufacturer determined to go one better and make the cutting of the stamp itself as rigidly mechanical as rule and compass could accomplish. [4]

We see here that concern with rigid geometry and mechanical repetition to which he gives increasing attention in 'The Arts of Painting and Sculpture' and *Last Lectures*. The opposition of repetition and change, the antithesis which Butler sees as the very basis of aesthetics, as of life, is of crucial importance in understanding the art of Virginia Woolf, as we shall see later. Fry relates it directly to the nature of society. Enslavement to a rigid order in society or to an unchanging religious belief, or, in modern life, enslavement to the machine, all produce 'finished', 'craftsmanlike' and essentially dead art. The Chinese mirror, much of the art of ancient Egypt, the modern 'opifacts', are linked together by this idea of mechanical repetition. The danger of craftsmanship is that it retains overtones

62

of 'guile' and dishonesty, for the craftsman can, by his skill, over-come our distaste for the mechanically perfect and shop-finished by simulating the organic work of art by employing an equally mechanical 'roughness'. The more exquisite and skilled the craftsmanship, the greater danger:

Working, as the Japanese did, under the influence of an indiscriminate admiration of their Chinese masters, the pedantry and falsification which connoisseurship induces was a constant bar to genuine aesthetic expression, and we find, alongside of the vulgar love of mere technical skill and shop-finish, a curious inverse phenomenon. The connoisseur is quick enough to see the vulgarity of shop-finish and to recognise the value of those irregularities of texture which are the result of the artist's sensibility. But this led him to an inconsiderate admiration for works of art in which these qualities were deliberately simulated. Many Japanese works of art were made by extremely skilled craftsmen, consciously giving an air of rough or primitive craftsmanship to their creations. This sentimental insincerity has been the bane of Japanese art. We are of course familiar with this phenomenon in modern Europe. It appears to arise as an inevitable commercial exploitation of the recognition on the part of any society of the importance of aesthetic feeling.[5]

He explains earlier how the craftsmanlike leads inevitably to the machine-made and the total exclusion of the artist's sensibility. The artist must open himself to the direct impact of sensation, to the pain of living, to the possibilities of change. By extension, this applies to all professions, to all those who protect and ossify themselves by the accumulation of facts or of expertise. In *A Sampler of Castile* Fry speaks of the 'profession' of beggar: '. . .all professions deform the character,' he says, 'and there are many which produce uglier distortions'.[6] His earlier praise of *Don Quixote* reminds us that the self-awareness, the consciousness of convention as convention, and the mockery of 'expertise' are all contained in that remarkable work. Since its very beginnings, in its new mockery of romance, the novel has attacked and undercut craftsmanship and so pointed the way to freedom and life-giving change. And the alternative to expertise is not necessarily dilettantism; it is, according to Fry, the deepest assimilation of tradition. It should be so much a part of the artist that it comes to him not as something external to be emulated, but as unconscious promptings which direct his sensibility, his own personal vision. Fry believes in Academicism in the best sense, which accounts for the bitterness of his attack on the Royal Academy, which he believed had betrayed the tradition of painting by promoting mere craftsmanship. Lawrence was explicitly hostile to the Bloomsbury set, yet in this urgent awareness of the dangers of mechanisation he is at one with Fry. If we look closely at, say, *Women in Love* I think that we can see a real similarity in their deep concern with this aspect of modern life.

There is in that novel an attack on the familiar notion of character and the employment of a technique of character drawing similar to that which we saw earlier in Conrad's *Victory* and Virginia Woolf's *Night and Day*. The characters become animals. Birkin is a chameleon,[7] and the young man whom he and Ursula meet in the market is a rat;[8] Gerald is a frozen rabbit,[9] and so on. The characters are related to each other by being compared to the same animals – they are of the same species. In this way, Loerke is also a rat, like the young man who is about to be married. The characters thus have a hidden or unconscious relationship to each other, against which is set the mechanical rigidity of society's demands – 'Mr mine-owner Crich', and so on – where one is defined by one's function as part of the machine. It is an antithesis of organic and mechanical similar to that of Fry's criticism. Birkin copies a Chinese goose, an art in which Fry would have seen the sensibility of the artist conveyed in the calligraphy, and thereby the vitality of the animal expressed. This is set against the geometrical, industrial art of Loerke, which is full of the sadistic expressionism which Fry saw and abhorred in much German art.[10]

Like Fry and Lawrence, Virginia Woolf sees the danger of mechanical craftsmanship. As we saw in an earlier chapter, even her early novels are far from being merely 'well-made' in the traditional sense, although they have often been read as though that were her intention. In an early review of *Mummery* by Gilbert Cannan, she points out the danger:

Nineteen volumes cannot be brought from start to finish without learning whatever you are capable of learning about writing books; but the risk of learning your lesson so thoroughly is that you may become in the process not an artist, but a professional writer. You may learn to write so easily that writing becomes a habit.[11]

In an essay called 'Craftsmanship', Virginia Woolf points out the incongruity of speaking of 'craft' in relation to language, for its connotations of 'usefulness' and 'cunning' do not apply to words:

They hang together, in sentences, in paragraphs, sometimes for whole pages at a time. They hate being useful; they hate making money; they hate being lectured about in public. In short, they hate anything that stamps them with one meaning or confines them to one attitude, for it is their nature to change.

Perhaps that is their most striking peculiarity – their need of change.[12]

Like Fry, she points out the role of the unconscious, for it we use words too rationally, 'they fold their wings and die'.[13] Her dislike of 'professional airs and graces' in the use of words and writing of novels applies, by extension, to all kinds of professionalism and craftsmanship. In his famous Preface to *Eminent Victorians* Strachey explains that the traditional professional biography must be abandoned:

With us, the most delicate and humane of all the branches of the art of writing has been relegated to the journeymen of letters; we do not reflect that it is perhaps as difficult to write a good life as to live one. Those two fat volumes, with which it is our custom to commemorate the dead – who does not know them, with their ill-digested masses of material, their slipshod style, their tone of tedious panegyric, their lamentable lack of selection, of detachment, of design?[14]

As with all attacks on professionalism, it is a plea for 'freedom of spirit'.[15] In her 'biography' of Orlando, Virginia Woolf follows Strachey's mockery of the tedious traditional 'life':

The biographer is now faced with a difficulty which it is better perhaps to confess than to gloss over. Up to this point in telling the story of Orlando's life, documents, both private and historical, have made it possible to fulfil the first duty of a biographer, which is to plod, without looking to right or left, in the indelible footprints of truth; unenticed by flowers; regardless of shade; on and on methodically till we fall plump into the grave and write *finis* on the tombstone above our heads.[16]

In *Flush*, the biography of the Brownings' dog, this is taken a stage further, and connected with an attack on other trades and specialisms. We are given a mock genealogy of the dog. The jargon of different crafts has always been a rich source of comedy, and heraldry, with its 'coronets and quarterings, couchant and rampant with how many lions and leopards',[17] has been a constant butt, certainly since the time of *Don Quixote*:

Now turn your eyes to this other side, and there you will see, in front of this other army, the victorious and never vanquished Timonal of Carcajona, prince of New Biscay, who comes clad in armor quartered azure, vert, argent, and or. He bears on his shield a cat or on a field gules with a scroll inscribed *Miau*, which is the beginning of his mistress' name – according to report – the peerless Miaulina, daughter of Alfeñiquén, duke of Algarbe.[18]

Each trade has its craftsmanship which can become empty form, and so the object of satire. So, in *Flush*, the butlers have their 'laws of livery'.[19] The craft of research thesis writing does not escape, as we see in the notes at the end of the biography:

Some hold that Byron's dog went mad in sympathy with Byron; others that Nero was driven to desperate melancholy by associating with Mr Carlyle. The whole question of dogs' relation to the spirit of the age, whether it is possible to call one dog Elizabethan, another Augustan, another Victorian, together with the influence upon dogs of the poetry and philosophy of their masters, deserves a fuller discussion than can here be given it.[20]

This is simply a light-hearted treatment of a theme which Virginia Woolf felt deeply. Her concern with the nature of convention and awareness that the mechanical could crush the life out of human beings was as deeply felt as Fry's and Lawrence's.

In her sketch 'The Mark on the Wall', Virginia Woolf rejects professional knowledge in favour of the beauty of the world of sensations. The underwater image here points forward to those images of scraping in *Mrs Dalloway* which we discussed earlier and also prefigures the theme of anti-professionalism in that novel:

And what is knowledge? What are our learned men save the descendants of witches and hermits who crouched in caves and in woods brewing herbs, interrogating shrew-mice and writing down the language of the stars? And the less we honour them as our superstitions dwindle and our respect for beauty and health of mind increases...Yes, one could imagine a very pleasant world. A quiet, spacious world, with the flowers so red and blue in the open fields. A world without professors or specialists or house-keepers with profiles of policemen, a world which one could slice with one's thought as a fish slices the water with his fin, grazing the stems of the water-lilies, hanging suspended over nests of white sea eggs...How peaceful it is down here, rooted in the centre of the world and gazing up through the grey waters, with their sudden gleams of light, and their reflections – if it were not for Whitaker's Almanack – if it were not for the Table of Precedency![21]

Throughout its history the novel has been a repository of anti-professional feeling, from the craft of knight errant and the writing of romance to the double profession of Mrs Gamp. In *Mrs Dalloway* it is specifically modern science and medicine which are attacked. Both in her creative writing and her criticism, Virginia Woolf admires the creation of space and freedom by variations of perspective and point of view. The exaggeration involved in changing perspectives is a quality she admires: a teacup is a mountain, a face becomes a landscape, and so on. A strict 'sense of proportion' is the pre-eminent scientific virtue, for everything is given its exact quantitative weight. In *Mrs Dalloway* the brain specialist, Sir William Bradshaw, is the personification of scientific balance and is the very type of the professional man. Because of its static perspective, 'proportion' prevents the free play of the human spirit:

Proportion, divine proportion, Sir William's goddess, was acquired by Sir William walking hospitals, catching salmon, begetting one son in Harley Street by Lady Bradshaw, who caught salmon herself and took photographs scarcely to be distinguished from the work of professionals. Worshipping proportion, Sir William not only prospered himself but made England prosper, secluded her lunatics, forbade childbirth, penalised despair, made it impossible for the unfit to propagate their views until they, too, shared his sense of proportion – his, if they were men, Lady Bradshaw's if they were women (she embroidered, knitted, spent four nights out of seven at home with her son), so that not only did his colleagues respect him, his subordinates fear him, but the friends and relations of his patients felt for him the keenest gratitude for insisting that these prophetic Christs and Christesses, who prophesied the end of the world, or the advent of God, should drink milk in bed, as Sir William ordered; Sir William with his thirty years' experience of these kinds of cases, and his infallible instinct, this is madness, this sense; his sense of proportion.[22]

The psychiatrist becomes for Virginia Woolf the figure of hate which the doctor was for Molière. Bradshaw moulds his wife into his own pattern, and she produces pale shadows, illusions – photographs of a 'professional' standard. Craftsmanship and verisimilitude in art often go hand in hand, as we have seen from Fry's criticism. Proportion is 'objective', it is by definition that which people have in common, but because it is entirely communicable it can also be enforced. Another specialism, the 'profession of faith' acts in the same way as scientific professionalism:

But Proportion has a sister, less smiling, more formidable, a Goddess even now engaged – in the heat and sands of India, the mud and swamp of Africa, the purlieus of London, wherever, in short, the climate or the devil tempts men to fall from the true belief which is her own... Conversion is her name and she feasts on the wills of the weakly, loving to impress, to impose, adoring her own features stamped on the face of the populace.[23]

Conversion may be of this religious kind, as practised by Miss Kilman, but an equal danger is the scientific law of Sir William, the salmon fisherman who becomes the fisher of men. The clash between objective law and subjective experience is seen in the insanity of Septimus Smith. When we first meet him, Septimus commits a non-sequitur: 'The sun became extraordinarily hot because the motor car had stopped outside Mulberry's shop window.'[24] His is the 'logical' madness which accords with the fact that it was science gone mad in the First World War which caused his illness, shell-shock: 'A marvellous discovery indeed – that the human voice in certain atmospheric conditions (for one must be scientific, above all scientific) can quicken trees into life!'[25] He makes a desperate attempt to put his subjective pain into an objective scientific framework:

But what was the scientific explanation (for one must be scientific above all things)? Why could he see through bodies, see into the future, when dogs will become men? It was the heat wave presumably, operating upon a brain made sensitive by eons of evolution. Scientifically speaking, the flesh was melted off the world. His body was macerated until only the nerve fibres were left. It was spread like a veil upon a rock.[26]

Here again the tension between the inner and the outer worlds is described. How can Septimus communicate his feelings? The only scientific, objective form of communication is the proportion of Bradshaw, and so Septimus can only mutter 'Communication is health;

communication is happiness.'[27] Clarissa, Septimus' double, over-comes the problem by holding a party in which people can come together, and Virginia Woolf herself overcomes the problem by constructing a keyboard of symbols which includes Clarissa's party. We can see that the obsessive circling of Septimus' mind is indicated by the repetitions 'for one must be scientific' and 'communication. . . communication'. The whole problem of repetition is inextricably bound up with this question of craftsmanship, for the danger of craft is that it leads to mechanical repetition which crushes human vitality and the free openness to the scraping and grazing of the world of sensation and intuition.

7
Colour

Roger Fry's idea of the importance of colour changed greatly as his criticism developed. In 'An Essay in Aesthetics' written in 1909, he sees painting in terms of five basic elements, namely, line mass, space, light and colour. The last he believed to be least important, 'the only one of our elements which is not of critical or universal importance to life, and its emotional effect is neither so deep nor so clearly determined as the others'.[1] About the time of this essay, Fry was translating an article by Maurice Denis on Cézanne. This was to have a profound effect on the rest of Fry's criticism, not least in this matter of the importance of colour. It undercuts the whole idea of those 'elements' of painting which Fry outlines above. A few quotations from this essay, which Fry in his introduction calls 'masterly and judicious', will indicate the radical change in direction which Denis sees as Cézanne's contribution to art:

'There is no such thing as line,' he said, 'no such thing as modelling, there are only contrasts. When colour attains its richness form attains its plenitude.' (Quoted by E. Bernard.)

Thus, in his essentially concrete perception of objects, form is not separated from colour; they condition one another, they are indissolubly united. And in consequence in his execution he wishes to realize them as he sees them, by a single brush-stroke... *Forms* are for him *volumes*.

Hence all objects were bound to tell for him according to their relief, and to be situated according to planes at different distances from the spectator within the supposed depth of the picture. A new antinomy, this, which threatens to render highly accidental 'that plane surface covered with colours arranged in a determined order'. Colorist before everything, as he was, Cézanne resolved this antinomy by chromatism – the transposition, that is, of values of black and white into values of colour.

...He replaces light by colour. This shadow is a colour, this light, this half-tone are colours...

70

Volume finds, then, its expression in Cézanne in a gamut of tints, a series of touches; these touches follow one another by contrast or analogy according as the form is interrupted or continuous. This was what he was fond of calling *modulating* instead of modelling.[2]

Denis can describe Cézanne's aims and methods, but in trying to describe the final *effect* of his art, the critic inevitably comes up against the problem of the relationship between colour and language and the wider relationship, between criticism and art:

The attempt here made is to *define* the work of the painter: not to express its poetry. All the magic of words would not suffice to translate, for one who has never had it, the unforgettable impression which the sight of a fine Cézanne arouses. The charm of Cézanne cannot be described; nor could one tell of the nobility of his landscapes, the freshness of his chords of green, the purity and profundity of his blues, the delicacy of his carnations, the velvety brilliance of his fruit.[3]

Denis links together Mallarmé and Cézanne as classic artists, saying that they both refused to overstep the limits of their arts. The writer worked within the domain of pure literature, with sonority of words and rhythm of phrase, and Cézanne worked strictly within the boundaries of painting.[4] He goes on to point out the origin of Cézanne's art in the Symbolist movement and quotes Cézanne's own intention in his use of colour:

'I wished to copy nature,' said Cézanne, 'I could not. But I was satisfied when I had discovered that the sun, for instance, could not be reproduced, but that it must be *represented* by something else...by colour.'[5]

Perhaps this helps to explain Roger Fry's passion for Mallarmé's poetry. The statement of the problem in terms of 'representation' by colour rather than 'reproduction' allows comparisons to be made with the way in which colour is used in literature. (We must remember here that the criticism of visual art is itself limited to language.) Both the critic and the artist must face the problem of representation. Orlando recognises this when he tries to write poetry: he finds that 'Green in nature is one thing, green in literature another'.[6] The way in which we see things, our 'reality', is bound up with our conventions, with the way, for example, in which artists have previously represented colour; colour-words depend upon the kind of language game we happen to be engaged in, as Orlando discovers:

So then he tried saying the grass is green and the sky is blue and so to propitiate the austere spirit of poetry whom still, though at a great distance, he could not help reverencing. 'The sky is blue,' he said, 'the grass is green.' Looking up, he saw that, on the contrary, the sky is like the veils which a thousand Madonnas have let fall from their hair; and the grass fleets and darkens like a flight of girls fleeing the embraces of hairy satyrs from enchanted woods. 'Upon my word,' he said, (for he had fallen into the bad habit of speaking aloud), 'I don't see that one's more true than another. Both are utterly false.' And he despaired of being able to solve the problem of what poetry is and what truth is and fell into a deep dejection.[7]

If the colours of nature are not put into a meaningful relation, they simply repeat themselves in the most boring way, becoming, in 'The Searchlight' a symbol of boredom:

It seemed as if the day would never end. And he had no one to talk to – nothing whatever to do. The whole world stretched before him. The moor rising and falling; the sky meeting the moor; green and blue, green and blue, for ever and ever.[8]

Whenever there is a lack of any other sort of relationship Virginia Woolf's world falls into that hideous aspect of repetition which we see throughout *Between the Acts*: 'The flat fields glared green yellow, blue yellow, red yellow, then blue again. The repetition was senseless, hideous, stupefying.'[9]

In *Last Lectures* Fry differentiates between colour used in an intellectual way and that which has a more direct 'physiological' effect:

We have seen here the kind of question and answer which formal relations provide; and the same holds of colour, which has so often been regarded as in some way a source only of an inferior kind of pleasure. There is of course an immediate sensual pleasure in some colours, a pleasure perhaps of a direct physiological kind – some of Titian's reds and blues may give us this; but this is a very small part of Titian's effect, and some great colourists give us very little of this direct pleasure. Our pleasure then is of this intellectual kind. We say, why is that colour in this place? and the answer comes, Oh, because of that other colour in that place, and we feel at once with a shock of pleasure that the answer satisfies us.[10]

In an earlier article he contrasts the art of Van Gogh with Cézanne in this matter of colour, following Denis in seeing the importance of colour as design in Cézanne in contrast with Van Gogh's 'physio-logical excitement':

Van Gogh is adequately, perhaps a little too generously, represented. The sunflowers give him at his very best, with his passionate abandon-ment to certain colour sensations. Colour is with him an almost physio-logical excitement rather than as with Cézanne an aspect of formal design. He values certain colours almost in and by themselves, as children do when they talk of their favourite colour, and not as part of a necessary system of relations.[11]

The savouring of colour in this way is connected with the child's idea of the world. It is comparable to the enjoyment of the mere sound of words. Virginia Woolf relates the two in the following passage:

The nurses after breakfast were trundling the perambulator up and down the terrace; and as they trundled they were talking – not shaping pellets of information or handing ideas from one to another; but rolling words, like sweets on their tongues; which, as they thinned to transparency, gave off pink, green, and sweetness.[12]

On this physiological level, our feeling for colour is not linguistic, it is purely sensory, like a taste. The mere sound of words is of the same order. Feelings and sensations cannot be directly given in language, they can only be indicated, for example by this synaes-thetic image of the child's sweet which changes colour and taste as it dissolves. We saw in the earlier examination of the relation be-tween language and sensation that the two join together in this ambiguous territory which is explored by the half-human animal Flush. There can be no relation established between smells, as Fry points out. With colour, however, we may move away from simple sensation if we wish, and some sort of keyboard of colours can be constructed, some 'system of relations' as in Cézanne's art. Cassirer explains the difference by seeing a hierarchy leading from the indeter-minate senses of taste and smell, through tactile sensation, to the highest objective senses, vision and hearing:

Where language seeks to designate determinate qualities of smell, it is usually compelled to proceed indirectly, through substances which it has coined on the basis of other sensory-intuitive data. A classification, such as that of colour, into 'universal' names – red, blue, yellow, and green etc. – is not possible.[13]

Thus Virginia Woolf can give two of her sketches these 'universal' titles, 'Blue' and 'Green' and proceed to give a list of things which fall under each heading. The same thing could not have been done with smell. The sketches do not 'mean' anything, they are simply indications of that universal classification of colour which Cassirer speaks of, and a demonstration that such classifications simplify an illimitable range of shades, of 'things which are green' or 'things which are blue'. These sketches are at one end of a scale at the other end of which is the use of colour merely as a signal. Virginia Woolf describes this in an essay on Sickert:

Thus when seven or eight people dined together the other night the first ten minutes went in saying how very difficult it is to get about London nowadays; was it quicker to walk or to drive; did the new system of coloured lights help or hinder? Just as dinner was announced, somebody asked: 'But when were picture galleries invented?', a question naturally arising, for the discussing about the value of coloured lights had led somebody to say that in the eyes of a motorist red is not a colour but simply a danger signal. We shall very soon lose our sense of colour, another added, exaggerating, of course. Colours are used so much as signals now that they will very soon suggest action merely – that is the worst of living in a highly organised community.[14]

There are many intermediate notes on this keyboard of colour. The nearest to the use of colour as a signal is its use as an emblem, as when 'black' means 'evil' and so on. Less definite than this is when colour is used meaningfully, but ambiguously, to stand for inter-related, or even opposite meanings. Eisenstein composes his own 'rhapsody in yellow' in order to indicate the relationship between emotion and colour. In the minor key, he says, yellow is negative, as in T. S. Eliot's early poetry, where it is connected with sin. In Whitman, the 'golden', positive, side of yellow is more in evidence. Eisenstein relates these ambiguities to the colour green:

It becomes apparent that many characteristics we ascribe to the colour yellow derive from its immediate neighbour in the spectrum – green. Green, on the other hand, is directly associated with the symbols of life – young leaf shoots, foliage and 'greenery' itself – just as firmly as it is with the symbols of death and decay – leaf-mould, slime, and the shadows on a dead face.[15]

He goes on to point out that colours in a work of art do not have a predetermined meaning:

74

In art it is not the *absolute* relationships that are decisive, but those *arbitrary* relationships within a system of images dictated by the particular work of art.

The problem is not, nor ever will be, solved by a fixed catalogue of colour-symbols, but *the emotional intelligibility and function of colour will rise from the natural order of establishing the colour imagery of the work, coincidental with the process of shaping the living movement of the whole work.*[16]

In her sketch 'An Unwritten Novel', Virginia Woolf experiments light-heartedly with the use of colour in literature. She pretends that the need for plausibility prevents her from introducing bright colours into the story:

The fronds of aspidistra only partly concealed the commercial traveller – Rhododendrons would conceal him utterly, and into the bargain give my fling of red and white, for which I starve and strive; but rhododendrons in Eastbourne – in December – on the Marshes' table – no, no, I dare not; it's all a matter of crusts and cruets, frills and ferns. Perhaps there'll be another moment later by the sea.[17]

The story-teller denies herself the 'fling of red and white', but in literature this kind of exclusion is an inclusion: the rhododendrons are 'there', just as the 'unwritten' novel exists. The implausibility of the inclusion of bright colour is a mock reason for its 'exclusion'. The colours are both included and withdrawn because although their inclusion would relieve the drabness of the story, it is precisely this drabness which the storyteller is trying to convey. Here we have in essence the tension between the desire for colour, a gratuitous desire, and the need for a consistent 'meaning' in literature. The sketch as a whole is 'washed over as with a painter's brush of liquid grey'.[18] Virginia Woolf tries to attain, perhaps, a visual effect something like that described by Fry in speaking of a Corot painting:

The greys of horse and rider are all nearly neutral greys, and yet by the subtle contrasts of cooler and warmer variations seen against the cold, bluish greens of the foliage, they are as deeply satisfying to our sense of colour as the richest and most luxuriant colour orchestration; and then the one minute touch of red, and even that not really bright, sounds a culminating note in the delicate but resonant harmony.[19]

Virginia Woolf's touch of red is less than 'not really bright', it is 'not really there'. She cannot give us the cooler and warmer variations of grey, she can only give the universal colour word attached to various objects, such as the grey wool[20] and the grey landscape dim as ashes.[21] The emotional significance which Eisenstein speaks of is clearly established here. Grey means drabness or dullness, but its significance is quite complex, for although it is a 'colour', in contrast with the 'fling of red and white', it means 'lack of colour'. The sketch exploits different kinds of colour language; 'grey' moves in that borderland between silence and speech which Virginia Woolf so often explores. In her essay on Sickert from which we quoted earlier, she describes this kind of connection between literature and visual art:

But here the speakers fell silent. Perhaps they were thinking that there is a vast distance between any poem and any picture; and that to compare them stretches words too far. At last, said one of them, we have reached the edge where painting breaks off and takes her way into the silent land. We shall have to set foot there soon, and all our words will fold their wings and sit huddled like rooks on the tops of the trees in winter.[22]

Here we have, to illustrate her point, the wonderful image of the starkly visual and utterly silent rooks. She goes on to explore this area which is the territory of the imagist poets, but also, as she points out, of all great writers:

But since we love words let us dally for a little on the verge, said the other. Let us hold painting by the hand a moment longer, for though they must part in the end, painting and writing have much to tell each other: they have much in common. The novelist after all wants to make us see. Gardens, rivers, skies, clouds changing, the colour of a woman's dress, landscapes that bask beneath lovers, twisted woods that people walk in when they quarrel – novels are full of pictures like these. The novelist is always saying to himself how can I bring the sun on to my page? How can I show the night and the moon rising? And he must often think that to describe a scene is the worst way to show it. It must be done with one word, or with one word in skilful contrast with an-other. For example, there is Shakespeare's 'Dear as the ruddy drops that visit this sad heart'. Does not 'ruddy' shine out partly because 'sad' comes after it; does not 'sad' convey to us a double sense of the gloom of the mind and the dullness of colour? They both speak at once, striking two notes to make one chord, stimulating the eye of the mind and of the body. Then again there is Herrick's

> More white than are the whitest creams,
> Or moonlight tinselling the streams.

where the word 'tinselling' adds to the simplicity of 'white' the glittering, sequined, fluid look of moonlit water. It is a very complex business,
the mixing and marrying of words that goes on, probably unconsciously,
in the poet's mind to feed the reader's eye. All great writers are great
colourists, just as they are musicians into the bargain; they always
contrive to make their scenes glow and darken and change to the eye.
Each of Shakespeare's plays has its dominant colour. And each writer
differs of course as a colourist. Pope has no great range of colours; he is
more draughtsman than colourist; clear washes of indigo, discreet blacks
and violets best suit his exquisite sharp outlines – save that in the
Elegy to an Unfortunate Lady there is a mass of funeral black; and the
great image of the Eastern King glows, fantastically, if you like, dark
crimson. Keats uses colour lavishly, lusciously, like a Venetian. In the
Eve of St. Agnes he paints for lines at a time, dipping his pen in mounds
of pure reds and blues. Tennyson on the other hand is never luscious;
he uses the hard brush and the pure bright tints of a miniature painter.
The Princess is illuminated like a monk's manuscript: there are whole
landscapes in the curves of the capital letters. You almost need a magni-
fying glass to see the minuteness of the detail.[23]

This essay does indicate how wide ranging and detailed was Virginia
Woolf's interest in the use of colour in literature. In the following
pages I will try to show that in her novel *The Waves* she uses colour
in quite a new way, a use which corresponds to Cézanne's art as
described in that article by Denis with which this discussion began.

As we saw earlier, Fry translated Denis's essay in 1909, and it
had a radical effect on his view of the importance of colour in art.
Many of the insights in that essay are incorporated in Fry's important later essay 'Plastic Colour' in *Transformations*. The important
function he there assigns to colour is helpful in interpreting Virginia
Woolf's use of colour in *The Waves*. Tennyson's colour is like a
monk's manuscript, her own is like that of the Post-Impressionists.
In his essay, Fry points out that Primitive artists did not regard
colour as anything more than mere decoration:

colour was hardly regarded as expressive of any feelings about the
visible three-dimensional world of actual life. So far as these were given
it was by the general disposition and character of the forms. Colour
was essentially an addition, an ornament and embroidery of the linear
design calculated to make it more attractive but not more expressive.[24]

Fry's great interest in Primitive art in the early part of his career might explain why he regarded colour as less important in his early criticism. The greater importance which he gradually attached to colour is reflected in his view of the overall development of art:

From that day to this one may trace a gradual tendency towards a view of colour as an inherent part of the expressive quality of form, a tendency to recombine into a single indissoluble whole all the aspects of form instead of proceeding by the schematic division into line, shade and colour. That tendency has doubtless suffered many fluctuations, but on the whole it has persisted.[25]

He finds that great artists even in early times had in fact instinctively used colour in a more important way, though they occasionally reverted to a 'childish delight in pure primary colours'.[26] But this general historical trend was not smooth and uninterrupted:

But this process of the gradual identification of colour with plastic and spatial design has always been liable to interruptions, and for a reason that is natural enough. There is almost inevitably a conflict between the decorative and plastic uses of colour. It is yet another aspect of the incessant tension between the organisation of a picture upon the surface and its organisation in space.[27]

Here again is the duality which is constant throughout Fry's criticism: that between 'the hollow and the boss', which, since his early edition of Reynolds' *Discourses* in 1905, he had seen as the basis of all visual art. The Impressionists used colour expressively but 'their extreme preoccupation with atmospheric effects tended to destroy any clear and logical articulation of volumes within the picture space'.[28] This gradual increasing importance of colour culminates in the art of Cézanne:

It was here that Cézanne intervened. He had actually learned from Pissaro the Impressionist doctrine and practice, but it did not satisfy his passionate curiosity about plastic expression. He allowed the Impressionist observations to influence him whenever they assisted the statement of plastic relations, but his central theme was never the *effect* but the harmonic sequences of planes. Undoubtedly Impressionism allowed him to rely on colour to express these to an extent which had never been possible before. He even gave the preference to colour transitions over transitions of light and dark in contradistinction to Rembrandt. In fact, he found certain colour sequences which expressed directly these

78

sequences wherever they approach the critical phase of the contour of a volume, and in his water-colours he often confines himself to a statement of them.

Thus with Cézanne colour has ceased to play any separate *rôle* from drawing. It is an integral part of plastic expression.[29]

Cézanne, then, uses colour to create space. Let us add to the discussion Mauron's opinion that the psychological complex in literature corresponds to volume in the visual arts. He states that 'as the painter creates a spatial being, the writer creates a psychological being'.[30] In *The Waves* Virginia Woolf uses colour in an attempt to create psychological volume and at the same time give the idea of organisation on the surface of the canvas by means of the interludes.

It might be interesting to look first at those aspects of the novel which are more simply Impressionist. In this kind of vision, forms and contours are distorted and eliminated. Detachment from the practical world is one of the first requirements of Impressionist art. According to Fry, 'they upheld, more categorically than ever before, the complete detachment of the artistic vision from the values imposed on vision by everyday life'.[31] This everyday vision gives us the familiar world of 'fact', whereas detachment gives us an unfamiliar vision which we feel to be closer to the reality of direct sensation. This feeling of detachment comes from the strange qualities of light which are exploited by the Impressionists. Fry discussed the way in which Monet looked at the unfamiliar aspects of things and noted the changes of local colour due to different sources of light.[32] In *The Waves* we see things in a half-light, as if beneath waves. Our vision seems to pierce through thick air as the light changes and objects lose their familiar contours:

'Look,' said Rhoda; 'listen. Look how the light becomes richer, second by second, and bloom and ripeness lie everywhere; and our eyes, as they range round this room with all its tables, seem to push through curtains of colour, red, orange, umber and queer ambiguous tints, which yield like veils and close behind them, and one thing melts into another.'[33]

The Impressionists regarded objects as being important only for the way in which they reflect or absorb light. Things are distorted by the angle of the light falling upon them: 'Here lay knife, fork and glass, but lengthened, swollen, and made portentous.'[34] Throughout the novel solid tableware is lengthened or converted into light in this way. The apparent distortion is in fact a close record of their bare visual appearance when we set aside our conceptual vision and no longer see objects as 'useful': 'And every moment he seems to pump into this room this prickly light, this intensity of being, so that things have lost their normal uses – this knife-blade is only a flash of light, not a thing to cut with. The normal is abolished.'[35] These impressionist elements do exist in the novel, but seen as a whole the visual effects go beyond this. The interludes in *The Waves* move, like Monet's *Water Lilies*, from morning to sunset, but they are only part of the novel. We can trace in the visual aspects of Virginia Woolf's novels that same development which Fry saw when he described the movement from Impressionism to Post-Impressionism; Monet was prepared to restate the visual complexity in *Water Lilies*, Cézanne wanted to use this complexity as a basis for new constructions.[36] It is these new constructions which I wish to examine now in terms of the novel.

As Bernard points out, the use of colour in literature involves the whole question of the relationship between language and 'reality':

But how describe the world seen without a self? There are no words. Blue, red – even they distract, even they hide with thickness instead of letting the light through. How describe or say anything in articulate words again? – save that it fades, save that it undergoes a gradual transformation, becomes, even in the course of one short walk, habitual – this scene also.[37]

The mere articulation of the words 'red' and 'blue' certainly does not 'let the light through', but language might be able to create a relation similar to that established by colours in a painting. This can be illustrated from *The Waves* by the different languages of colour used by the characters. The relationship between these characters, between their 'psychological volumes', is indicated by their first speeches. Susan sees simple slabs of colour merely juxtaposed: '"I see a slab of pale yellow," said Susan, "spreading away until it meets a purple stripe."'[38] Jinny, on the other hand, uses words which have overtones of richness, and they are here twisted into an object which itself suggests decorative opulence: '"I see a crimson tassel," said Jinny, "twisted with gold threads."'[39] This use of colour accords with the nature of these characters. Susan has simple loves and hates. She is close to nature in her life on the farm and the simple repetitions of farm life and of the seasons find expression in the primary green and yellow which are the essential landscape colours. The repetition of these colours is described in *Between the Acts* as 'hideous' and 'stupefying'[40] but Susan is lulled into a sense of secure contentment. Her simple child-like preference for slabs of colour is similar to that ascribed by Fry to Primitive artists, or to Van Gogh, perhaps. Susan's attitude is contrasted with Bernard's phrase-making: '"I see the beetle," said Susan, "It is black, I see; it is green, I see; I am tied down with single words. But you wander off; you slip away; you rise up higher, with words and words in phrases."'[41] Susan describes abstract qualities in terms of these simple colours: 'yellow warmth',[42] 'green air'[43] and 'blue view'.[44] When she uses a compound colour word it is connected with her life on the farm, as in 'snail-green'.[45] Jinny, on the other hand, frequently uses compounds, but these are not connected with nature. On the rare occasion when she does use such a description, 'grass-green',[46] it is in order to describe *Susan*'s eyes. Jinny prefers the city to the country, and loves the trappings of society life. Her colours are associated, then, not with nature and sensations, but with society and objects, as in 'pearl-grey',[47] 'coffee-coloured'[48] and 'wine coloured'.[49]

The establishment of this relationship between Jinny and Susan is only one of the uses of colour in the novel. The predominant colours associated with Rhoda are white and grey. Like the 'grey' which we examined in 'An Unwritten Novel', this is more an absence of colour than an actual colour. 'White' is extremely ambiguous, implying purity, but also sterility and death. Bernard in his summing up at the end of the novel, connects Rhoda simply with grey:

Rhoda came wandering vaguely. She would take advantage of any scholar in a blowing gown, or donkey rolling the turf with slippered feet to hide behind. What fear wavered and hid itself and blew to a flame in the depths of her grey, her startled, her dreaming eyes?...The willow as she saw it grew on the verge of a grey desert where no bird sang.[50]

But we should remember that Bernard's picture of the characters at the end of the novel must be checked against the experience which we have shared with each of them throughout the novel. Rhoda herself anticipates Bernard's treatment:

What dissolution of the soul you demanded in order to get through one day, what lies, bowings, scrapings, fluency and servility! How you chained me to one spot, one hour, one chair, and sat yourselves down opposite! How you snatched from me the white spaces that lie between hour and hour and rolled them into dirty pellets and tossed them into the waste-paper basket with your greasy paws. Yet those were my life.[51]

We remember here that Bernard, the phrase-maker, had rolled his bread into grey pellets and called them people.[52] He neglects the white spaces in Rhoda's life, and these are much more important to her than the grey; but the white moments can be lived only for a brief spell, and then the deadly grey returns:

June was white. I see the fields white with daisies, and white with dresses; and tennis courts marked with white. Then there was wind and violent thunder. There was a star riding through clouds one night, and I said to the star, 'Consume me.' That was at midsummer, after the garden party and my humiliation at the garden party. Wind and storm coloured July. Also, in the middle, cadaverous, awful, lay the grey puddle in the courtyard, when, holding an envelope in my hand, I carried a message. I came to the puddle. I could not cross it. Identity failed me. We are nothing, I said, and fell. I was blown like a feather, I was wafted down tunnels. Then very gingerly, I pushed my foot across. I laid my hand against a brick wall. I returned very painfully, drawing myself back into my body over the grey, cadaverous space of the puddle. This is life then to which I am committed.[53]

Grey and white are connected by other characters with death, Bernard seeing an elephant 'white with maggots'[54] and Neville, the dead man whose 'jowl was white as a dead codfish'.[55] This is the deathly aspect of whiteness, for Bernard and Neville fail to see the hard purity of Rhoda's attitude. Louis, on the other hand has a secret affinity with her, and understands this emptiness which is at once pure sterility and yet pure freedom:

And as she stares at the chalk figures, her mind lodges in those white circles; it steps through those white loops into emptiness, alone. They have no meaning for her. She has no answer for them. She has no body as the others have. And I, who speak with an Australian accent, whose father is a banker in Brisbane, do not fear her as I fear the others.[56]

In her use of white in connection with Rhoda, Virginia Woolf is

82

exploiting the area between emptiness and purity which Mallarmé explores in his poems. In his introduction to Fry's translations of the poems, Mauron explains this use of white. Speaking of 'Nénuphar Blanc' he says:

Like the Faun, the oarsman (wearing, no doubt, a 'boater', that 'straw halo') obtains no real satisfaction; like the Faun, he is consoled by the 'hollow whiteness' of a dream. And once more the name of Freud rises to our lips. Observe by what incomparable sleight of artistic genius the whiteness, silence, emptiness, painful obsession of the early poems, at the period when the 'virgin paper' cruelly represented to the poet his own sterility, are transformed to the supreme ideal. The obsession persists, but its sign is changed; from painful it has become pleasant.[57]

Rhoda is obsessed, like Mallarmé, with *absence*. As a child, she had shaken white petals in a bowl of water, imagining their wreck,[58] and this symbolises her own sense of herself as being the spume of the waves which stamp and stamp throughout the novel: 'I am the foam that sweeps and fills the uttermost rims of the rocks with whiteness; I am also a girl, here in this room.'[59] Eventually she is overwhelmed in the bareness and whiteness of suicide. Throughout we are reminded of the poem of Mallarmé which Fry translates as 'To the Overwhelming Blackness Husht':

> To the overwhelming blackness husht
> Base of lava and basalt
> Up to the echoes enslaved
> By a virtueless trump
>
> What sepulchral shipwreck (you
> Know it, foam, but only slaver)
> Supreme one among the flotsam
> Abolished the disclad mast
>
> Or that which furious (in default
> Of some high perdition
> With all the vain abyss let loose)
>
> In the so white dragging hair
> Will have drowned in niggard wise
> Some young siren's infant flank.[60]

Mauron's commentary on the poem helps to illuminate the role of

Rhoda in *The Waves*. He says 'The fundamental construction, with an assured poetic logic, gives an impression of silence and overwhelming disaster, an impression preceding any explanation.'[61]

In the constant tension between the flat canvas and the created picture space, Fry sees colour as performing a double function – it can be both 'plastic' and 'decorative'. We have been investigating the plastic use of colour in *The Waves*, colour used to establish what Mauron and Fry call 'psychological volumes'. The interludes in the novel are in part an attempt to assert the surface of the canvas, where colour is used 'decoratively'. In the following interlude the same colours, white and grey, are clearly associated with Rhoda, but by being placed in an interlude, they are removed from psychological depth and are seen as a 'surface' pattern: 'Now the sun had sunk. Sky and sea were indistinguishable. The waves breaking spread their white fans far out over the shore, sent white shadows into the recesses of sonorous caves and then rolled back sighing over the shingle.'[62] The interlude is then related to the impressionist element of light:

The precise brush stroke was swollen and lop-sided; cupboards and chairs melted their brown masses into one huge obscurity. The height from floor to ceiling was hung with vast curtains of shaking darkness. The looking-glass was pale as the mouth of a cave shadowed by hanging creepers.[63]

As the sun sinks we are again in the realm of absence, here, of the absence of colour which is established and reinforced by the repetition of the word 'darkness':

As if there were waves of darkness in the air, darkness moved on, covering houses, hills, trees, as waves of water wash round the sides of some sunken ship. Darkness washed down streets, eddying round single figures, engulfing them; blotting out couples clasped under the showery darkness of elm trees in full summer foliage. Darkness rolled its waves along grassy rides and over the wrinkled skin of the turf, enveloping the solitary thorn tree and the empty snail shells at its foot. Mounting higher, darkness blew along the bare upland slopes, and met the fretted and abraded pinnacles of the mountain where the snow lodges for ever on the hard rock even when the valleys are full of running streams and yellow vine leaves, and girls, sitting on verandahs, look up at the snow, shading their faces with their fans. Them, too, darkness covered.[64]

8

Space: 'hollowing out a canvas'

A number of critics have pointed out the spatial effects in Virginia Woolf's work. William Troy, for example, makes the following unfavourable remarks on her first novel, *The Voyage Out*:

But already one can observe a failure or reluctance to project character through a progressive representation of motives, which provides the structure in such a novelist as Jane Austen, for example, whom Mrs Woolf happens to resemble most in this novel. For an ordered pattern of action unfolding in time Mrs Woolf substitutes a kind of spatial unity (the setting is a yacht at sea and later a Portuguese hotel), a *cadre*, so to speak, within which everything – characters, scenes and ideas – tends to remain fixed and self-contained.[1]

Troy is quite right in seeing a spatial element in the novel, but his interpretation is not adequate. In *The Voyage Out* space and perspective are linked with the development of the main character, Rachel. Her voyage out towards an understanding of the narrowness of her past life is symbolised by changes in her spatial perspective. Her education begins with a simple dose of relativism:

The people in ships, however, took an equally singular view of England. Not only did it appear to them to be an island, and very small island, but it was a shrinking island in which people were imprisoned. One figured them first swarming about like aimless ants, and almost pressing each other over the edge; and then, as the ship withdrew, one figured them making a vain clamour, which, being unheard, either ceased, or rose into a brawl. Finally, when the ship was out of sight of land, it became plain that the people of England were completely mute. The disease attacked other parts of the earth; Europe shrank, Asia shrank, Africa and America shrank, until it seemed doubtful whether the ship would ever run against any of those wrinkled little rocks again. But, on the other hand, an immense dignity had descended upon her; she was an inhabitant of the great world, which has so few inhabitants, travelling all day across an empty universe, with veils drawn before her and behind.[2]

The passengers on the great liners see the *Euphrosyne* as a wretched little boat, and the people on board as insects.[3] But when it comes into harbour it is a ship overshadowing much smaller boats. This simple juxtaposition of the large and the small symbolises a change in the heroine's psychological point of view; for Rachel, 'the end of the voyage meant a complete change of perspective'.[4] Helen Ambrose, Rachel's guide in the voyage towards maturity, sees landscapes in the fire, a constant symbol of the large in the small.[5] Rachel moves in this direction as she puts civilisation into perspective:

'Towns are very small,' Rachel remarked, obscuring the whole of Santa Marina and its suburbs with one hand. The sea filled in all the angles of the coast smoothly, breaking in a white frill, and here and there ships were set firmly in the blue.[6]

The spatial effects in this novel, then, have the clear psychological function of illustrating the broadening of Rachel's mind. Troy goes on in his article to contrast the symbolic novel with the traditional novel which has a clear chronological development and a story:

The objection to the lyrical method in narrative is that it renders impossible the peculiar kind of interest which the latter is designed to supply. By the lyrical method is meant the substitution of a group of symbols for the orderly working-out of a motive or a set of motives which has constituted the immemorial pattern of narrative art. Perhaps the simplest definition of symbols is that they are things used to stand for other things; and undoubtedly the most part of such a definition is the word 'stand'. Whatever operations of the imagination have gone on to produce them, symbols themselves become fixed, constant, and static. They may be considered as the end-results of the effort of the imagination to fix itself somewhere in space. The symbol may be considered as something *spatial*.[7]

The achievement of the sense of the 'moment', of the instantaneous effect of a picture is clearly one of Virginia Woolf's aims and to do this she has to break up the temporal sequence. In her work, with help from Roger Fry's criticism, we have a unique opportunity of examining spatial form and symbolism in the novel.

The title of this chapter is taken from a remark of Seurat which Fry often quotes, that painting is 'the art of hollowing out a canvas'.[8] Seurat's real subject, says Fry, is space, which he creates partly by his use of painted frames. 'The function of a frame', says Fry, 'is to cut off the imagined picture space from the actual space of the room.'[9] This idea of 'picture space' is in accord with what Susanne Langer calls 'virtual space':

The answer is, I think, that the space in which we live and act is not what is treated in art at all. The harmoniously organised space in a picture is not experiential space, known by sight and touch, by free motion and restraint, far and near sounds, voices lost or re-echoed. It is an entirely visual affair; for touch and hearing and muscular action it does not exist. For them there is a flat canvas, relatively small, or a cool blank wall, where for the eye there is deep space full of shapes. This purely visual space is an illusion, for our sensory experiences do not agree on it in their report. Pictorial space is not only organised by means of colour (including black and white and the gamut of grays between them), it is created; without the organising shapes it is simply not there. Like the space 'behind' the surface of a mirror, it is what the physicists call 'virtual space' – an intangible image.[10]

Of course, space is not the same thing in literature as in visual art. But as we saw in the last chapter, on colour, Virginia Woolf tries to find a literary equivalent for visual effects. Literal space in literature can only be created by a typographical trick, as in the following passage from *Orlando*:

For it has come about, by the wise economy of nature, that our modern spirit can almost dispense with language; the commonest expressions do, since no expressions do; hence the most ordinary conversation is often the most poetic, and the most poetic is precisely that which cannot be written down. For which reasons we leave a great blank here, which must be taken to indicate that the space is filled to repletion.

After some days more of this kind of talk...[11]

This, of course, is not 'virtual' or picture space. It is simply another way of saying, as Virginia Woolf does in an essay, that 'There is an astonishing number of things that never get into novels at all and yet are of the salt of life...'[12] Like Sterne's devices, it is a way of marking the boundaries of language.

Another typographical device is the use of dots. Like the blank space in *Orlando* it is used in an unserious way in *A Room of One's Own*: 'For truth...these dots mark the spot where, in search of truth, I missed my turning up to Fernham.' Shiv Kumar[13] sees the use of dots as one of the typical devices of the stream-of-consciousness novel. He is thinking of their use, not in the spatial sense we are describing here, but in the way which Virginia Woolf herself describes in her review of Vernon Lee's *The Sentimental Traveller*. There, she sees dots as a way of opening the mind to impressions:

The dots are a characteristic device, and part of an artistic system that prevails throughout. If only, in travelling, you will open your mind to receive all impressions and force your imagination to track down the most fugitive of suggestions, something charming and valuable, because original, will be recorded. This is perhaps the course that any sensitive mind adopts naturally though it does not always go on to trace it out upon paper.[14]

Dorothy Richardson also uses the device in this psychological manner, to suggest the tenuousness with which one thought is joined to another. Virginia Woolf often uses dots, however, in a different manner, to suggest space. The idea of disconnected movements within a landscape is given in this passage from *Jacob's Room*, a novel full of the evocation of space:

A window tinged yellow about two feet across alone combated the white fields and the black trees...At six o'clock a man's figure carrying a lantern crossed the field...A raft of twigs stayed upon a stone, suddenly detached itself, and floated towards the culvert...A load of snow slipped and fell from a fir branch...Later there was a mournful cry...A motor car came along the road shoving the dark before it... The dark shut down behind it... Spaces of complete immobility separated each of these movements.[15]

Here, Virginia Woolf's use of dots is clearly visual, temporal and spatial rather than psychological. Her sketch 'The Searchlight' contains a striking illustration of this. Here the dots simulate the movement of a telescope across a landscape:

'He focussed it,' she said. 'He focussed it upon the earth. He focussed it upon a dark mass of wood upon the horizon. He focussed it so that he could see...each tree...each tree separate...and the birds...rising and falling...and a stem of smoke...there...in the midst of the

trees...And then...lower...lower...(she lowered her eyes)...
there was a house...[16]

This passage contains two of the images which Virginia Woolf uses
throughout her work to present the idea of space: birds rising and
falling and smoke drifting. We must examine now the significance
of space, and once again the writings of Fry are of assistance here.

The function of colour in literature and painting was investigated
in the last chapter where I suggested its underlying significance in
the two arts. In Fry's criticism it was clear that colour was primarily
important in establishing a *relation*, either in depth or on the surface
of the canvas, and this helped to explain Virginia Woolf's use of
colour. We can use a similar method here. According to Fry, the
importance of space in a painting is that it creates a sense of *freedom*.
He speaks of this in his essay on Fra Bartolommeo:

But, above all, Fra Bartolommeo's discoveries tend to the clearest
realisation of the picture space and of the relation of the volumes to
that space, their situation within it and the vivid evocation of the circulation of air around them which is, in fact, the consummation of their
plastic freedom.[17]

In his writing this creation of space is continually linked in this
way with the idea of freedom. Space can be created by the use of
colour:

Here we feel the space around each of the figures and we realise fully
their relatively greater or less recession from the eye...And this
realisation of space implies a sense of colour as a plastic function...Now
nothing was more striking than the way in which here the various colours
maintained their position and thereby aroused a feeling of spacial freedom.[18]

But the price of this freedom is the 'emptiness' of space. In this
respect it is similar to 'whiteness', showing the kind of ambiguity
which we discussed in the last chapter. Like repetition also, space
has a double nature, for it can be seen as a reassuring freedom or a
frightening negation. Virginia Woolf's deep concern with the
ambiguity of these ideas can be seen in the equation she often makes
between space and silence. In her essay on Sickert, the painter, she
discovers 'a silence at the heart of art', just as Clarissa Dalloway,
the society hostess, discovers an 'emptiness at the heart of life'.

There is the silence of space and the emptiness of speech. Seurat's empty landscapes and Virginia Woolf's silent interludes in *The Waves* achieve their emptiness by banishing human beings. Fry describes Seurat's landscapes in a way which could apply to Virginia Woolf's 'interludes':

Who before Seurat ever conceived exactly the pictorial possibilities of empty space? Whoever before conceived that such vast areas of flat, unbroken surfaces as we see in his *Gravelines* could become the elements of a plastic design? And yet nothing less 'empty', pictorially speaking, can be imagined. There is such a tense, imaginative conviction in these subtly-built-up statements of surface that one can well believe that Seurat's own definition of the art of painting, as 'the art of hollowing out a canvas', was so evident to him as to make the effort of the imagination in cutting away so much material proportional to the vastness and emptiness of the space thus excavated.[19]

This silence and emptiness Virginia Woolf sees in all art, and therefore in life itself. This is especially noticeable in her last novel, *Between the Acts*, where emptiness and silence are insistently evoked.[20] The sense of freedom and yet of emptiness given by space is often symbolised in her novels by the drifting of smoke through the air, as in *The Years*, where the wind which blows throughout the novel carries smoke with it. The mist and fog which were part of the theme of 'illusion' in *Night and Day* become in *The Years* the acrid smoke of the burning of the leaves, drifting into the emptiness of space. The image of the birds rising and falling is also a recurrent image in her work. There, we have the freedom yet restraint of space, for the birds are seen acting in a group as if they were tied with invisible thread. In *Mrs Dalloway* the smoke and birds come together to establish the spatial effect: '...looking at the flowers, at the trees with smoke winding off them and the rooks rising, falling...'[21] This rising and falling of rooks is one of those obsessive 'private' images which Virginia Woolf makes public and meaningful in the course of her work. We can see this difficult transformation in her diary:

Even now, I have to watch the rooks beating up against the wind, which is high, and still I say to myself instinctively 'What's the phrase for that?' and try to make more and more vivid the roughness of the air current and the tremor of the rook's wing slicing as if the air were full of ridges and ripples and roughnesses. They rise and sink, up and down, as if the exercise rubbed and braced them like swimmers in rough water. But what a little I can get down into my pen of what is so vivid to my eyes, and not only to my eyes; also to some nervous fibre, or fanlike membrane in my species.[22]

The idea of space, then, leads on naturally to a feeling of solidarity, of connectedness, with nature and with the rest of humanity. This accounts for the Wordsworthian 'solitary traveller' episode in *Mrs Dalloway*. The grey car and the aeroplane in the novel bind together the various viewpoints; they are spatial, but their significance is wider than Troy understands in the criticism quoted above. The car, the aeroplane and the spider's web in the novel are at once spatial and psychological symbols. The connection between space and 'point of view' or perspective can be seen in that sketch which we have found so useful in helping to understand Virginia Woolf's methods, 'An Unwritten Novel'. Minnie's life is an emptiness which must be filled. The mending of a hole in her glove is an image of the dullness of her life – she encloses herself in a thick grey web, the opposite of the soft mesh of free space which Virginia Woolf sees as the true vista and vision.

Fry complained of those critics of visual art who put psychological above spatial values:

If I am right, the constant criticism of Courbet to the effect that though he was manifestly a great painter his art was purely material, that it revealed nothing of the spirit, and was therefore inferior, falls to the ground. It was based on a false assumption that spiritual values could only be attained through psychological structures, that spatial and plastic ones had no such function.

This habit of putting psychological above spatial values in graphic art comes, of course, only too naturally to men of letters who occupy themselves with plastic art.[23]

In many ways Virginia Woolf tries to right the balance between the literary and the visual by allowing a great deal of the spatial element in her art – as much, indeed, as words can accomplish in this direction. She never forgets the visual, spatial metaphor involved in speaking of 'point of view' or 'perspective'; they are never merely psychological. Her alert visual awareness is shown in this passage from her diary:

Proportions changed

That in the evening, or on colourless days, the proportions of the land-scape change suddenly, I saw people playing stoolball in the meadow; they appeared sunk far down on a flat board; and the downs raised high up and mountainous round them. Detail was smoothed out. This was an extremely beautiful effect: the colours of women's dresses also showing very bright and pure in the almost untinted surroundings. I knew, also, that the proportions were abnormal – as if I were looking between my legs.[24]

Earlier in her diary she had spoken of a new theory of fiction: 'The one I have in view is about *perspective*. But I do not know. My brain may not last me out.'[25] The psychological and visual space are inter-woven in her essay on Lawrence,[26] where she speaks of her own 'angle of approach' to his works, an angle which 'shuts off many views and distorts others'. His upbringing, we are told, 'set his gaze at an angle'. At all points the spatial metaphors are used in this double way to indicate the difference in temperament between Lawrence and herself and at the same time indicate a different visual sensibility. She mentions the classic anecdote about the cherries painted so realistically that birds pecked them, and goes on to say that behind Lawrence's apparent verisimilitude there is a hidden arrangement. In his work we must not linger over a scene, as we do over the famous hawthorn hedge in Proust, but must hurry on. This is very revealing for the light it casts on Virginia Woolf's own works. The 'lingering' of Proust at certain significant moments is what she tries to attain in her novels at certain points. This is achieved partly by the use of a frame, the function of which Fry often discussed, and which the passage from Proust to which she refers in her essay, illustrates:

And then I returned to my hawthorns, and stood before them as one stands before those masterpieces of painting which, one imagines, one will be better able to 'take in' when one has looked away, for a moment, at something else; but in vain did I shape my fingers into a frame, so as to have nothing but the hawthorns before my eyes; the sentiment which they aroused in me remained obscure and vague, struggling and failing to free itself, to float across and become one with the flowers. They themselves offered me no enlightenment, and I could not call upon any other flowers to satisfy this mysterious longing. And then, inspiring me with that rapture which we feel on seeing a work by our favourite painter quite different from any of those that we already know, or, better still, when some one has taken us and set us down in front of a picture of which we have hitherto seen no more than a pencilled sketch...[27]

Lawrence, she believes, does not 'linger', but moves restlessly on. The scene which she singles out as having intrinsic value in his work, the swing scene in *Sons and Lovers*, itself illustrates this sense of movement. It might be argued that by being 'unaware of the present save as it affects the future', Lawrence is giving us an idea of the dynamic possibilities of life. Virginia Woolf's lack of sympathy, her temperamental reading of Lawrence, arises, I think, partly from the fact that in her own work she seeks freedom in Proust's way, by the past crystallised in the present, and for that to occur a certain static quality is necessary. But there must be some rhythm in that moment of stillness; her own movement is not from present to future as in Lawrence, but from the near to the far and the large to the small. Her special moments are instantaneous and spatial.

This spatial feeling can be illustrated from her essay on *Robinson Crusoe* in which she tries to work out some of the ideas about perspective which she first touched upon in her diary. Defoe is discussed in terms of point of view:

Our first task, and it is often formidable enough, is to master his perspective...All alone we must climb upon the novelist's shoulders and gaze through his eyes until we, too, understand in what order he ranges the large common objects upon which novelists are fated to gaze...[28]

When this visual or spatial metaphor is stressed, any movement is not from present to future, but from large to small, as Virginia Woolf describes in the same essay:

Here is Scott, for example, with his mountains looming huge and his men therefore drawn to scale; Jane Austen picking out the roses on her teacups to match the wit of her dialogues; while Peacock bends over heaven and earth one fantastic distorting mirror in which a tea-cup may be Vesuvius or Vesuvius a tea-cup...It is in their perspective that they are different.[29]

Virginia Woolf ends her essay with a wonderful evocation of space; the passage is an imagist poem in prose:[30]

Thus Defoe, by reiterating that nothing but a plain earthenware pot stands in the foreground, persuades us to see remote islands and the solitudes of the human soul. By believing fixedly in the solidity of the pot and its earthiness, he has subdued every other element to his design; he has roped the whole universe into harmony. And is there any reason, we ask as we shut the book, why the perspective that a plain earthenware pot exacts should not satisfy us as completely, once we grasp it, as man himself in all his sublimity standing against a background of broken mountains and tumbling oceans with the stars flaming in the sky?[31]

The free play of perspective, the ability to see infinity in a grain of sand is a child-like virtue. A landscape is projected on to a nurse's face in her recently discovered children's story *Nurse Lugton's Golden Thimble*; a dish of water becomes a seascape in *The Waves*, and a snail shell a cathedral.[32] These new perspectives create our human freedom. The sense of space is evoked most strikingly in *To the Lighthouse*.

Part Two: Repetition and Rhythm

9

An introduction to the problem

SAMUEL BUTLER

We saw earlier how Butler's thinking in the *Note-Books* was based explicitly on a number of antitheses, all bound up with one another, and all transferable to different areas of study, such as music, biology, literature, and so on. The antithesis I would like to isolate here, because it is of great aesthetic importance, is that of repetition and change. In biological terms, repetition is a question of reproduction, and we are in that ambiguous area of Blake's 'Crystal Cabinet':

Given a single creature capable of reproducing itself and it must go on reproducing itself for ever, for it would not reproduce itself, unless it produced a creature that was going to reproduce itself, and so on ad infinitum.

Then comes Descent with Modification. Similarity tempered with dissimilarity, and dissimilarity tempered with similarity – a contradiction in terms, like almost everything else that is true or useful or indeed intelligible at all.[1]

The development of the species is exactly the same in this respect, as memory in the individual, although we should not say *exactly* the same here:

Memory vanishes with extremes of resemblance or difference. Things which put us in mind of others must be neither too like nor too unlike them. It is our sense that a position is not quite the same which makes us find it so nearly the same. We remember by the aid of differences as much as by that of samenesses. If there could be no difference there would be no memory, for the two positions would become absolutely one and the same, and the universe would repeat itself for ever and ever as between these two points.[2]

Butler goes on in his characteristic way to apply this antithesis to the field of artistic creation. The repetition and variation which is true of evolution and of memory must be true of the arts. He describes the arts of the musician, painter, and writer as essentially the same, as the creation of something new and nothing new at the same time. The way in which these novel things arise out of things which are repeated is a mystery. We come back again and again to the paradox which Butler sees as meeting us at the end of every inquiry: 'we do not know the cause of the variations whose accumulation results in species and any explanation which leaves this out of sight ignores the whole difficulty'.[3]

REPETITION IN THE NOVEL

Novel criticism: E. K. Brown and D. Lodge

The importance of repetition in the novel is discussed by E. K. Brown in his excellent study *Rhythm in the Novel*. He takes as his starting point E. M. Forster's definition of rhythm as repetition with variation. Brown is concerned with a small part of the area which lies between exact repetition and unlimited variation, 'the part where repetition is exceptionally strong, and variation is related to it in some fashion especially artful, pleasing, or powerful'.[4] He goes on to say that repetition can be seen in word and phrase, sequences of incident and grouping of characters, symbol, and the rhythmic interweaving of themes. He argues that repetition achieves much more than the creation of unity and intensification, which is all that Zola had claimed for it. Brown's discussion of expanding symbols and the interweaving of themes is of great interest, and his examination of the rhythmical aspects of Forster's work is excellent. But he does not push his insights far enough to reach that area of paradox and antithesis which we see when we consider Forster's inheritance from Butler. Brown stops short of a more general analysis of what is involved in the idea of repetition. His final remarks are just, and closely resemble Butler's idea of antithesis:

To express what is both an order and a mystery rhythmic processes, repetitions with intricate variations, are the most appropriate of idioms. Repetition is the strongest assurance an author can give of order; the extraordinary complexity of the variations is the reminder that the order is so involute that it must remain a mystery.[5]

Repetition in Virginia Woolf's work involves more than the

'employment' of rhythm which Brown notes in the 'interweaving of themes' in *To the Lighthouse*. Brown does not distinguish adequately between those works in which there are repetitive devices and those which are self-consciously concerned with repetition itself. To examine this self-consciousness we must look at the wider significance of repetition; although it is a constant element in literary work, it is in certain writers a conscious interest, at times an obsession. We may, at the end of our inquiry, come to Brown's 'mystery' and Butler's paradox, but we must look first at some of the implications of repetition, at what is involved in the emptiness of the Marabar caves and the emptiness which Clarissa Dalloway sees at the heart of life.

David Lodge in his excellent study *Language of Fiction* states that 'the perception of repetition is the first step towards offering an account of the way language works in extended literary texts such as novels'. It is certainly true, as he goes on to say, that 'the significance of repetition in a given text is not conditional on its being a deliberate and conscious device on the author's part'.[6] Virginia Woolf's concern with repetition itself means that our analysis must go beyond a consideration of 'devices' and must begin with a more general introduction to the problem of repetition and rhythm.

Two 'stream-of-consciousness' writers: Gertrude Stein and Dorothy Richardson

Virginia Woolf shares this concern with other 'stream-of-consciousness' writers, notably Gertrude Stein and Dorothy Richardson. In speaking of Gertrude Stein, one can hardly avoid discussing her repetitious style. She believed that a writer must 'begin again and again' to 'maintain a continuous present'. (This definition appeared in *Composition as Explanation* which was published by Leonard and Virginia Woolf.) F. J. Hoffman describes her use of repetition like this:

Repetition is an essential strategy in composition; it guarantees similarity and forces the consciousness upon the nature of the thing seen while at the same time it provides the avenue along which movement and change may occur. Hence Miss Stein's writing is often accused of being monotonous and wearisomely repetitious; but it is deliberately so, to preserve it from being superficial.[7]

D. Sutherland explains how Gertrude Stein's notion of character leads to repetition, and his description comes close to Virginia Woolf's idea of character:

If the character does not change, if its interior and exterior history has no important influence upon it, and if it is the definition and description of types of character and the demonstration of these types that interest the writer, the problem is one of projecting character in time without a sequence of events and all the context of irrelevant accidents. This leads naturally to repetition, the constantly new assertion and realisation of the same simple thing, an existence with its typical qualities, not an event. As actually that is, on this view, what the character does, constantly asserting and insisting on its same existence from moment to moment and from day to day, the repetitions in *The Making of Americans* are an accurate expression of it.[8]

He goes on to quote Gertrude Stein's request to 'read me by repetition'. Elizabeth Sprigge relates Gertrude Stein's use of repetition to another important concept bound up with repetition, namely rhythm. Stein, says Sprigge, was aware of 'people's variety of emphasis in repetition. For her this was the rhythm of personality, and later as a writer, working out the pattern of recurrence in human behaviour, she used rhythm to clarify repetition'.[9] If, as I hope to show, Virginia Woolf was explicitly concerned with repetition, then clearly all this is of great interest, and the relationship between these writers is clearer than if we simply relate them through the vaguer idea of 'stream-of-consciousness' writing. There is a further link between them in their mutual friend Roger Fry. Sprigge quotes in this connection one of Gertrude Stein's letters, written in 1913: 'Roger Fry is being awfully good about my work. It seems that he read 3 Lives long ago and was much impressed with it and so he is doing his best to get me published.'[10] We may be certain, then, that Virginia Woolf was acquainted with the work of Gertrude Stein before she rejected *The Making of Americans* and accepted *Composition as Explanation* for the Hogarth Press in 1926. These critics certainly show a sympathetic understanding of the reasons for Gertrude Stein's employment of repetition, but is she artistically successful? Clive Hart believes that what he considers to be her failure stems from the fact that she does not transmute her repetitions into a rhythm: 'Even Gertrude Stein, who, with the possible exception of Péguy, must be the greatest devotee of repetitiveness western literature has ever known, cannot raise pure repetition to the status of *leitmotif*.'[11] He indicates that Joyce's difficulty in this matter is one shared with all repetitive writers: 'The more repetition a book contains, the less easy it must obviously be for the writer to create motifs whose recurrence will arrest the attention of the reader.'[12] The problem of avoiding deadening habit, of transmuting repetition into a vital rhythm is the basis of Bergson's philosophy, as we shall see later.

This kind of Bergsonian transformation is clearly one of Dorothy Richardson's more important themes. What many critics have considered monotonous and boring in her work C. R. Blake sees as a deliberate attempt to give a sense of the continuity of consciousness, in that the parallel repetitions secure an even and continuous rhythm. This also helps the writer to achieve a Proustian fusion of past and present when the reader is reminded by image, phrase and allusion, of prior events. Past and present are in this way linked together in the reader's mind. Because this is a fundamental process of consciousness, says Blake, it is a fundamental element in the structure of *Pilgrimage*. The following passage from *Deadlock* gives us, I think, an idea of what Dorothy Richardson was trying to achieve in the work as a whole:

Speech did something to things; set them in a mould that was apt to come up again; repeated, it would be dead; but perhaps one need never repeat oneself? To say the same things to different people would give them a sort of fresh life; but there would be death in oneself as one spoke. Perhaps the same thing could be said over and over again, with other things with it, so that it had a different shape, sang a different song and laughed all round itself in amongst different things.[13]

Mechanical autonomy: D. H. Lawrence

As in the earlier chapter on autonomy, we can turn to Lawrence for help in this matter. We mentioned there the 'Lady of Shalott' theme in *The Virgin and the Gipsy*. In *Women in Love* Birkin criticises Hermione's over-cerebral outlook like this:

'It's all that Lady of Shalott business,' he said, in his strong abstract voice. He seemed to be charging her before the unseeing air. 'You've got that mirror, your own fixed will, your immortal understanding, your own tight conscious world, and there is nothing beyond it. There, in the mirror, you must have everything.[14]

This egoistic repetition of the self is an illusion, a repetition which does not improve the quality of life. Birkin answers Gerald's argument that the miner with his piano is attempting to find something 'higher':

'Higher!' cried Birkin. 'Yes. Amazing heights of upright grandeur. It makes him so much higher in his neighbouring collier's eyes. He sees himself reflected in the neighbouring opinion, like in a Brocken mist, several feet taller on the strength of the pianoforte, and he is satisfied. He lives for the sake of that Brocken spectre, the reflection of himself in the human opinion. You do the same. If you are of high importance to humanity you are of high importance to yourself. That is why you work so hard at the mines. If you can produce coal to cook five thousand dinners a day, you are five thousand times more important than if you cooked only your own dinner.'[15]

This repetition of the self occurs on a small scale in the smoke and mirrors of the Pompadour café, the meeting place of self-regarding artists.[16] The problem is one of connecting ourselves to the rest of humanity and yet retaining our sense of identity. Egoistic separateness sees merely the repetition of the self in everything, but equally false is the mixing and merging of sentimental attachments or the wallowing in the life of the instincts. Set against Birkin's idea of rhythmical, flame-like movement is a life dominated by routine and by machinery, by hateful repetition:

But better die than live mechanically a life that is a repetition of repetitions. To die is to move on with the invisible. To die is also a joy, a joy of submitting to that which is greater than the known; namely, the pure unknown. That is a joy. But to live mechanised and cut off within the motion of the will, to live as an entity absolved from the unknown, that is shameful and ignominious. There is no ignominy in death. There is complete ignominy in an unreplenished, mechanised life. Life indeed may be ignominious, shameful to the soul. But death is never a shame. Death itself, like the illimitable space, is beyond our sullying.[17]

The repetitions of Ursula's meditation here work against the repetitions which she rejects. It is modified repetition, the pulsing rhythm of her anger and of life itself, which is repetition with variation. And this is typical of Lawrence's style generally, as he explains in his Foreword to *Women in Love*: 'In point of style, fault is often found with the continual, slightly modified repetition. The only answer is that it is natural to the author: and that every natural crisis in emotion or passion or understanding comes from this pulsing, frictional to-and-fro, which works up to culmination.'[18] The obsession with unrhythmic repetition leads to an intense awareness of clock time, as Gudrun discovers towards the end of the novel:

The thought of the mechanical succession of day following day, day following day, *ad infinitum*, was one of the things that made her heart palpitate with a real approach of madness. The terrible bondage of this tick-tack of time, this twitching of the hands of the clock, this eternal repetition of hours and days – oh God, it was too awful to contemplate. And there was no escape from it, no escape.[19]

Gerald, as 'mine-owner Crich' symbolises the dehumanisation, the mechanical and repetitive aspects of modern civilisation. He swings between 'marshy' childishness and machine-like hardness:

So manly by day, yet all the while, such a crying of infants in the night. Let them turn into mechanisms, let them. Let them become instruments, pure machines, pure wills, that work like clockwork, in perpetual repetition. Let them be this, let them be taken up entirely in their work, let them be perfect parts of a great machine, having a slumber of constant repetition. Let Gerald manage his firm. There he would be satisfied, as satisfied as a wheel-barrow that goes backwards and forwards along a plank all day – she had seen it.[20]

There are two aspects of repetition in Lawrence's work, then, the mechanical and the organic, the latter being precisely those repetitions with variations which Forster terms 'rhythmical'. But how do these variations come about? Do they have their own hidden order? Indeed, it seems to be inevitable that they should, otherwise they would be 'irrelevant', gratuitous, outside that unity which we might expect in a work of art. This is important for understanding the novel as a whole, for the question of accident or design, 'luck or cunning' is one of the themes of *Women in Love*:

Gerald as a boy had accidentally killed his brother. What then? Why seek to draw a brand and a curse across the life that had caused the accident? A man can live by accident, and die by accident. Or can he not? Is every man's life subject to pure accident, is it only the race, the genus, the species, that has a universal reference? Or is this not true, is there no such thing as pure accident? Has *everything* that happens a universal significance? Has it? Birkin, pondering as he stood there, had forgotten Mrs Crich, as she had forgotten him.

He did not believe that there was any such thing as accident. It all hung together, in the deepest sense.[21]

For there to be a murderer, perhaps there needs to be a murderee,[22] and the connection lies in the subconscious, beneath the surface of the lake in which Gerald's sister drowns, beneath the earth where the Crich family send their workers to heap up their wealth and their tips of waste. (Clearly these questions remind us of certain of Freud's ideas. Of especial interest in this connection is the notion of 'compulsion toward repetition' which he describes in *Beyond the Pleasure Principle*.) Perhaps it would be appropriate at this point to look at this problem from a broadly psychological point of view.

REPETITION AND PSYCHOLOGY

Kierkegaard on the concept of repetition

Kierkegaard indicates the importance of repetition in his 'Essay in Experimental Psychology' called *Repetition*. In his introduction to the work, Walter Lowrie includes an article written by Kierkegaard in defence of his essay. Kierkegaard explains that if we seek to gain freedom through either (A) pleasure or (B) shrewdness, then repetition will be seen as undesirable, for repetition takes away pleasure, and if we use shrewdness to avoid repetition we will eventually be forced to repeat the trick whereby repetition was avoided. Seeking freedom through shrewdness or pleasure therefore leads us to despair. But if we seek (C) 'freedom in its highest form', freedom defined in relation to itself, then repetition is welcomed and we fear change, which might 'alter the eternal nature' of freedom. This true freedom is constantly being obscured:

As when one is in the street and hears the least little part of a flute-player's piece, and then at that moment the rumbling of wagons and noise of traffic makes it necessary even for the market-woman to cry in a loud voice if Madame who stands beside her is to hear the price of her cabbage, and then again there is quiet for an instant, and again one hears the flute-player – so in the first part of *Repetition*, (C) is heard at intervals and is drowned by the noise of life.[23]

Kierkegaard is trying to make us see repetition in all its abstractness, and so he rejects particular repetitions such as the cycle of the seasons or of history. Virginia Woolf, as an artist, must give repetition a substance to work in, just as a wave needs its medium.

Therefore particular repetitions of memory or history must be used in order to point towards the concept of repetition. In the passage above, Kierkegaard himself finds it necessary to use imagery and analogy. Throughout *The Years* we hear the traffic of London, the street criers and musicians:

Against the dull background of traffic noises, of wheels turning and brakes squeaking, there rose near at hand the cry of a woman suddenly alarmed for her child; the monotonous cry of a man selling vegetables; and far away a barrel organ was playing. It stopped; it began again.[24]

Because this is a slightly modified repetition of the descriptive passages which have gone before, and because it fits into a complex pattern of repetitions in the novel as a whole, what we hear when the barrel organ stops and then begins again, is repetition itself.

Hubert Waley on repetition and the subconscious

The relationship between repetition and the subconscious is discussed by Hubert Waley in a series of essays which appeared in *The Burlington Magazine* in 1923 and were later published by Leonard and Virginia Woolf as one of the Hogarth Essays, *The Revival of Aesthetics*. Waley says that repetitive structure is common to all art, and comes to the conclusion that the artist employs repetition in order to get down to that level of the mind at which, in Lawrence's phrase, things 'hang together in the deepest sense':

Now the problem with which we are faced is this: Why is rhythm in our sense omnipresent in art? The answer which I suggest is that the creative mind employs rhythm to produce in itself a state in which the aesthetic faculty can function freely, that, in a word, every bout of aesthetic activity must be accompanied by a sort of self-hypnotism.[25]

He sees repetition as a means of getting round our usual intellectual reasoning:

The musician repeats over and over to himself the phrase he finds obsessing his mind. The artist imposes first upon one part of his subject and then upon another his obsessive configurations of form and colour. The poet reiterates his obsessive cadences. I envisage the process as a sort of circular system involving the mutual reinforcement of the agencies at work, obsession leading to repetition and repetition stimulating the forces which lead to obsession.[26]

The importance which Waley here ascribes to repetition is con-
firmed in the autobiographies of two poets. In his book *The Strings
Are False* Louis MacNeice speaks of the way in which he made a
liturgy out of the passing train which seemed to repeat 'Hickleton,
Hickleton, Hickleton'; and C. Day Lewis in *The Buried Day* says:
'I enjoyed the repetitive rhythm which children and poets thrive
on.' This repetition, according to Waley, is a means of avoiding the
utilitarian emphasis in the normal functioning of the intellect. He
goes on to speak of other states of mind which are pleasurable and
devoid of use, such as a certain stage of being stunned or the first
moments of an epileptic fit, as described by Dostoevsky. Waley is
describing 'moments of vision' similar to those which Virginia
Woolf sees in the works of Conrad, and which are of course important in her own novels. Waley brings together in his psychological
explanation these two phenomena, the pleasure of rhythm and the
sense of a 'special moment':

We have already noticed in some detail the hypnotic effect of such
impressions, and we have had occasion to mention the fact that similar
results can be obtained by fastening attention down to a single point,
as in Buddhist meditation, rather than stimulating it repetitively. That
the intellect can be affected by a bang on the head or a dose of some
drug seems to us natural enough but its sensitivity to anything so
intangible as mere repetition or immobilisation of impressions appears
somehow paradoxical. May not the explanation be something of this
kind – that irregular movement is the natural gait of intellectual functioning, and that it is unable either to progress with measured regularity
or to stay still. If you compel it to do either of these things it simply
breaks down. Mere matter, on the other hand, has of course immobility,
of a sort, as its natural state, and when this immobility is disturbed the
next most natural state seems to be one of rhythmical movement.[27]

'Déjà vu'

Waley's mention of Dostoevsky reminds us that epileptic fits are
often accompanied by a sense of *déjà vu*, due to a simultaneous
neural discharge rather than the normal random firing. This sense
of 'having been here before' is the basis of J. B. Priestley's *Time-
Plays*.[28] In his introduction to the 1947 edition Priestley writes of
his indebtedness to the books of J. W. Dunne, who claimed that
dreams are glimpses into the future. Dunne builds up a philosophical

system to explain the 'gigantic pattern' which Eleanor speaks of in *The Years*:

And suddenly it seemed to Eleanor that it had all happened before. So a girl had come in that night in the restaurant; had stood, vibrating, in the door. She knew exactly what he was going to say. He had said it before, in the restaurant. He is going to say, She is like a ball on the top of a fishmonger's fountain. As she thought it, he said it. Does everything then come over again a little differently? she thought. If so, is there a pattern; a theme, recurring, like music; half remembered, half foreseen?...a gigantic pattern, momentarily perceptible?[29]

The psychological explanation is that this apparent premonition is a form of hysteria known as *déjà vu*. (I would suggest from my own testing of Dunne's experiment that his method, of waking oneself up unduly rapidly for the purpose of recording dreams, results not in premonition of the future, but in this kind of hysteria, here self-induced.)[30] I. M. L. Hunter in his book on memory quotes a passage from *David Copperfield* to illustrate this phenomenon and goes on to describe it in the following way:

In its strongest form, *déjà vu* saturates all present experience with recollective familiarity. The person feels that he has already experienced all that is happening at this moment and all that is going to happen next. It is rather like witnessing a second showing of the same cinefilm, except that the person knows he has not experienced the present events before. When this experience takes place, it usually lasts, at most, for a minute or two. But in that brief time, the activities of recognising are, as it were, out of hand so that everything which occurs is reacted to as having been witnessed previously. There is a tendency for this strong form of *déjà vu* to occur in people who suffer from a certain kind of brain dysfunction. In these people there is, from time to time, a period of spontaneous neural discharge from the temporal lobe region of the brain. During the temporal-lobe fits, the person experiences, without necessarily either fear or pleasure, this intense feeling that everything around him has happened in the same way before. He may come to know *déjà vu* well as a symptom of his fits. Now it must be emphasised that the occurrence of *déjà vu*, even in its strongest form, is not confined to people with brain dysfunction. Indeed many people, especially those who are sensitive to their own states of conscious awareness, have experienced this paradoxical recognising at one time or another.[31]

Virginia Woolf is certainly one of 'those who are sensitive to their own states of conscious awareness' described by Hunter and we have here a partial explanation for the disturbing, almost hysterical effect which we feel in some of her work.

Verbal repetition: semantic satiation and verbal transformation

Virginia Woolf often tries to indicate the boundaries of language. An awareness of the gap between words and what they represent stems from the realisation that language does not copy a given reality. Words can jingle together quite regardless of meaning, and out of context they lose their transparency and seem strangely opaque, as we see in this passage from *The Years* 'and the next word he heard was "adenoids" – which is a good word, he said to himself, separating it from its context; wasp-waisted; pinched in the middle; with a hard, shining, metallic abdomen, useful to describe the appearance of an insect...'[32] The best way to show a word out of context and so take away its meaning is to repeat it over and over. I. M. L. Hunter describes this phenomenon, known as 'semantic satiation';

Before concluding our general survey of repetition, brief mention may be made of some curious effects which arise when repetitions are carried out in close succession. If we pronounce a word over and over again, rapidly and without pause, then the word is felt to lose meaning. Take any word, say, CHIMNEY. Say it repeatedly and in rapid succession. Within some seconds, the word loses meaning. This loss is referred to as 'semantic satiation'. What seems to happen is that the word forms a kind of closed loop with itself. One utterance leads into a second utterance of the same word, this leads in to a third, and so on. Now this is a highly unusual sequence of events. Normally, when a word is used it has meaning in the sense that it is a momentary component of some developing theme. The word normally arises in the course of a train of activity and leads on, through some of its attributes, to further related attributes and a continuation of the theme. But after repeated pronunciation, this meaningful continuation of the word is blocked since, now, the word leads only to its own recurrence.[33]

In the following passage from *The Years* Virginia Woolf uses something like semantic satiation. The objects (spoons) and the word 'spoons' seem to part company and take on a separate life of their own:

'Spoons! Spoons! Spoons!' cried Delia, brandishing her arms in a rhetorical manner as if she were still declaiming to someone inside. She caught sight of her nephew and niece. 'Be an angel, North, and fetch spoons!' she cried, throwing her hands out towards him.

'Spoons for the widow of the Governor-General!...

'Spoons are coming,' she said to Lady Lasswade...[34]

and so on until the word is thoroughly emptied of meaning. The triple repetition of words, a constant feature of Virginia Woolf's writing, is the 'triple melody' and the 'three-fold ply' which give a minimum coherence to life 'between the acts'. At the centre of art and of life there is a silence and emptiness.[35] Virginia Woolf's interest in the repeated rhythm of phrases can be understood again with the help of Hunter, who describes the 'verbal transformation effect' in the following way:

Another effect of massed repetition is akin to semantic satiation. But this time, the person simply listens to the speech of someone else. A phrase is recorded on tape, e.g., 'drop salt into milk'. And the tape is formed into a loop so that the same phrase is played over and over again, rather like a gramophone when the needle is stuck in a groove. Now if we listen to this repeated utterance, it seems to change. We hear other words, we hear nonsense sounds, it is difficult to believe that we are merely listening to the same phrase over and over.[36]

The rhythm of a phrase can have an effect even when the phrase itself has no meaning. The repeated cry of the street hawker in *The Years* is unintelligible; the rhythm persists, but the words are 'almost rubbed out'.[37] This lack of meaning can also free the phrases and allow them to become pure pattern. If exact words and phrases to some extent falsify, then the truth might be contained in the modified repetition, the rhythm of language. This pattern we can see in a foreign language which we do not understand: 'Latin was it? He broke off a sentence and let it swim in his mind. There the words lay, beautiful, yet meaningless, yet composed in a pattern – *nox est perpetua una dormienda*.'[38] Nonsense and music are closely connected. Of the children's song in *The Years* 'not a word was recognisable',[39] yet it is a kind of 'pure poetry'. (We are reminded here, perhaps, of the chorus in Dorothy Richardson's *Honeycomb*.)[40] When language is divested of meaning it becomes as free as music. There remains only the basic structure of a modified repetition or rhythm, which Susanne Langer sees as the very basis of music:

And what about repetition of forms, equal divisions, if recurrence is not the real basis of rhythm? What is the function of the countless regularities of accent, phrase, figure and bar in the greatest master-pieces?

Repetition is another structural principle – deeply involved with rhythm, as all basic principles are with each other – that gives musical composition the appearance of vital growth. For what we receive, in the passage of sound, with a sense of recognition, i.e. as recurrence, is oftentimes a fairly free variant of what came before, a mere analogy, and only logically a repetition; but it is just the sort of play on a basic pattern, especially the reflection of the over-all plan in the structure of each part, that is characteristic of organic forms.[41]

Virginia Woolf closely associates meaningless phrases with music because this brings to the surface a sense of underlying repetition. It is this recurrence which comes closest to the apparent repetitions of the non-human world. The old lady who sings her incomprehensible song in *Mrs Dalloway* represents all that repeats and persists.[42]

KARIN STEPHEN ON BERGSON

Shiv Kumar in his study of Bergson and the stream-of-consciousness writers quotes Leonard Woolf as his authority for believing that Virginia Woolf probably never read her sister-in-law's book, *The Misuse of Mind*. If we ignore questions of derivation, influence, and indebtedness, and concentrate on the similarity of ideas and helpful-ness in discussing the central problem of repetition and change, then Karin Stephen's book is very useful.

First, she argues that objects are not known separately from their qualities; grass, for example, cannot be separated from its 'green-ness' and so on. Perhaps, then, these qualities are directly known. She exposes this fallacy by considering the nature of change. The spectrum might be a series of successive colours, but this she con-siders to be an abstraction, since the fact which we know forms a continuous 'becoming' which is not made up of any fixed stages; we fall back on saying that the 'colour' changes. But this is obviously an abstraction, since there is no 'colour' over and above the red, orange, green and so on. Similarly there is no 'red' apart from the changing process with which we are directly acquainted. Having shown 'change' to be reality she is now faced with the problem of dealing with its counterpart, repetition. To help her analysis, she uses the example of music:

This means that in change such as this, change, that is, which has duration repetition is out of the question. Take a song in which the last line is sung twice over as a refrain: the notes, we say, are repeated, but the second time the line occurs the actual effect produced is different, and that, indeed, is the whole point of a refrain. This illustrates the second important difference which Bergson wants to bring out between the forms of change which belong respectively to non-logical facts and to the logical abstractions by which we describe them, that is between duration as contrasted with a logical series of stages. The notes are abstractions assumed to explain the effect produced which is the actual fact directly known. The notes are stages in a logical series of change, but their effect, the actual fact, changes as a process of duration. From this difference in their ways of changing there follows an important difference between fact and abstraction, namely that, while the notes can be repeated over again, the effect will never be the same as before. This is because the notes, being abstractions, are not affected by their relations which give them their position in the logical series which they form, while their effect, being a changing process, depends for its flavour upon its position in the whole duration to which it belongs: this flavour grows out of the whole of what has gone before, and since this whole is itself always growing by the addition of more and more 'later stages', the effect which it goes to produce can never be the same twice over.[43]

Now clearly this has a direct bearing on the topic we have been considering, and gives us an insight into the reason for Bergson's use of metaphor rather than logical discourse. Karin Stephen points out that an abstract term is as much a substitution for reality as a metaphor. Bergson is placed in the paradoxical position of noting repetitions (that is, seeing connections) while at the same time denying their existence and indeed condemning as pernicious the intellect which abuses itself in such an occupation. It is for this reason that he uses, in Stephen's words, 'self-contradictory terms'.[44] She points out that although repetitions are necessary in explanation, they do not occur in reality:

No 'two' positions in a creative process of duration can have an identical past history, every 'later' one will have more history, every 'earlier' one less. In a logical series, on the other hand, there is no reason why the same term should not occur over and over again at different points in the course of the series, since in a logical series every term, being distinct from every other and only joined to it by external relations, is what it is independently of its position.

111

If Bergson is right therefore in saying that abstractions change as a logical series while the actual facts change as a creative process of duration, it follows that, while our descriptions and explanations may contain repetitions the actual fact to which we intend these explanations to apply, cannot. This, if true, is a very important difference between facts and abstractions which common sense entirely overlooks when it assumes that we are directly acquainted with common qualities.[45]

How can we classify, how can we construct general laws when the actual fact itself does not contain repetitions? Bergson cannot without contradiction say that there are relations of similarity between past and present facts. How then, does he deal with memory? He believes that we must overcome our habit of thinking of abstractions as having an independent existence if we are to understand memory:

Whenever there is actual fact there is memory, and memory creates duration which excludes repetition. Perceived familiarity depends upon memory but memory, according to Bergson, does not work by preserving a series of repetitions for future reference. If we say that memory connects 'the past' with 'the present' we must add that it destroys their logical distinctness. But of course this is putting it very badly: there is no 'logical distinctness' in the actual fact for memory to 'destroy': our language suggests that first there was matter, forming a logical series of distinct qualities recurring over and over, and then memory occurred and telescoped the series, squeezing 'earlier' and 'later' moments into one another to make a creative duration. Such a view is suggested by our strong bias towards regarding abstractions as having independent existence apart from the real fact from which they have been abstracted: if we can overcome this bias the description will do well enough.[46]

And so the discussion turns again around the question of repetition. Karin Stephen advocates a new balance between repetition and immediate experience. But the problem of communicating this experience to others, or indeed, of remembering it ourselves, raises the same problem and paradox as before:

Now the directly known forms a creative duration whose special characteristics are that it is non-logical (i.e. is not made up of distinct mutually exclusive terms united by external relations) and does not contain parts which can be repeated over and over, while on the other hand the terms which we have to substitute for it if we want to describe it only stand for repetitions and have the logical form. It looks, therefore, as if our descriptions could not, as they stand, be very successful in conveying to others the fact known to us directly, or in recalling it to ourselves.[47]

She goes on to suggest alternate acquaintance and analysis, but it is difficult to see how these are to be related if repetition is treated with such distaste. Gertrude Stein and Dorothy Richardson seem to be trying to overcome repetition by embracing it, and so inevitably including its opposite, change. The repetition and change is the rhythm of their art.

Early in her discussion, Karin Stephen makes the distinction between the two ways of seeing the world:

In whatever situation he finds himself a man may take up one of two attitudes, he may either adopt a practical attitude, in which case he will set to work to explain the situation in order that he may know what to do under the circumstances, or he may take a speculative interest in it and then he will devote himself to knowing it simply for the sake of knowing.[48]

Roger Fry makes the same point in *Vision and Design*, in a passage which is very close to Bergson's ideas:

First with regard to the greater clearness of perception. The needs of our actual life are so imperative, that the sense of vision becomes highly specialised in their service. With an admirable economy we learn to see only so much as is needful for our purposes; but this is in fact very little, just enough to recognise and identify each object or person; that done, they go into an entry in our mental catalogue and are no more really seen. In actual life the normal person really only reads the labels as it were on the objects around him and troubles no further. Almost all things which are useful in any way put on more or less this cap of invisibility.[49]

We might now turn to Roger Fry for his notions of 'repetition' and 'rhythm'.

ROGER FRY

In her biography of Fry, Virginia Woolf speaks of his essay 'Art and Life', which was written in 1917 and she goes on to say that 'the word "rhythm" was henceforth to occur frequently in his writing'.[50] She is quite right in seeing 'rhythm' as an increasing element in his criticism, but he had written of this connection between art and life in terms of rhythm much earlier than she suggests, in fact as early as 1904, as we can see from this passage:

The history of the development of an art may be looked at from two points of view. It may be looked on as a gradual conquest of the forms of nature, a gradual discovery of how things appear to the eye; or, on the other hand, as the logical and internally necessitated evolution of a rhythm; a process in which the rhythm of one generation of artists is bound, by its very nature, to generate the rhythm of the next. There come certain moments in this process when the rhythm which the artist inherits is more, others when it is less, propitious to the expression of the highest truths about the external universe: but always the rhythm tends to move along the lines of its own separate and predestined course. In French gothic art this seems to be particularly marked. We can trace how the lines of the Romanesque sculptors became more and more flexible without apparently approaching any nearer to natural form until suddenly the rhythm arrives at a point where it becomes perfectly adapted to the expression of life. At such a moment of the relaxation of a too rigid formula we get the generalised heroic naturalism of the early thirteenth century. To such a moment the silver king belongs. But the rhythm of rhythms moves on inevitably; it is but a moment, and the rhythm, here so suavely austere, becomes, by the inevitable accentuation of its new character, by its own internal impetus, year by year too fluent and too elegantly involved.[51]

This historical movement, the way in which one convention reaches a peak and then decays is seen as the 'rhythm of rhythms'; it is the larger rhythm within which the rhythms of individual works develop. Virginia Woolf rightly points out that rhythm becomes increasingly important in Fry's criticism, but she does not describe the way in which the idea changes. What happens in Fry's later criticism, I am suggesting, is not the greater use of the word 'rhythm' in this general historical sense, but an examination of what is involved in the idea of rhythm. And this involves, as in Waley's discussion, an understanding of the relationship between rhythm and repetition. Fry became more and more introspectively concerned with repetition and rhythm until, in *Last Lectures* this becomes one of his main themes. Previous critics have in general been very much concerned with the swing of the pendulum between the formal and representational elements in Fry's criticism, and have neglected this other theoretical interest. Yet it is of great importance,

114

for his idea of rhythm draws together his other concerns, with craftsmanship, science, law, representation, autonomy, and literary problems, such as the form of the novel. I am not imposing a false coherence on Fry's work – his many self-contradictions have been indicated by previous critics, and by Fry himself – I am simply pointing out a unity in the *problems* which he chose to tackle, and by doing this perhaps making clear a community of interest with Virginia Woolf and other twentieth-century writers.

We can see this importance of rhythm in his articles on 'line' in the *Burlington Magazine* and the debate with D. S. MacColl which followed. Their articles and letters cover the whole question of the place of representation in art, and cannot be simply summarised here. I would like to select the question of repetition which is raised in these articles and which was to occupy Fry to an increasing extent in his subsequent work. MacColl wonders what the 'new quality of rhythm' is which Fry sees in Piccasso and Matisse:

'Quality' in this connection I do not follow: I take it what is meant is a new rhythm. And this, so far as it is expounded depends on the use of 'a larger unit'. There is no merit in a large unit as such: nor is the rhythm necessarily altered, e.g. by writing in semibreves instead of quavers. The surface of a sheet of paper may be squared up into units measuring one inch by one and a half, or two by three, or in other ratios; and happiness of scale depends on the proportion of this unit to the size of the sheet. But I doubt whether Mr Fry means 'unit'.[52]

MacColl goes on to point out that a unit must be the same as another unit, not similar to it. Fry had compared this new rhythm to the change from regular to free verse, and MacColl comments:

But I conjecture that what Mr Fry really means is that modern drawing does not, like the stricter forms of verse, take the shape of repeated pattern. That is true enough; but it is not true only of modern drawing; it is equally true of Renaissance design. Repeated pattern belongs to things like wall-papers and textiles. These are the analogue of strict verse, in which metrical design takes the upper hand; though the analogy is not complete, since the repeated units in verse take on, with words, a changing *meaning*. But painting and pictorial drawing have never had this strict constitution; they have only approached it in frieze composition, or in closely symmetrical composition, which is one special case of the general law of rhythmical balance. The analogy throughout for drawing has been with the structure of prose, that is to say, a

115

structure in which metrical rhythm is in the background and phrase rhythm takes the lead.[53]

He points out in a footnote that no one has discovered the laws of this prose rhythm. But the analogy with prose leads him to oppose Fry on the question of representation: 'And this brings us up once more against the element that Mr Fry and his friends exclude from the art of drawing. Prose rhythm is moulded upon *meaning* as strict verse rhythm is not.'[54] As we saw in an earlier chapter, Fry's position on the question of representation is much more balanced than critics have assumed. (Note that MacColl here finds it necessary to speak of 'Mr Fry and his friends'.) In his reply Fry dissociates himself from Clive Bell's absolute rejection of representation. What is of special interest here, however, is his comment on the question of 'unit' in a work of art. He disposes of the question of representation and goes on:

Secondly, my use of the word 'unit'. Here at last I can gratefully acknowledge Mr MacColl's assistance. I used the word loosely to describe the subordinate unities in the whole texture of a design. I have sometimes used for this the word division, but this hardly suggests sufficiently the idea of repetition or recurrence. I said that the modern artist had increased the size of the unit of design, meaning that the whole pictorial unity was built up with a smaller number of such subordinate unities...Phrase might be a better word on the analogy of literature and music, or perhaps the rather vague word division will have to suffice. I think that, other things being equal, there is an aesthetic merit in reducing the number and amplifying the sweep of the divisions in that the unity thereby attained is more immediately apprehended.[55]

From this time, Fry notes the repetitions in the paintings he is discussing, a trend in his criticism intensified perhaps by the parallel work of Hubert Waley.

Fry's essay 'On Some Modern Drawings' in *Transformations* is a modified version of these essays in *The Burlington Magazine*. He tempers the duality of the earlier articles, but does not abandon it:

It would be foolish to over emphasise too much the distinction which I have here indicated between calligraphic and Impressionist drawing. Undoubtedly the freedom of hand of the calligraphic training, if it has not produced too fixed a formula, will serve the artist's turn when he is concentrated upon the vision, and it is not irrelevant that Rembrandt had one of the most beautiful, if not the most beautiful, handwriting that we know.[56]

He sees art as either based on practised repetitions which are subconsciously modified or based upon variations which are given an underlying form by the subconscious which brings out hidden repetitions. His work on handwriting showed the importance of the unconscious in modifying regularity:

The frequent repetition, then, of any form tends to make possible its rhythmic or calligraphic expression. This is the method in the case of handwriting, where the shapes of letters and even words have, by constant repetition, become ingrained in our nervous system, and can be called forth without any idea of these shapes rising to consciousness. A somewhat similar result is produced by the training of students in that system of figure-drawing which derives from Michelangelo and Raphael. The student repeats so constantly certain sequences of typical curves in a somewhat similar order that they become unconscious habits, and, according to the individual's capacity, rhythmic.

But there is another method by which the artist may withdraw his consciousness from his gesture sufficiently to allow of his line being rhythmical. This is attained if, before an actual appearance, he becomes so concentrated upon the interpretation of a contour as to be unconscious of what goes on between his hand and the paper.[57]

He still makes the comparison between prose and verse in this connection[58] and sees the dangers of each of these aspects of art as, on the one hand incoherence, and on the other, monotony. Fry's argument with MacColl, in general terms, can be seen as an opposition between dualism and transition. Fry in his articles makes a sharp division between calligraphic and impressionist art; MacColl denies this strict opposition and instead suggests a scale of gradual development. Fry himself had previously used the same kind of argument as MacColl when he denied Reynolds' strong antithesis between the grand and the ornamental styles:

The sharp line between the grand and ornamental styles seems rather arbitrary; and a classification which separates Tintoretto entirely from Titian, and places them alongside of Teniers, is something of a shock to our feelings. It might be fairer to say that there are infinite gradations in the degree of imaginative intensity of a conception, and that what is required of a work of art is the exact correspondence of the expression to the imaginative key.[59]

There seems to be in aesthetics this constant to and fro between the assertion of duality, and rejection of it in favour of a series of finer gradations. (This is itself a duality.) And the movement in aesthetics is true to what Fry sees as the development of art itself. So, in his study of Cézanne he says:

> true Impressionists... were more concerned to seize the full complexity of the coloured mosaic of vision than to isolate and emphasise those indications in the total complex which are evocative of plastic form... The intellect is bound to seek for articulations. In order to handle nature's continuity it has to be conceived as discontinuous; without organisation, without articulation the intellect gets no leverage.[60]

In this problem of continuity and discontinuity, we come back again, as Butler predicted we would at the end of every inquiry, to a contradiction. The continuous can be articulated only if it is seen as discontinuous. The continuity 'intuited' by Bergson can be chopped in pieces by the discontinuity, of, say, Wyndham Lewis. Roger Shattuck in his excellent book *The Banquet Years* misuses Fry's phrase 'luxury effect', but understands the central dualism in his criticism:

> Rousseau's decorative sense is almost as sure as his sense of colour and, like it, serves the luxury effect as well as the need for order. (The terms are Roger Fry's.) In both colour and form, decorative styles fall into two general categories: repetition and variation (complication). The former tends toward simple rhythmical patterns, like a row of trees; the latter tends toward what Focillon called the 'system of labyrinth' – Arabic decorative borders, baroque devices, and old fashioned stencils. Most 'primitive' art favours repetitive decoration; Rousseau employed both techniques.[61]

Shattuck should perhaps have used the term 'surface' or 'decorative' effect here rather than 'luxury' effect, for Fry used this only in the most derogatory way to describe mechanical or shop finish, whereas by 'decorative' he simply meant the pattern on the surface of the canvas. Shattuck obviously has this latter idea in mind here. In his study of Cézanne Fry stresses the importance of formal repetitions:

> One notes how few the forms are. How the sphere is repeated again and again in varied quantities. To this is added the rounded oblong shapes which are repeated...If we add the continually repeated right

lines and the frequently repeated but identical forms of the leaves on the wallpaper...[62]

Against this repetition Cézanne balances the irregular shifting data of Impressionism. His art is that of 'holding together in a single rhythmical scheme such an immense number of small and often closely repetitive movements'.[63] And the fruitful tension seen in each canvas is repeated in his whole development, which is an exploration and a growth like that of life itself:

It is evident that all his life he was continually brooding over one tormenting question; how to conciliate the data of Impressionism with – what he regarded as an essential to style – a perfect structural organisation...It was this determination to arrive at a perfect synthesis of opposing principles, perhaps, that kept Cézanne's sensibility at such a high tension, that prevented him ever repeating himself, from ever executing a picture as a performance. Each canvas had to be a new investigation and a new solution.[64]

Fry admires Matisse's work for the same qualities. His repetition and variation Fry describes as:

an astonishing sense of linear rhythm, a rhythm which is at once extremely continuous and extremely elastic, that is to say it is capable of extraordinary variations from the norm without loss of continuity. The phrase can be held through all its changes. Imagine the rhythm rendered the least bit tight and mechanical in its regularity and the whole system of allusion and ellipsis would break down and become ridiculous.[65]

And Matisse avoids repetition in his work as a whole: 'If we sense he is making use of the same effect, he scents the danger and throws away a suspiciously easy tool.'[66] Many of the implications of this idea of repetition and variation as the basis of art are worked out in Fry's *Last Lectures*. His dislike of the machine-made and of the kind of 'craftsmanship' which crushes human vitality and individuality is clearly in line with our discussion of *Women in Love*. Also close to Lawrence is his idea that freedom from repetition does not come from mere chance, but from the unconscious.[67] The extremes are the endless repetition of Buddhas and confusing abundance of variation in Indian art which for Fry 'lacks syntax'. Both extremes are in his view caused by the intrusion of religion into art. This is interesting in its relation to Forster's *A Passage to India*. There can

119

be no connection between the two extremes; there is nothing to connect India with the West, and nothing, perhaps, to connect one human being with another. There is simply a juxtaposition, an emptiness at the heart of the canvas, the stillness which comes from the three-fold 'come, come, come'.

This ability of repetition to suggest stillness Fry notes in his comments on Seurat's *La Parade*:

This transmutation results from the extreme simplification of all the forms according to certain conscious and deliberate principles. Thus we note that across the elaborate rectilinear framework of the design are played two main formal elements, an ovoid exemplified in the two blue patches on the *affiche* repeated in the numbers behind the central figure and again and again in the bowler hats and shoulders of the men and, in contradiction to this, the conical shapes of the trombone-player's head and hat, inverted in his legs and again in several of the women's hats. It is perhaps this continuous repetition of a few simple forms that gives to the picture its strange fixity and stillness.[68]

Roger Shattuck throughout his book emphasises the importance of repetition and variation, and of transition and juxtaposition, in art, and this 'strange fixity and stillness' which Fry sees in Seurat's work, Shattuck believes might be the chief characteristic which future ages will see in our century: 'Contrary to all expectation, this century may one day be known as the age of stillness, of arrest.'[69] Roger Fry was of course in close contact with the French avant-garde which Shattuck studies, and many of the insights into their art in *The Banquet Years* help us to understand Fry's ideas and Virginia Woolf's art. Shattuck's remarks on Satie's music are particularly interesting:

Socrate is that rare phenomenon, utterly *white* music, which denies its own existence as it goes along by an absolute refusal of development. Both rhythm and melody in Western tradition rely on a fine balance between repetition and variation. Satie wrote *Socrate* in figures that are endlessly repeated and scarcely varied at all. Yet the music never stands still...Satie attempted in *Socrate* a new balance between monotony and variety.[70]

This concern with boredom and repetition is not simply a vague parallel with the work of Virginia Woolf, for it results in a strange formal similarity. Satie was obsessed by what Virginia Woolf in *Between the Acts* calls the 'triple melody' and the 'three-fold ply'.

Triple melody

Shattuck uses one of Fry's favourite terms to describe the effect of this three-fold structure in Satie's music, it is 'plastic':

There is a trivial feature of Satie's music that takes on significance in this context. His first major sets of pieces all contain three parts: three *Sarabandes*, three *Gymnopédies*, three *Gnossiennes*. Of the fifty-odd works that followed, almost half are similarly threefold. This trinitarian obsession was a quirk which became part of his musical pose. But in about eight works – clearly in the three mentioned above – the arrangement stands for a formal approach to his material. Satie takes one musical idea and, instead of developing it at length and working variations on it, regards it briefly from three different directions. He varies only the bare contour, the notes in the melody but not its general shape, the chords in the accompaniment but not its dominant mood. An artist drawing a head from three different sides could obtain the same effect. There are obvious grounds for comparison of this procedure with that of the cubists. They investigated the complexity in time and space of a simple object studied simultaneously from several points of view. Satie frequently scrutinizes a very simple musical object: a short, unchanging *ostinato* accompaniment plus a fragmentary melody. Out of this sameness comes subtle variety. Far from being a mere trick, this serial construction illustrates one of Satie's principal resources – brevity as pure form...Brevity in music is inescapably comic and, as Satie employed it by threes, inescapably plastic.[71]

What is this fascination with three? Edmund Wilson sees the Marxist dialectic as part of this obsession, which is shared by many writers:

But in what way does this prove the dialectical Trinity? In what way is that Trinity proved when Professor Haldane maps out the processes of mutation and selection as triads any more than it was proved by Hegel when he arranged all his arguments in three parts – or, for that matter, for Vico, when he persisted in seeing everything in threes: three kinds of languages, three systems of law, three kinds of government, etc., or by Dante, when he divided his poem into three sections with thirty-three cantos each?[72]

The particular triad which we invoke depends on the kind of

discourse we are engaged in. Here, we might say that three is significant in art and aesthetics because it is the smallest number which
allows repetition and variation.

We can see this triple melody in Dorothy Richardson's *Deadlock*.
Gerald, Harriet and Miriam make three attempts to get a record
going at the right speed on an old gramophone. At first it is too fast,
then too slow, but finally the song comes out at the correct speed
and pitch:

The march of the refrain came lilting across the stream of days, joyfully
beating out the common recognition of the three listeners. She restrained
her desire to take it up, flinging out her will to hold back the others,
that they might face out the moment and let it make its full mark. In
the next refrain they could all take the relief of shouting their acknow-
ledgement, a hymn to the threefold life. The last verse was coming
successfully through; in an instant the chorus refrain would be there.
It was old and familiar, woven securely into experience, beginning its
life as memory. She listened eagerly.[73]

Earlier in the novel Miriam and Shatov had visited the British
Museum and looked at a translation of *Anna Karenina*. Miriam likes
the sound of the tri-syllabic Russian name, and the Russian custom
of having three names:

But Anna Karenine was not what Tolstoi had written. Behind the ugly
feebleness of the substituted word was something quite different, strong
and beautiful; a whole legend in itself. Why had the translator altered
the surname? Anna Karaynina was a line of Russian poetry. His word
was nothing, neither English nor French, and sounded like a face-cream.
She scanned sceptically up and down the pages of English words, chilled
by the fear of detecting the trail of the translator.
   Mr Shatov read steadily, breathing his enthusiasm in gusts, pausing
as each fresh name appeared, to pronounce it in Russian and to explain
the three names belonging to each character. They were all expressive;
easy to remember because of their expressiveness. The threefold name,
giving each character three faces, each turned towards a different part
of his world, fascinating...[74]

Later, she translates into English from a German translation a
trilogy of Russian short stories. The process of translation is itself
a threefold activity: 'The knowledge that it could, by three stages,
laborious but unchanging and certain in their operation, reach a life
of its own, the same in its whole effect, and yet in each detail so

different from the original, radiated joy through the whole slow process.'[75] The gradual unfolding from one language to another to a third, from the literal translation through the rough draft to the finished translation, and from the first story to the completed sequence, is the movement of life itself:

The second story lay untouched, wrapped in its magic. Contemplating the way, with its difference, it enhanced the first and was enhanced by it, she longed to see the two side by side and found, while she hesitated before the slow scattering process of translation, a third that set her headlong at work towards the perfect finished group. There was no weariness in this second stretch of labour. Behind her lay the first story, a rampart, of achievement and promise, and ahead, calling her on, the one that was yet to be attempted, difficult and strange, a little thread of story upon a background of dark thoughts, like a voice heard through a storm. Even the heaviest parts of the afternoon could be used, in an engrossed forgetfulness of time and place. Time pressed. The year was widening and lifting too rapidly towards the heights of June when everything but the green world, fresh gleaming in parks and squares through the London swelter, sweeping with the tones of spring and summer mingled amongst the changing trees, towards September, would fade from her grasp and disappear.[76]

Virginia Woolf uses triple form in her book *Three Guineas*. It is used as a very crude rhetorical device to overcome resistance to her arguments about the place of women in society. In her diary she says that it should be read in conjunction with *The Years*.[77] She was thinking perhaps of the feminist argument contained in both works, but of more interest here is the use of repetition. It would be pointless to instance all the uses of triple repetition and three-fold examples in the book, but *Three Guineas* is interesting in that it points forward to *Between the Acts* in this respect, as in the passage in which she asks how long women will have to endure 'the old tune which human nature, like a gramophone whose needle has stuck, is now grinding out with such disastrous unanimity? "Here we go round the mulberry tree, the mulberry tree, the mulberry tree..."'[78] We are reminded here of the gramophone in *Between the Acts* which repeats over and over 'dispersed are we'. Virginia Woolf differs from Dorothy Richardson in that she insists on the repetition involved in triple form, whereas Dorothy Richardson gives equal weight to change, to repetition with variation. The effect of this is to give

Virginia Woolf's work in comparison a highly-strung, hysterical feeling, a sense of brittleness, of the hollowness of The Hollow Men, who sing 'Here we go round the prickly pear, prickly pear, prickly pear...' Dorothy Richardson uses three to show the movement, the rhythm of life's development, whereas Virginia Woolf's trinities enforce her perception of repetition.

Repetition itself has a double aspect. Once again Shattuck's discussion of Satie is of help here. Satie uses repetition to make us see the glory and horror of boredom:

'The public venerates boredom', Satie wrote. 'For boredom is mysterious and profound.' And elsewhere: 'The listener is defenseless against boredom. Boredom subdues him.' Satie's need for self-effacement springs from his fascination with boredom – fear of it and knowledge of its power...Satie challenges us not to be impressed but to be bored. He says in effect: Here are the naked features of our world. If they provoke you or bore, you will have reacted constructively, for either way you will be forced to move. This is the meaning of a staggering sentence that describes his entire being: 'Experience is one of the forms of paralysis'....If experience is a form of paralysis, satisfaction is a form of death. In his hands music never became an exercise in self-contentment. It was a means of upholding our freedom.[79]

This double nature of boredom, or of repetition, is one of Virginia Woolf's continuing obsessions, especially in *The Waves*.

REPETITION AND STILLNESS: 'JACOB'S ROOM'

J. K. Johnstone sees *Jacob's Room* as somewhat incoherent and lacking in unity. It is, he says, 'a number of vivid but loosely related episodes, surrounded, sometimes separated from one another, by vast and indefinite tracts of time and space'.[80] He is correct in saying that the novel points the way to Virginia Woolf's more mature works, but I believe he over-emphasises the fragmentary aspect of its construction, and fails to see the underlying implications of the repetitions. He recognises certain repeated phrases, but does not relate these satisfactorily to the other repetitions in the novel:

She wishes to convince us that the whole of Jacob's life, from the scene on the Cornish beach to the final scene in Jacob's room (which are related by the reiterations of Jacob's name, and by the presence of Mrs Flanders, worried and helpless), existed from the beginning in the real world – which is outside the limitations of time and space – and only remained to be fulfilled in present time. This conception, which accords with Virginia Woolf's view of life, attracts by its very daring: if it could be accomplished, Jacob's life would be given an inevitability that would be absolute. But the most that the artist can do in this respect, so it seems, is to foreshadow, as Strachey does in his biographies, the future course of events. And this is fortunate; for art, though it may aim at the absolute, should never attain it: if it did, it would be too far removed from life. At any rate, when the incident in Piccadilly is described for the second time, and when sentences from earlier descriptions of Jacob's rooms at Cambridge and in Bloomsbury are repeated verbatim in the last chapter, we may have for a moment the feeling, which we sometimes know in life, that all this has happened before – but only for a moment: then we see through the device, and reflect upon the mechanics of the novel, rather than upon the inevitability of Jacob's life.[81]

It might be argued that Virginia Woolf did want her readers to reflect upon the 'mechanics of the novel', which she would not consider to be separate from the 'inevitability of Jacob's life'. The whole question of the distance between art and life is much more complex than Johnstone implies in his discussion. Jacob is a very shadowy figure: 'And this is a serious weakness in the novel; for its centre, the character who might unite all its various scenes, is – not there.'[82] This comes about because in *Jacob's Room* Virginia Woolf puts into practice her theory of character – 'that it is impossible to sum a person up, that there is nothing more ludicrous than one person's opinion of another person'.[83] Johnstone's remarks are valid, but he does not deal fully with the principle of repetition which gives a kind of unity to the work. The theme of 'absence' develops from her previous novel *Night and Day*, and the hero's absence in *Jacob's Room* is an essential part of the novel's meaning. We saw the way in which the characters in the earlier novel were wrapped in mist; *Jacob's Room* is a development of this kind of vision. We might illustrate this by quoting one of the descriptions which Johnstone rightly points out are repeated verbatim in the last chapter: 'Listless is the air in an empty room, just swelling the curtain; the flowers in the jar shift. One fibre in the wicker armchair creaks, though no one sits there.'[84] The ghostly sitter in the chair is as real as the other characters in the novel, who are, as Leonard Woolf immediately recognised, all ghosts.

Virginia Woolf uses repeated phrases to 'copy' in a stylised way certain sounds. This is done quite subtly in the following passage: 'Back from the Chapel, back from the Hall, back from the Library, came the sound of his footsteps, as if the old stone echoed with magisterial authority: "The young man – the young man – the young man – back to his rooms."'[85] This repetition represents the echoes of Jacob's footfall in the empty court, but it also points to the fact that Jacob is typical of all the other young men who were once at Cambridge. The idea of uniqueness within repetition, central to Virginia Woolf's art, is here given expression with fine economy.

One of the themes of the novel is the connection between the spiritual and material, or mind and body. Jacob, as Johnstone points out, is 'not there', but what the novel attempts is to clear a space between the fixity of a statue and the elusiveness of an 'absence'; between these final terms of the scale the human spirit moves. This movement is made up of repetitions, but they can be interwoven with variations and so become a rhythm. Here, the repetition of a phrase expresses the movement of the mind as it circles around the problem of connecting the mind and body: 'The problem is insoluble. The body is harnessed to a brain. Beauty goes hand in hand with stupidity...The problem is insoluble.'[86] In this case the repeated phrase also forms a kind of parenthesis around the meditation, and gives it a sense of stillness.

To these dichotomies which we have mentioned others can be added, such as that between the 'real' and the 'ideal', but most important perhaps is that between 'art' and 'reality'. The idea of infinite regression, of mirror on mirror, once more haunts the page. The pictures which hang in Jacob's room are even more unreal than visual art as described by Plato, for they are copies of copies: 'Then there were photographs from the Greeks, and a mezzotint from Sir Joshua – all very English.'[87] This kind of illusion is also involved in the idea of history or tradition: our idea of the Greeks is an illusion:

But it is the governesses who start the Greek myth. Look at that for a head (they say) – nose, you see, straight as a dart, curls, eyebrows – everything appropriate to manly beauty; while his legs and arms have lines on them which indicate a perfect degree of development – the Greeks caring for the body as much as for the face. And the Greeks could paint fruit so that birds pecked at it. First you read Xenophon;

then Euripides. One day – that was an occasion, by God – what people have said appears to have sense in it; 'the Greek spirit'; the Greek this, that and the other; though it is absurd, by the way, to say that any Greek comes near Shakespeare. The point is, however, that we have been brought up in an illusion.[88]

Byron is in the shade of the Greeks, but Jacob is a shadow of this shade. The repetition involved in tradition gives rise to the mock-heroic element in the novel. In this way, Mother Stuart is a debased oracle, something like Madame Sosostris of *The Waste Land*:

Stuart, as the lady would point out, is the name of a Royal house; but what that signified, and what her business was, no one knew; only that Mrs Stuart got postal orders every Monday morning, kept a parrot, believed in the transmigration of souls, and could read the future in tea leaves. Dirty lodging-house wallpaper she was behind the chastity of Florinda.[89]

The repetition of phrases is an element in this mock-epic style. The repeated 'eternal conspiracy of hush' gives a sense of false solemnity to Mrs Flanders' baby-sitting.[90] Later in the novel the repetition of 'the boy Curnow' is a mocking elevation of the urchin to the status of epic hero. The constant use of inversion is an attempt to convey a sense of solemnity. The first words of the inverted phrases convey the sense intended – 'gravely', 'solemnly' and so on. The unchanging nature of the religious ceremony is associated with the solemnity of the Homeric simile:

As the sides of a lantern protect the flame so that it burns steady even in the wildest night – burns steady and gravely illumines the tree-trunks – so inside the Chapel all was orderly. Gravely sounded the voices; wisely the organ replied, as if buttressing human faith with the assent of the elements.[91]

This gives a sense of stillness to the novel. One of the final repetitions in the last chapter is an inversion of this kind, giving Jacob's room a sculptured quality in contrast with his 'character', which is all movement like a flickering light. The repetition and inversion enforce this contrast: 'Listless is the air in an empty room, just swelling the curtain; the flowers in the jar shift. One fibre in the wicker arm-chair creaks, though no one sits there.'[92] Once more Jacob is a ghost.

127

10

The double nature of repetition:
'The Waves'

Repetition is one of the most basic patterns of meaning or significance. Human beings in the most degrading situations can give a
limited meaning to their lives by repetition. The soldiers in David
Jones's *In Parenthesis* create a kind of liturgy in this way:

> The repeated passing back of aidful messages
> assumes a cadency.
> Mind the hole
> mind the hole
> mind the hole to left
> hole right
> step over
> keep left, left.
> 　　　　　One grovelling, precipitated, with his
> gear tangled, struggles to feet again:
> Left be buggered.
> 　　　　　Sorry mate – you all right china ? – lift
> us yer rifle – an' don't take on so Honey – but
> rather, mind
> the wire here
> mind the wire
> mind the wire
> mind the wire.[1]

Although this liturgical repetition gives assurance and is an assertion of humanity, repetition can become empty and mechanical, a
true reflection of the machine, or the machine-gun. It is this aspect
which Virginia Woolf points to in the figure of Septimus in *Mrs
Dalloway*. Some critics regard Virginia Woolf as an ivory-tower
aesthete, a descendant of the nineties. C. Campos criticises all the
Bloomsbury Group in this way: 'The Great War had if anything a
negative influence on these writers: in trying to act as if what had

happened between 1914 and 1918 could be forgotten, they emphasised all the more a state of mind really belonging to an age that had ended in 1918.'[2] By concentrating on problems of form, including repetition, Virginia Woolf is able to include at the same time other, wider, problems. Septimus Smith's 'state of mind' is only pre-war in the sense that Virginia Woolf uses her own experience of mental disturbance, which had begun before the War, in his portrayal. He is a victim of the War, suffering from shell-shock,[3] but his lack of feeling also indicates a general deadness in society in a machine age. 'He felt nothing' is constantly reiterated in the novel. He sees events from the outside, without emotion, and so even his wife's sobs become banausic repetition and his own actions are empty and mechanical:

Far away he heard her sobbing; he heard it accurately, he noticed it distinctly; he compared it to a piston thumping. But he felt nothing.

His wife was crying, and he felt nothing; only each time she sobbed in this profound, this silent, this hopeless way, he descended another step into the pit.

At last, with a melodramatic gesture which he assumed mechanically and with complete consciousness of its insincerity, he dropped his head on his hands.[4]

David Jones recognises the inhuman aspect of repetition and its wider significance, as shown, for example by his allusion to T. S. Eliot's poem *The Hollow Men*, in the repetition of 'Prickly Pear Prickly Pear'.[5] Virginia Woolf shares with David Jones and T. S. Eliot a sense of the glory, boredom and horror of modern life. It is in her use of repetition that these elements come together. Repetition can be boring or terrifying, but it is also a source of glory, for through its action, men can achieve the kind of defiance of their circumstances which the soldiers accomplish in *In Parenthesis*.

A closer examination of *The Waves* will indicate how the whole design arises from the idea of repetition and rhythm. But this is not simply a question of artistic 'technique'; for the artist, a passionate interest in aesthetic problems cannot be separated from an interest in 'life'. The accusation that Virginia Woolf is a mere aesthete is as absurd as such an accusation would be against, say, T. S. Eliot.

Yeats also was interested in repetition and rhythm. He believed that there were two sorts of repetition, the rhythmical and the abstract. He calls them Cain and Abel, the noise of a machine and the coming and going of breath. Virginia Woolf sees these two kinds of repetition as depending on our point of view, rather than inherent in the repetition itself. Even 'the coming and going of breath' is not necessarily rhythmical, as Neville points out: 'We grew; we changed; for, of course, we are animals. We are not always aware by any means; we breathe, eat, sleep automatically.'[6] The breaking of waves on the beach is often regarded as rhythmical, as repetition with variation. Susanne Langer uses this example in order to define rhythm:

But the most impressive example of rhythm known to most people is the breaking of waves in a steady surf. Each new comber rolling in is shaped by the undertow flowing back, and in its turn actually hurries the recession of the previous wave by suction. There is no dividing line between the two events. Yet a breaking wave is as definite an event as one could wish to find – a true dynamic *Gestalt*.

Such phenomena in the inanimate world are powerful *symbols* of living form, just because they are not life processes themselves. The contrast between the apparently vital behaviour and the obviously inorganic structure of ocean waves, for instance, emphasises the pure semblance of life, and makes the first abstractions of its rhythm for our intellectual intuition. That is the prime function of symbols. Their second function is to allow us to manipulate the concepts we have achieved. This requires more than a recognition of what may be termed 'natural symbols', it demands the deliberate making of expressive forms that may be deployed in various ways to reveal new meanings. And such created *Gestalten*, that give us logical insight into feeling, vitality and emotional life, are works of art.[7]

Langer sees the difference between inorganic structure and organic behaviour as a kind of gap which allows distancing and so the possibility of manipulation. This distance corresponds to that which Cassirer sees between sensation and language. The waves in *The Waves* move in an area which lies between organic and inorganic, and a further ambiguity is created by the fact that they are perceived from different points of view. Susanne Langer speaks of the breaking of waves as an 'example of rhythm', but for Louis it is an example, not of rhythm but of repetition, for he sees it as 'the chained beast' which 'stamps and stamps on the shore'.[8] The neutral observer of the interludes, a kind of chorus, describes the tide in the following way: 'The wave paused, and then drew out again, sighing like a sleeper whose breath comes and goes unconsciously.'[9] This hits exactly the middle ground between organic and inorganic. In waves we see vital behaviour in an inorganic structure, in a sleeping person the reverse is the case. The interludes continually aim at this ambiguous area between the animate and inanimate (which incidentally is one of the themes of Butler's *Note-Books*). In the following passage, the tide is an 'engine', a mechanical and artificial creation, but it has 'muscularity', a natural and organic attribute. Further, the waves are compared with men on horseback, but men engaging in the 'inhuman' act of war:

They fell with a regular thud. They fell with the concussion of horses' hooves on the turf. Their spray rose like the tossing of lances and assegais over the riders' heads. They swept the beach with steel blue and diamond-tipped water. They drew in and out with the energy, the muscularity, of an engine which sweeps its force out and in again.[10]

The same repetition can be either abstract or rhythmical depending on the way we look at it; how it strikes us at a particular moment or in a certain context. In this way, repetition can be either comforting or terrifying, organic or mechanical, boring or rhythmical depending on our point of view. In *The Waves* there are six points of view, and each has its own relation to the problem of repetition and rhythm.

Something which has rhythm when we are a part of it becomes empty and repetitious if we see it from the outside. The café may become the centre of communal life in big cities and Dorothy Richardson's heroine, Miriam, can allow herself to feel the gregarious warmth of such places:

She could understand a life that spent all its leisure in a café; every day ending in warm brilliance, forgetfulness amongst strangers near and intimate, sharing the freedom and forgetfulness of the everlasting unchanging café, all together in a common life. It was like a sort of dance, every one coming and going poised and buoyant, separate and free, united in freedom. It was heaven...That old man sitting alone with a grey face and an extinguished eye was the end of it, but even now the café held him up; he would come till death came too near to allow him movement. He was horrible, but less horrible than he would be alone in a room. He had to keep the rules and manage to behave. As long as he could come he was still in life...[11]

Louis, however, cannot submerge himself in the habitual life of the café. He does not see freedom, only machine-like activity:

Yet I cannot. (They go on passing, they go on passing in disorderly procession.) I cannot read my book, or order my beef, with conviction. I repeat 'I am an average Englishman; I am an average clerk,' yet I look at the little men at the next table to be sure that I do what they do. Supple-faced, with rippling skins, that are always twitching with the multiplicity of their sensations, prehensile like monkeys, greased to this particular moment, they are discussing with all the right gestures the sale of a piano. It blocks up the hall; so he would take a Tenner. People go on passing; they go on passing against the spires of the church and the plates of ham sandwiches. The streamers of my consciousness waver out and are perpetually torn and distressed by their disorder. I cannot therefore concentrate on my dinner. 'I would take a tenner. The case is handsome; but it blocks up the hall.' They dive and plunge like guillemots whose feathers are slippery with oil. All excesses beyond that norm are vanity. That is the mean; that is the average. Meanwhile the hats bob up and down; the door perpetually shuts and opens. I am conscious of flux, of disorder; of annihilation and despair. If this is all, this is worthless. Yet I feel, too, the rhythm of the eating-house. It is like a waltz tune, eddying in and out, round and round. The waitresses, balancing trays, swing in and out, round and round, dealing plates of greens, of apricot and custard, dealing them at the right time, to the right customers. The average men, including her rhythm in their rhythm ('I would take a tenner; for it blocks up the hall') take their greens, take their apricots and custard. Where then is the break in this continuity? What the fissure through which one sees disaster? The circle is unbroken; the harmony complete. Here is the central rhythm; here the common mainspring. I watch it expand, contract; and then expand again. Yet I am not included.[12]

Like Miriam Henderson, he can see the eating-house as a 'sort of dance', a 'waltz tune'. The 'rhythm of the eating-house' is organic and reassuring to everyone who is included in it. From his position as an outsider, however, there is a sense of meaningless repetition; there is an endless bobbing up and down as the man discusses interminably the sale of his piano. He is like a gramophone with the needle stuck in one groove: 'I would take a tenner; for it blocks up the hall.' The people who come and go are reduced to their hats: 'The hats bob up and down'. The whole scene is like a piece of clockwork '...here the common mainspring, I watch it expand, contract; and then expand again.' This outside view, however, which all of Virginia Woolf's artists have to some extent, enables them to see the form and pattern of their experience. Louis goes on to speak of his task as an artist:

To me is addressed the plaint of the wandering and distracted spirit (a woman with bad teeth falters at the counter), 'Bring us back to the fold, we who pass so disjectedly, bobbing up and down, past windows with plates of ham sandwiches in the foreground.' Yes; I will reduce you to order.[13]

Repetition is a source of value and comfort, yet it can be seen as the denial of human value, for people can become like machines. Repetition is the basis of 'structure' and 'form' in art and yet too intense an awareness of repetition, such as Louis has, can give a sense of emptiness and disorder. Louis' response is to reduce the repetitions to some sort of coherence. From his earliest days Louis is very sensitive to repetitions: '"That is the first stroke of the church bell," said Louis. "Then the others follow; one, two; one two; one, two."'[14] His attitude towards time is governed by an obsession with repetition; he refuses 'to come to the top and live in the light of this great clock, yellow-faced, which ticks and ticks.'[15] He is glad to escape from the repetitions of childhood: 'We shall not always give out a sound like a beaten gong as one sensation strikes and then another. Children, our lives have been gongs striking; clamour and boasting; cries of despair; blows on the nape of the neck in gardens.'[16] He will try to escape by forging poetry into a 'ring of steel',[17] which is an image repeated with slight variations throughout Louis' soliloquies. It is a ring to tame 'the beast which stamps and stamps', the repeated concussion of the waves that haunts him throughout his life. Springing from his sense of repetition, and an answer to it, is his sense of tradition and history. J. Schaefer comments:

Louis longs to cut himself free from the past and future and to live in the present which prompts him to action. His chief personal problem revolves around the difficulty of reconciling his actual physical existence in the present moment with his mental and emotional existence in history. Louis resembles T. S. Eliot's Prufrock in many ways, perhaps most of all in his awareness of the discrepancy between the scope of history and the role he has to play in it.[18]

Schaefer goes on to point out that 'His whole attitude to history seems a parody of T. S. Eliot's ideas as formulated in "Tradition and the Individual Talent"'.[19] The critic is right in seeing Eliot's influence in the novel, and particularly in the portrayal of Louis, but to describe him as Prufrock and his ideas as *parodies* of Eliot seems to me to miss the mark. The landscape of Louis' poems is similar to that of Eliot in the 'Preludes' or 'Prufrock', being full of the squalor of city life: 'there I see the broken windows in poor people's houses; the lean cats; some slattern squinting in a cracked looking-glass as she arranges her face for the street corner...'[20] This is a parody only in the sense that a parody may be the product of a deep assimilation of another artist's work. If we follow one specific image echoed from Eliot, we will see that the novel as a whole does not parody Eliot, it enlarges on certain of his images and ideas; and so forms a criticism of Eliot's position, and perhaps finds a place for itself in his 'tradition'. The image of the nightingale links Louis with Eliot:

Sealed and blind, with earth stopping my ears, I have yet heard rumours of wars; and the nightingale; have felt the hurrying of many troops of men flocking hither and thither in quest of civilisation like flocks of birds migrating seeking the summer; I have seen women carrying red pitchers to the banks of the Nile.[21]

Louis returns to the image of the nightingale later in the novel, and sets it in juxtaposition to the sordid nature of city life: '"Listen," I say, "to the nightingale, who sings among the trampling feet; the conquests and migrations. Believe–" and then am twitched asunder. Over broken tiles and splinters of glass I pick my way.'[22] On the surface this is a mere copy of Eliot, and apparently justifies Schaefer's criticism that Louis sounds 'alarmingly like Prufrock at times'. But here we see the problem of abstracting characters one by one from this novel. They are 'one person' in a sense, but they also complement and criticise and are influenced by each other – just as Virginia Woolf, Eliot's publisher and friend, would be influenced by him. Louis feels that he hears the nightingale in spite of the 'earth stopping my ears', in spite of the 'dirty ears' which have reduced the nightingale's song to the conventional representation of it in the traditional ballad, 'Jug, jug'. From a position of the full enjoyment of her sexuality, Jinny explains the transcription of the nightingale's song in quite a different way: 'Now let us sing our love song –

Come, come, come. Now my gold signal is like a dragon-fly flying taut. Jug, jug, jug, I sing like the nightingale whose melody is crowded in the too narrow passage of her throat.'[23] The song of the nightingale is powerful because it is compressed by passion. Eliot's sexual disgust is here implicitly criticised, as Virginia Woolf had explicitly criticised him for being 'anaemic'.[24] Further, it is Neville, not Louis, who contrasts Shakespeare's vision with the everyday scene in Eliot's manner:

It is better to look at a rose, or to read Shakespeare as I read him here in Shaftesbury Avenue. Here's the fool, here's the villain, here in a car comes Cleopatra, burning on her barge. Here are figures of the damned too, noseless men by the police-court wall, standing with their feet in fire, howling. This is poetry if we do not write it.[25]

Eliot's influence is clearly much more diffuse than Schaefer seems to suggest, much wider than simply Louis as a parody of Prufrock. If we see Louis as concerned not simply with history, but with history as a kind of escape from repetition, then this becomes a useful and profound way of looking at the work of Eliot himself – something which goes beyond parody. The relationship of history or tradition to the repetitions of the ego are made clear in the following passage:

'I have signed my name,' said Louis, 'already twenty times. I, and again I, and again I. Clear, firm, unequivocal, there it stands, my name. Clear-cut and unequivocal am I too. Yet a vast inheritance of experience is packed in me. I have lived thousands of years. I am like a worm that has eaten its way through the wood of a very old oak beam. But now I am compact; now I am gathered together this fine morning.[26]

So Eliot's phrases and ideas and images echo and re-echo through-out the novel, centred mainly, but not exclusively on Louis. A typical passage is the following – clearly this is Eliot's 'world':

This is the arch and ironical manner in which I hope to distract you from my shivering, my tender, and infinitely young and unprotected soul...I luxuriate in gold and purple vestments. Yet I prefer a view over chimney-pots; cats scraping their mangy sides upon blistered chimney-stacks; broken windows; and the hoarse clangour of bells from the steeple of some brick chapel.[27]

The idea of Louis being obsessed particularly by repetition, hating

it yet attracted to it and finding it inevitable, can help us to appreciate certain elements in Eliot's poetry. Some understanding of this
kind is certainly necessary for a full appreciation of his *Four
Quartets*. The vision of a metropolitan Hades in that poem is
anticipated by Jinny:

'Here I stand,' said Jinny, 'in the Tube station where everything that
is desirable meets – Piccadilly South Side, Piccadilly North Side, Regent
Street and the Haymarket. I stand for a moment under the pavement
in the heart of London. Innumerable wheels rush and feet press just
over my head. The great avenues of civilisation meet here and strike
this way and that. I am in the heart of life. But look – there is my body
in that looking glass. How solitary, how shrunk, how aged! I am no
longer young. I am no longer part of procession. Millions descend
those stairs in a terrible descent.[28]

Rhoda, in her solitude, is very much like Louis. Like him, she
lives in the waste land, the land of the hollow men. She hates the
organic nature of life: 'Walking on the embankment, I prayed that
I might thunder for ever on the verge of the world where there is no
vegetation, but here and there a marble pillar.'[29] She has perception
of repetition like that of Louis:

The human face is hideous. This is to my liking. I want publicity and
violence and to be dashed like a stone on the rocks. I like factory
chimneys and cranes and lorries. I like the passing of face and face and
face, deformed, indifferent. I am sick of prettiness; I am sick of privacy.
I ride rough waters and shall sink with no one to save me.
  Percival, by his death, has made me this present, has revealed this
terror, has left me to undergo this humiliation – faces and faces, served
out like soup-plates by scullions...[30]

We are reminded here of Louis in the café, but whereas Louis'
repetition comes from an extension of his awareness of self ('I,
I and again I'), with Rhoda it comes from her lack of self. She dislikes the individual human face, and declares that she herself has 'no
face'. This lack of physiognomic perception is important in trying
to understand repetition and rhythm. Human faces are much the
same, in general outline, or seen from a distance, yet no two faces
are ever exactly alike. In this respect, then, human faces are
rhythmical, for we have repetition with variations. But Rhoda hates
these variations which become obvious on closer examination, she

hates 'all details of the individual life'.[31] This is made clear when
Rhoda and Louis see the others in the distance. Louis asks 'Are they
men or are they women? They still wear the ambiguous draperies
of the flowing tide in which they have been immersed.'[32] Rhoda
admires the distant, statuesque view, but her disappointment grows
as they come nearer and become individual, detailed and various:

'Now,' said Rhoda, 'as they pass that tree, they regain their natural
size. They are only men, only women. Wonder and awe change as they
put off the draperies of the flowing tide. Pity returns, as they emerge
into the moonlight, like the relics of an army, our representatives, going
every night (here or in Greece) to battle, and coming back every night
with their wounds, their ravaged faces. Now light falls on them again.
They have faces. They become Susan and Bernard, Jinny and Neville,
people we know. Now what a shrinkage takes place! Now what a
shrivelling, what an humiliation! The old shivers run through me,
hatred and terror, as I feel myself grappled to one spot by these hooks
they cast on us; these greetings, recognitions, pluckings of the finger
and searchings of the eyes. Yet they have only to speak, and their first
words, with the remembered tone and the perpetual deviation from
what one expects, and their hands moving and making a thousand past
days rise again in the darkness, shake my purpose.'[33]

Rhoda hates this 'deviation from what one expects', the 'antics of
the individual'.[34] She is uncompromising in her love of the geometrical, abstract, and dehumanised. In music it is the static architectural aspects which she admires, the square on the oblong.[35]
This implies a distance from life; she is an outsider, like Louis:

Coming up from the station, refusing to accept the shadow of the trees
and the pillar-boxes, I perceived, from your coats and umbrellas, even
at a distance, how you stand embedded in a substance made of repeated
moments run together; are committed, have an attitude, with children,
authority, fame, love, society; where I have nothing. I have no face.[36]

Whereas Louis has an acute consciousness of repetitions in time,
Rhoda has a perception of spatial distance, of emptiness, and of
repetitions within this emptiness, and so she creates the small
worlds with her basin of water, and sees landscapes in people's faces.

For Neville, unlike Louis and Rhoda, there are no repetitions. In
terms of painting, Rhoda is interested in the geometry, Neville in
the trembling brushstroke which is entirely personal to the artist

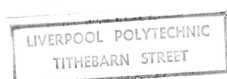

and so reveals his sensibility. His perception is exclusively physiognomic, for each love is different and has its own private images. The
images in the following passage are unique; they are not repeated
and made into motifs as are most of the other images in the novel. He
contrasts his constant change with Susan's unchanging repetition:

When someone comes in at breakfast, even the embroidered fruit on
on my curtain swells so that parrots can peck it; one can break it off
between one's thumb and finger. The thin, skimmed milk of early morning turns opal, blue, rose. At that hour your husband – the man who
slapped his gaiters, pointing with his whip at the barren cow – grumbles.
You say nothing. You see nothing. Custom blinds your eyes. At that
hour your relationship is mute, null, dun-coloured. Mine at that hour
is warm and various. There are no repetitions for me. Each day is
dangerous. Smooth on the surface, we are all bone beneath like snakes
coiling.[37]

He goes on to describe unique incidents which are not explained or
expanded even in his own soliloquies. They are private and quite
incapable of repetition:

Suppose we read *The Times*; suppose we argue. It is an experience.
Suppose it is winter. The snow falling loads down the roof and seals
us together in a red cave. The pipes have burst. We stand a yellow tin
bath in the middle of the room. We rush helter-skelter for basins.
Look there – it has burst again over the bookcase. We shout with
laughter at the sight of ruin. Let solidity be destroyed. Let us have no
possessions. Or is it summer? We may wander to a lake and watch
Chinese geese waddling flat-footed to the water's edge, or see a bone-
like city church with young green trembling before it. (I choose at
random; I choose the obvious.)[38]

The Chinese goose leads on to the idea of calligraphy. Here
'character' also has the meaning 'ideograph' as in Chinese writing:

Each sight is an arabesque scrawled suddenly to illustrate some hazard
and marvel of intimacy. The snow, the burst pipe, the tin bath, the
Chinese goose – these are signs which swung high aloft upon which,
looking back, I read the character of each love; how each was different.[39]

We remember that Roger Fry described the single brushstroke as
the 'record of a gesture'. In keeping with this, Neville carefully
notes and treasures the particular gestures of people, those actions
which can never be reproduced: 'But look – he flicks his hand to the

back of his neck. For such gestures one falls hopelessly in love for a lifetime. Dalton, Jones, Edgar and Bateman flick their hands to the backs of their necks likewise. But they do not succeed.'[40] But behind all this change lies an unchanging desire – sexual need is the unchanging repetition upon which the variations are worked:

And since I am, in one respect, deluded, since the person is always changing, though not the desire, and I do not know in the morning by whom I shall sit at night, I am never stagnant; I rise from my worst disasters, I turn, I change.[41]

He claims that there are no repetitions for him, but his pederastic dream never changes and never leaves him: the naked boys squirting hosepipes at each other.[42] The emphasis on particularity is an attempt to give variety to this repeated dream, just as his insistence on the 'moment', is an attempt to oppose an emotional time against the repetitious clock-time:

They did not wrinkle their noses and scratch their foreheads with your precise gesture. You are you. That is what consoles me for the lack of many things – I am ugly, I am weak – and the depravity of the world, and the flight of youth and Percival's death, and bitterness and rancour and envies innumerable.

But if one day you do not come after breakfast, if one day I see you in some looking-glass perhaps looking after another, if the telephone buzzes and buzzes in your empty room, I shall then, after unspeakable anguish, I shall then – for there is no end to the folly of the human heart – seek another, find another, you. Meanwhile, let us abolish the ticking of time's clock with one blow. Come closer.[43]

This accounts for his absorption in the 'ordinary scene',[44] and his rejection of plot, for he opposes the single unrepeatable moment against Bernard's love of 'story'. A moment of this kind is complete in itself, like a gesture:

'Bernard's stories amuse me,' said Neville, 'at the start. But when they tail off absurdly and he gapes, twiddling a bit of string, I feel my own solitude. He sees everyone with blurred edges. Hence I cannot talk to him of Percival. I cannot expose my absurd and violent passion to his sympathetic understanding. It too would make a "story". I need someone whose mind falls like a chopper on a block; to whom the pitch of absurdity is sublime, and a shoe-string adorable. To whom can I expose the urgency of my own passion?[45]

Like many of Virginia Woolf's characters, he has a moment of vision, which is a triumph over clock time:

Yet I am struck still as I walk by sudden premonitions of what is to come. Yesterday, passing the open door leading into the private garden, I saw Fenwick with his mallet raised. The steam from the tea-urn rose in the middle of the lawn. There were banks of blue flowers. Then suddenly descended upon me the obscure, the mystic sense of adoration, of completeness that triumphed over chaos. Nobody saw my poised and intent figure as I stood at the open door. Nobody guessed the need I had to offer my being to one god; and perish, and disappear. His mallet descended; the vision broke.[46]

This dissatisfaction with 'story' helps to explain Virginia Woolf's own rejection of the traditional plot in her novels.

Neville opposes against the march of the clock, the single moment, the unique gesture, the 'one trembling star'. Jinny, like Neville is in the grip of the constant repetition of her sexual needs, but against time she sets the cosmetic details of social life: '"The iron gates have rolled back," said Jinny. "Time's fangs have ceased their devouring. We have triumphed over the abysses of space, with rouge, with powder, with flimsy pocket-handkerchiefs."'[47] The gilt chairs and precious stones, the constant images of her speeches, form an unchanging background to her constantly changing partners. Many people live a life of change and excitement when they are young, then become static, like the man at the party:

That man there, by the cabinet; he lives you say, surrounded by china pots. Break one and you shatter a thousand pounds. And he loved a girl in Rome and she left him. Hence the pots, old junk found in lodging-houses or dug from the desert sands. And since beauty must be broken daily to remain beautiful, and he is static, his life stagnates in a china sea. It is strange though; for once as a young man, he sat on damp ground and drank rum with soldiers.[48]

Just as Neville's rejection of story throws light on Virginia Woolf's similar rejection, so here does Jinny's dissatisfaction with characters who can be summed up 'with facts and again with facts'. These little summaries of people soon grow boring:

I cannot remain seated for long. I must jump up and go. The coach may start from Piccadilly. I drop all these facts – diamonds, withered hands, china pots and the rest of it – as a monkey drops nuts from its naked paws. I cannot tell you if life is this or that. I am going to push out into the heterogeneous crowd. I am going to be buffeted; to be flung up, and flung down, among men, like a ship on the sea.[49]

Jinny stands for a moment outside the machine of the big city, and sees the Underground as a sort of hell, but unlike Louis, she can allow herself to be taken up by these repetitions, she can be 'inside': 'Lifts rise and fall; trains stop, trains start as regularly as the waves of the sea. This is what has my adhesion. I am a native of this world, I follow its banners.'[50]

Certain natural repetitions we must all recognise. But if we are not fully alert, these can have simply a narcotic effect, as they do here on Susan:

I shall lie like a field bearing crops in rotation; in the summer heat will dance over me; in the winter I shall be cracked with cold. But heat and cold will follow each other naturally without my willing or unwilling. My children will carry me on; their teething, their crying, their going to school and coming back will be like the waves of the sea under me. No day will be without its movement. I shall be lifted higher than any of you on the backs of the seasons.[51]

Susan welcomes the repetitions of nature, which she finds soothing and comforting. But these cycles, the rotation of crops, the movement of the seasons, and especially the repetition of birth and death, can be seen as cruel and remorseless unless they are given form and so transmuted into a rhythm. She moves on from the movement of the seasons and sinks herself in another rhythm, that of her own fruitfulness:

'Summer comes, and winter,' said Susan. 'The seasons pass. The pear fills itself and drops from the tree. The dead leaf rests on its edge. But steam has obscured the window. I sit by the fire watching the kettle boil. I see the pear tree through the streaked steam on the window-pane.[52]

Here the image of the steam on the window links this passage with feelings of repetition in the other characters; for example, Louis has a similar vision in the 'mechanical café'. The soporific effect of Susan's attitude is reinforced in this passage by the constantly repeated 'sleep':

Sleep, sleep, I croon, whether it is summer or winter, May or November.

Sleep I sing – I, who am unmelodious and hear no music save rustic music when a dog barks, a bell tinkles, or wheels crunch upon the gravel. I sing my song by the fire like an old shell murmuring on the beach. Sleep, sleep, I say, warning off with my voice all who rattle milk-cans, fire at rooks, shoot rabbits, or in any way bring the shock of destruction near this wicker cradle, laden with soft limbs, curled under a pink coverlet.[53]

But Susan feels that something is missing from her life, for this kind of immersion is only possible when she is in her prime. Age inevitably brings its over-ripeness, its dissatisfaction with the body. Schaefer believes that Susan's self-consciousness is at odds with her absorption into the natural rhythm, but her dissatisfaction arises quite naturally from the process of ageing and the loss of her child-bearing function:

I ask now, standing with my scissors among my flowers, Where can the shadow enter? What shock can loosen my laboriously gathered, relentlessly pressed down life? Yet sometimes I am sick of natural happiness, and fruit growing, and children scattering the house with oars, guns, skulls, books won for prizes and other trophies. I am sick of the body, I am sick of my own craft, industry and cunning, of the unscrupulous ways of the mother who protects, who collects under her jealous eyes at one long table her own children, always her own.[54]

As she grows older she realises that this sleepy life of simple natural repetition has something missing from it: 'Still I gape,' said Susan, 'like a young bird, unsatisfied, for something that has escaped me.'[55]

Bernard comforts himself with refrains, but his attitude changes as he matures, and in this development we can see the movement from one aspect of repetition to another. He talks about the formation of a refrain and its significance:

On the outskirts of every agony sits some observant fellow who points; who whispers as he whispered to me that summer morning in the house where the corn comes up to the window, 'The willow grows on the turf by the river. The gardeners sweep with great brooms and the lady sits writing.' Thus he directed me to that which is beyond and outside our own predicament; to that which is symbolic, and thus perhaps permanent, if there is any permanence in our sleeping, eating, breathing, so animal, so spiritual and tumultuous lives.[56]

Later, Bernard returns to his refrain but the further repetition of death works against the 'permanence' he spoke of in the passage above:

And by some flick of a scent or a sound on a nerve, the old image – the gardeners sweeping, the lady writing – returned. I saw the figures beneath the beech trees at Elvedon. The gardeners swept; the lady at the table sat writing. But I now made the contribution of maturity to childhood's intuitions – satiety and doom; the sense of what is unescapable in our lot; death...[57]

He later becomes disillusioned with the refrain, for it has become empty and mechanical, referring only to shadows. It is merely the recording of change, not a symbol of permanence:

those fabulous presences, men with brooms, women writing, the willow tree by the river – clouds and phantoms made of dust too...I, carrying a notebook, making phrases, had recorded mere changes; a shadow, I had been sedulous to take note of shadows.[58]

In tracing this change in Bernard's attitude towards his refrain, we can see the movement from the bright to the dark side of repetition. Bernard, the writer, is especially interesting in his attitude towards repetitions, and this could be looked at more closely, for it helps us to understand Virginia Woolf's art. In the following passage, the making and repeating of phrases stems from self-consciousness and embarrassment:

Now the awful portals of the station gape; 'the moon-faced clock regards me.' I must make phrases and phrases and so interpose something hard between myself and the stare of housemaids, the stare of clocks, staring faces, indifferent faces, or I shall cry.[59]

The creation of phrases with which to face a new situation reminds us of Miriam Henderson's similar reaction. For her, it is an attempt to fix the moment, to give it some sort of permanence:

'How lovely the air is here.'...The phrase repeated itself again and again, going with her up the platform towards the group of lights. It was all she could summon to meet the new situation. It satisfied her; it made her happy. It was enough; but no one would think it was enough.[60]

Bernard is conscious of the repetitions of life, but whether he feels included or excluded depends on whether he has an audience:

But soliloquies in back streets soon pall. I need an audience. That is my downfall. That always ruffles the edge of the final statement and prevents it from forming. I cannot seat myself in some sordid eating-house and order the same glass day after day and imbue myself entirely in one fluid – this life. I make my phrase and run off with it to some furnished room where it will be lit by dozens of candles. I need eyes on me to draw out these frills and furbelows. To be myself (I note) I need the the illumination of other people's eyes, and therefore cannot be entirely sure what is my self. The authentics, like Louis, like Rhoda, exist most completely in solitude. They resent illumination, reduplication.[61]

He feels outside the machine of daily life when he hears of Percival's death:

This then is the world that Percival sees no longer. Let me look. The butcher delivers meat next door; two old men stumble along the pavement; sparrows alight. The machine then works; I note the rhythm, the throb, but as a thing in which I have no part, since he sees it no longer.[62]

But the repeated signals of everyday life arouse his curiosity again: 'Yet already signals begin, beckonings, attempts to lure me back. Curiosity is knocked out only for a short time. One cannot live outside the machine for more perhaps than half an hour.'[63] Only by looking at the paintings in the gallery can he remain in his detached condition, on the outside of life. Such detachment, Louis' normal condition, Bernard finds a strain even for a short time: 'I am exhausted with the strain and the long, long time – twenty-five minutes, half an hour – that I have held myself alone outside the machine.'[64] We see in Bernard a constant effort to remake himself. At certain moments, like that of Percival's death, he feels momentarily outside the repetitions of daily life. He feels this again in middle age: 'For many years I crooned complacently, "My children...my wife...my house...my dog". As I let myself in with my latch-key I would go through that familiar ritual and wrap myself in these warm coverings. Now that lovely veil has fallen.'[65] He goes to Rome and is again 'outside the machine' for a while but then he becomes caught up once more 'in the general sequence when one thing follows another'.[66] Bernard is aware of the two worlds of repetition and rhythm. He has an ambivalent feeling towards repetition. There is an emptiness in one thing following another, it is boring, and to Louis, horrifying. But although we may 'pretend to revile it', we often feel borne along by its soothing hypnotic effect. Bernard recognises the double nature of repetition:

That goes on. Listen. There is a sound like the knocking of railway trucks in a siding. That is the happy concatenation of one event following another in our lives. Knock, knock, knock. Must, must, must. Must go, must sleep, must wake, must get up – sober, merciful word which we pretend to revile, which we press tight to our hearts, without which we should be undone. How we worship that sound like the knocking together of trucks in a siding![67]

Bernard's sense of the two kinds of repetition and the taste for story and for phrases which goes hand in hand with this, makes it fitting that he should do the summing up at the end of the novel, this final section being a recapitulation, a repetition in 'fictional' form of what has gone before. Schaefer criticises the strict adherence to the interior monologue throughout, finding that the self-consciousness required is out of keeping with the character, especially, of Susan, because her attitude does not allow the distancing necessary for self-awareness. If we accept that criterion then the whole of the childhood section stands condemned. Besides, Virginia Woolf can indicate self-awareness by making a character 'doubly' aware. This is the case with Bernard, who is given the distance to stand back and comment on the rest of the characters, while at the same time pointing out the dangers of abstracting from their context 'the characters of our friends'.[68] This double awareness is shown in his appreciation of the two types of repetition, but on a more fundamental level, in his attitude to the language which he himself employs. This can be illustrated in his comments on Percival:

As he was not in the least precocious, he read whatever was written up for our edification without any comment, and thought with that magnificent equanimity (Latin words come naturally) that was to preserve him from so many meannesses and humiliations, that Lucy's flaxen pigtails and pink cheeks were the height of female beauty.[69]

This detailed concern with language and what it is able to express, its connection with emotion and sensation, its overtones of meaning, are interests which Bernard and Virginia Woolf have in common. This kind of awareness can be seen in the following passage, where

Bernard describes the inadequacy of language to describe the feeling of being in and out of love:

and then the mystic sense of completion and then that rasping, dog-fish skin-like roughness – those black arrows of shivering sensation, when she misses the post, when she does not come. Out rush a bristle of horned suspicions, horror, horror, horror – but what is the use of painfully elaborating these consecutive sentences when what one needs is nothing consecutive but a bark, a groan? And years later to see a middle-aged woman in a restaurant taking off her cloak.[70]

There is an attempt to give that 'scraping' effect which we saw earlier in the analysis of *Mrs Dalloway*. (The same 'fish-scale' image is used here.) The arrows of sensation which Bernard speaks of are not a vague image, they remind us specifically of the similar feeling which he had as a child when a sponge was squeezed over him. The blackness of the arrows reminds us of Jinny's black 'No'. Then there is the etymological play on 'bristle', 'horned' and 'horror', with the added suggestion of the horned cuckold. Finally there is the three-fold repetition of 'horror', linking it with the other three-fold repetitions in the novel, and indeed throughout the work of Virginia Woolf.

Bernard has emotions and passions, but there is part of him which is always the voyeur, as he recognises himself: 'On the outskirts of every agony sits some observant fellow who points'. This allows him to stand back and assess the lives of the others, which are inter-twined with his own. The natural repetition of Susan's life, which even she comes to see as lacking in something, Bernard criticises in the following way:

When, for example, I went to Lincolnshire that summer to see Susan and she advanced towards me across the garden with the lazy move-ment of a half-filled sail, with the swaying movement of a woman with child, I thought, 'It goes on; but why?' We sat in the garden; the farm carts came up dripping with hay; there was the usual country gabble of rooks and doves; fruit was netted and covered over; the gardener dug. Bees boomed down the purple tunnels of flowers; bees embedded themselves on the golden shields of sunflowers. Little twigs were blown across the grass. How rhythmical, and half-conscious and like something wrapped in mist it was; but to me hateful, like a net folding one's limbs in its meshes, cramping. She who had refused Percival lent her-self to this, to this covering over.[71]

The precision of Louis' repetition is too constricting also, and his religion, like Susan's 'Nature', is an opiate, a lullaby:

I thought how Louis would mount those steps in his neat suit with his cane in his hand and his angular, rather detached gait. With his Australian accent ('My father, a banker at Brisbane') he would come, I thought, with greater respect to these old ceremonies than I do, who have heard the same lullabies for a thousand years.[72]

Against this, Bernard puts some particular detail, in the manner of Neville:

But then like the lost and wailing dove, I find myself failing, fluttering, descending and perching upon some curious gargoyle, some battered nose or absurd tombstone, with humour, with wonder, and so again watch the sightseers with their Baedekers shuffling past, while the boy's voice soars in the dome and the organ now and then indulges in a moment of elephantine triumph. How then, I asked, would Louis roof us all in? How would he confine us, make us one, with his red ink, with his very fine nib? The voice petered out in the dome, wailing.[73]

The elephantine triumph of the organ reminds us of Louis' beast, the waves which stamp and stamp on the shore, and death, the elephant white with maggots. Bernard cannot accept the repetition of Louis, which is too neat, although he can understand it and even borrow Louis' image of the clockwork mechanism:

Muscles, nerves, intestines, blood-vessels, all that makes the coil and spring of our being, the unconscious hum of the engine, as well as the dart and flicker of the tongue, functioned superbly. Opening, shutting; shutting, opening; eating, drinking; sometimes speaking – the whole mechanism seemed to expand, to contract, like the mainspring of a clock.[74]

And this mechanical life of Tuesday following Monday is pleasant enough, but from Neville he has learnt a different sort of time, emotional time:

Yes, but suddenly one hears a clock tick. We who had been immersed in this world became aware of another. It is painful. It was Neville who changed our time. He, who had been thinking with the unlimited time of the mind, which stretches in a flash from Shakespeare to ourselves, poked the fire and began to live by that other clock which marks the approach of a particular person.[75]

147

As Bernard points out, it is impossible to separate his life from those of the other characters. He is not overwhelmed by repetition as are Louis and Susan, or committed to constant change like Jinny and Neville, or to the empty space between these two like Rhoda. Bernard manages to bring these things together in the idea of the slowly forming drop. It is made up of repetitions run together, the moment of its falling is unique, and it leaves behind it a space, in which a new drop can be formed. Virginia Woolf is seeking in her art, like Bernard, a fully conscious acceptance of this rhythm of repeated creation and dissolution which is 'the eternal renewal, the incessant rise and fall and fall and rise again'.[76]

11

The symbolic keyboard; 'Mrs Dalloway'

The title of this chapter was inspired by Charles Mauron's introduction to Roger Fry's translations of Mallarmé. Virginia Woolf's
sense of emptiness is similar to that of Mallarmé, and she attempts
to create from it an art similar to that described by Mauron in his
introduction to Fry's translation:

The discovery of 'something else' has altered everything, at least in
appearance – for we know nothing of the psychological depths of the
question. Something other than reality, however, in the last resort is –
nothing. And the whole of literature (as Mallarmé, henceforth perfectly
lucid, was to explain to the English public in a style at first sight
incomprehensible) consists in the play of modulations between these two
extremes.
    A capital discovery: for if one thinks at all about the conditions of
what Roger Fry calls pure art, one cannot fail to see that the first of
these conditions is the establishment of a keyboard. There can be no
architecture without fixed points and subtle methods of passing from
one to another: without the modal system, no Gregorian music: without 'tempered' keyboard, no Bach: without depth and scale of luminous
values, no true painting. And the great creators are those who not
merely perform and construct, but in the first place cast their instru-
ment to suit the kind of performance which is proper to them. Mallarmé
from the very first knew the two extremes of his own range – crude
reality and 'grudging silence'; he suffered because he found himself
rejected by each in turn. What he wanted was to write, that is, to make
free play from one extremity to the other. A key board is nothing but a
system of transitions.[1]

The transitions between the recurrent images and symbols in *Mrs
Dalloway* form a keyboard of this kind. In his excellent essay on
Mrs Dalloway, Reuben Brower points out that the recurrent imagery
in that novel indicates an artistic integrity and an underlying consistent vision. He stresses the use of repetitive devices:

149

The unity of her design depends on the building up of symbolic meta-phors through an exquisite management of verbal devices: through exact repetitions, reminiscent variations, the use of related eye and ear imagery, and the recurrence of similar phrase and sentence rhythms.[2]

The integrity which Brower sees in the imagery of *Mrs Dalloway* is also evident in Virginia Woolf's works as a whole. Bernard Black-stone points out that her work is a whole, in that each scene and image is related to other scenes and images throughout all the novels.[3] An image of this type is the spider's web – the idea of people being attached to each other by an invisible thread constantly recurs throughout her works. In *Mrs Dalloway*, this example is typical:

And they went further and further from her, being attached to her by a thin thread (since they had lunched with her) which would stretch and stretch, get thinner and thinner as they walked across London; as if one's friends were attached to one's body, after lunching with them, by a thin thread...[4]

Similarly, Virginia Woolf's novels are linked to each other by various strands of imagery. (Another of these characteristic recurrent images, that of the parrot, also occurs in *Mrs Dalloway*.) Limiting himself to the complexity of the imagery within *Mrs Dalloway* itself, Brower brings out the significance of certain key words such as 'plunge' and 'party'. He examines the use of the word 'solemn' and finds that its full significance is built up by repetition in different contexts. He sees a two-fold sense of life in the novel, the enjoyment of being included and the fear of exclusion: 'But the sense of being absorbed in the process is inseparable from a fear of being excluded, from the dread that the process may be interrupted.'[5] This poise between inclusion and exclusion is in some ways a better expression of the 'double nature of repetition' which I have been speaking of. The dual value of the 'moment' can indeed be seen from the point of view of inclusion and exclusion from life, but if we persist in our investiga-tion of repetition, I think that it is possible to see certain aspects of *Mrs Dalloway* in a more favourable light than does Brower; it is possible to see a greater coherence in the keyboard of its images and symbols.

Our starting point in this analysis of the novel is a full recognition of Virginia Woolf's self-consciousness in her use of symbols and images. This involves an investigation into the nature of language and repetition, and not simply a description of her employment of recurrent images and symbols as rhetorical devices or decoration. This is a different emphasis from that of Brower, for he claims to detect in *Mrs Dalloway* a certain amount of apparently irrelevant adornment. He argues that on occasion Virginia Woolf 'elaborates the metaphor out of all proportion to its expressive value' and he instances 'the interlude of the "solitary traveller".'[6] If we bear in mind Virginia Woolf's introspective interest in language, then this apparent irrelevance becomes part of the complex meaning of the novel. As we saw in the earlier discussion, language does not repeat a given reality. This solitary traveller interlude is part of Virginia Woolf's investigation of the nature of image and metaphor. Brower's second objection is directly related to this theme: 'Perhaps the most obvious examples of metaphorical elaboration for its own sake are the super-literary, pseudo-Homeric similes which adorn various pages of *Mrs Dalloway*'.[7] If we look at the novel with an approach similar to that of Mauron's to Mallarmé's poetry, then these two 'irrelevances' which Brower notes can be seen as bound up with each other as part of that 'integrity' which he finds in the rest of the novel. What we have in *Mrs Dalloway* is the establishment of a keyboard, a 'system of transitions' which moves from the complete fusion to the complete separation of the human and the natural. If we take as our starting point the question 'in what way are the image and symbol connected with each other and with external reality?' then the apparently irrelevant imagery becomes directly relevant.

Our symbolic keyboard is made up of images which range from the subterranean (the fish, physical sensation) to the aerial (the aeroplane, science); the third term in the triad is the terrestrial (the tree, myth and metaphor). Within this overall keyboard, Virginia Woolf constructs various scales. We saw in an earlier chapter the scale which runs from the 'scraping' images to those of 'cutting'. We can understand this process better, perhaps, if we concentrate on the three key symbols mentioned, the fish, the tree and the aeroplane. But it must be borne in mind that this is only one of the tunes played in the novel. This scale is one ranging from the complete fusion of internal and external reality in the scraping of the fish, to the complete separation of the human and the natural in the latest scientific marvel, the aeroplane. The old woman singing marks a

traveller and taking away from him the sense of the earth, the wish to return, and giving him for substitute a general peace, as if (so he thinks as he advances down the forest ride) all this fever of living were simplicity itself...[11]

Elizabeth, being further removed from 'nature' in her concern with religious myth, rather than the myth of 'mother nature', strongly objects to being compared to a tree, or having her beauty compared with the beauty of nature: 'People were beginning to compare her to poplar trees, early dawn, hyacinths, fawns, running water, and garden lilies; and it made her life a burden to her...'[12] The next transition is from the use of cliché, in which nature is merely coinage, to the scientific attitude, in which nature is seen as 'data'. Between the two comes Septimus, who is 'connected' with the trees, but in a way which, like the rest of his madness, is a pseudo-scientific relationship of apparent cause and effect: 'But they beckoned; leaves were alive; trees were alive. And the leaves being connected by millions of fibres with his own body, there on the seat, fanned it up and down; when the branch stretched he, too, made that statement.'[13] This is also clearly part of the 'thread' imagery which was mentioned earlier. On the blinds of the official car, the tree has been converted into a sign, it is simply a pattern 'like a tree'. But it triggers some hidden war-horror in Septimus' memory, it is 'as if some horror had come almost to the surface and was about to burst into flames...The world wavered and quivered and threatened to burst into flames'.[14] The same complex of tree, 'grey' and fire is evoked later by the image of an artificial tree created by an indoor firework, a harmless employment of the gunpowder which had given Septimus shell-shock: 'as if he had set light to a grey pellet on a plate and there had risen a lovely tree in the brisk sea-salted air of their intimacy...'[15]

In *Mrs Dalloway* Virginia Woolf examines some of the meanings of 'symbol'. The symbolic vision and the establishment of a keyboard run counter to the science of Bradshaw and Holmes. For them, symbolism is evidence of disease, as their diagnosis of Septimus indicates: 'He was attaching meanings to words of a symbolical kind. A serious symptom to be noted on the card.'[16] In the novel, the aeroplane is the symbol of symbols. For Mr Bentley it is a triumph of scientific achievement:

Away and away the aeroplane shot, till it was nothing but a bright spark; an aspiration; a concentration; a symbol (so it seemed to Mr Bentley, vigorously rolling his strip of turf at Greenwich) of man's soul; of his determination, thought Mr Bentley, sweeping round the cedar tree, to get outside his body, beyond his house, by means of thought, Einstein, speculation, mathematics, the Mendelian theory – away the aeroplane shot.[17]

For the scientific man Nature has become a strip of turf to be vigorously rolled, just as Septimus, according to Bradshaw, must be crushed into submission, and for Miss Kilman, human nature must be religiously 'converted'. Mr Bentley sees Man's achievements as mathematical and scientific, and so his interpretation of what is meant by a symbol is scientific. For different characters the aeroplane has various meanings. This symbol of man's soul, as Bentley calls it, is used for the trivial purpose of advertising some product or other (and people differ in their interpretation of what the plane is writing in the sky). It is not a straightforward symbol, simply standing for something else in an allegorical way. We must not go to the other extreme, as some critics are in danger of doing, of seeing it as completely meaningless, as simply a technical device which enables the writer to relate spatially separated characters and to jump from one mind to another. It is neither an allegory nor a technical device, but a symbol in a wider sense. It is related to religious symbolism:

Then, while a seedy-looking nondescript man carrying a leather bag stood on the steps of St Paul's Cathedral, and hesitated, for within was what balm, how great a welcome, how many tombs with banners waving over them, tokens of victories not over armies, but over, he thought, that plaguy spirit of truth seeking which leaves me at present without a situation, and more than that, the cathedral offers company, he thought, invites you to membership of a society; great men belong to it; martyrs have died for it; why not enter in, he thought, put this leather bag stuffed with pamphlets before an altar, a cross, the symbol of something which has soared beyond seeking and questing and knocking of words together and has become all spirit, disembodied, ghostly – why not enter in? he thought, and while he hesitated out flew the aeroplane over Ludgate Circus.[18]

The religious, scientific and martial attitudes form a mutual criticism here; the three faiths are undercut and we are left with a trivial advertisement, and even that is ineffective:

It was strange; it was still. Not a sound was to be heard above the traffic. Unguided it seemed; sped of its own free will. And now, curving up and up, straight up, like something mounting in ecstasy, in pure delight, out from behind poured white smoke looping, writing a T, and O, an F.[19]

We have seen how the solitary traveller episode fits into the rest of the novel, but there remains Brower's other objection, to the 'pseudo-Homeric similes'. Clearly, these are part of our keyboard, part of the transition between simile, metaphor and symbol which we have been tracing, and so a passage like the following has its place:

As a person who has dropped some grain of pearl or diamond into the grass and parts the tall blades very carefully, this way and that, and searches here and there vainly, and at last spies it there at the roots, so she went through one thing and another...[20]

The dislocation here, the separation between vehicle and tenor, is clearly deliberate. Further, the similes are not 'pseudo-Homeric' they are mock-heroic, for they fit into their own pattern of allusion and display the disjunction between the traditional martial values and the actual squalor and waste of the First World War, which is personified in Septimus. Brower has failed to sense the ironic tone of much of the novel, a tone and attitude close to Eliot's *Waste Land* which the Hogarth press had published four years earlier. So, Clarissa Dalloway shores against her ruin the song from *Cymbeline*:

> Fear no more the heat o' the sun
> Nor the furious winter's rages.[21]

Brower's objection, then, to the Homeric similes and to the so-called 'interlude' of the solitary traveller, on the grounds that they are irrelevant, is not tenable, for they are both aspects of that web of allusion which binds the novel together.

On the scale which we have established, the following passage marks the transition from myth to metaphor. This is the world of Ceres and Mother Nature, of Sirens and Mermaids:

Such are the visions which proffer great cornucopias full of fruit to the solitary traveller, or murmur in his ear like sirens lolloping away on the green sea waves, or are dashed in his face like bunches of roses, or rise to the surface like pale faces which fishermen flounder through floods to embrace.[22]

The mock-epic element in *Mrs Dalloway* has often been compared with Joyce's use of epic in *Ulysses*. It is evident how much more general are Virginia Woolf's allusions. Her framework is not a particular epic, but, as I have tried to establish, a keyboard of symbols. She is much more concerned with the general type of simile or theme in epic poetry, and particularly with the glorification of war which led to the sickening waste of the First World War. This waste and degradation is conveyed in the irony of the allusion to Ceres in the following passage:

Something was up, Mr Brewer knew; Mr Brewer, managing clerk at Sibley's and Arrowsmith's, auctioneers, valuers, land and estate agents; something was up, he thought, and, being paternal with his young men, and thinking very highly of Smith's abilities, and prophesying that he would, in ten or fifteen years, succeed to the leather arm-chair in the inner room under the skylight with the deed-boxes around him, 'if he keeps his health,' said Mr Brewer, and that was the danger – he looked weakly; advised football, invited him to supper and was seeing his way to consider recommending a rise of salary, when something happened which threw out many of Mr Brewer's calculations, took away his ablest young fellows, and eventually, so prying and insidious were the fingers of the European War, smashed the plaster cast of Ceres, ploughed a hole in the geranium beds, and utterly ruined the cook's nerves at Mr Brewer's establishment at Muswell Hill.[23]

The gods and heroes of the novel are made of plaster. Hugh Whitbread is not 'the stout-hearted', he is 'the admirable', and his role is simply that of a sycophant at court. 'By Jove' is simply a mild expression of surprise: 'How they loved dressing up in gold lace and doing homage! There! That must be – by Jove it was – Hugh Whitbread, snuffing round the precincts of the great, grown rather fatter, rather whiter, the admirable Hugh!'[24] The threefold repetition of a name a little earlier establishes the mock-heroic undertone of these pages:

But alas, Wilkins; Wilkins wanted her; Wilkins was emitting in a voice of commanding authority, as if the whole company must be admonished and the hostess reclaimed from frivolity, one name:
'The Prime Minister,' said Peter Walsh.[25]

The military aspect of the epic is never forgotten. For example,

Clarissa's parasol is seen as the sacred weapon of a goddess[26] and Richard Dalloway comes 'bearing his flowers like a weapon'.[27] The general ironic light of the novel plays over the symbols of public life:

As for Buckingham Palace (like an old prima donna facing the audience all in white) you can't deny it a certain dignity, he considered, nor despise what does, after all, stand to millions of people (a little crowd was waiting at the gate to see the King drive out) for a symbol, absurd though it is; a child with a box of bricks could have done better, he thought; looking at the memorial to Queen Victoria (whom he could remember in her horn spectacles driving through Kensington), its white mound, its billowing motherliness; but he liked being ruled by the descendant of Horsa; he liked continuity; and the sense of handing on the traditions of the past.[28]

Scientific, religious, and heroic faiths have been smashed by the First World War. The cross, the aeroplane, the monument of Queen Victoria are no longer acceptable whole-heartedly, for they no longer bring human beings together. All that Clarissa Dalloway can do is literally bring them together at a party, so that for one moment they feel their common humanity. This is itself only a symbolic gesture, a greeting to other beings across the emptiness which she sees at the heart of life. Septimus is there only in spirit, and represents all that has been lost in the War. The news of his death puts Clarissa's party into a Classical setting, with the theme of 'Et in Arcadia Ego', and in an undertone is the Anglican Service for the Burial of the Dead:

Oh! thought Clarissa, in the middle of my party, here's death, she thought.[29]

12

Plot, history and memory: 'The Years'

In her essay 'The Historian and the Gibbon', Virginia Woolf quotes
J. B. Bury to support her idea of the subjectivity of history, which,
he says, 'is in the last resort somebody's image of the past, and the
image is conditioned by the mind and experience of the person who
forms it'.[1] Given Virginia Woolf's interest in repetition, it follows
that her idea of history will reflect this, for a keen sense of the
repetitions of life has often found expression in a cyclical view of
history. To say that 'history repeats itself' is the historical equivalent
of Valéry's more embracing declaration that the universe is the
'parrot of parrots'. J. B. Bury describes an extreme version of such
a cyclical theory in his book *The Idea of Progress*:

The theory of world-cycles was so widely current that it may almost be
described as the orthodox theory of cosmic time among the Greeks,
and it passed from them to the Romans. According to some of the
Pythagoreans each cycle repeated to the minutest particular the course
and events of the preceding. If the universe dissolves into the original
chaos, there appeared to them to be no reason why the second chaos
should produce a world differing in the least respect from its predecessor.
The nth cycle would be indeed numerically distinct from the first, but
otherwise would be identical with it, and no man could possibly discover the number of the cycle in which he was living. As no end seems
to have been assigned to the whole process, the course of the world's
history would contain an endless number of Trojan Wars, for instance;
an endless number of Platos would write an endless number of *Re-
publics*.[2]

Such is her perception of repetition in human things, especially the
repetitive inevitability of death, that Virginia Woolf's view of history, or its fictional equivalent, plot, is bound to be to some extent
repetitive. This kind of cyclical view forms the framework of *The
Years*. Events are repeated in the same pattern with only slight

variations throughout the novel. In the 1891 chapter the news of Parnell's death is given:

She looked at a placard that was crumpled across a boy's legs. 'Death' was written in very large black letters. Then the placard blew straight, and she read another word: 'Parnell.'
'Dead'. . . she repeated. 'Parnell.' She was dazed for a moment. How could he be dead – Parnell? She bought a paper. They said so. . .
'Parnell is dead!' she said aloud.[3]

The death of the King nineteen years later, in the 1910 chapter, is only a slight variation of this:

The voice came nearer and nearer.
'Death. . . ?' she said.
'Death. . . ?' said Sara. They leant out. But they could not hear the rest of the sentence. Then a man who was wheeling a barrow along the street shouted up to them:
'The King's dead!'[4]

Before the constant repetition of death all human and historical difference is obliterated.

In an article called 'The Pageant of History', Leonard Woolf notes the sense of security which an unchanging climate gives, a kind of background against which various historical events are acted out: 'The climate, you may say, is not a part of social history. . . at any rate, this note of the rain and mist recurring through twenty centuries and six hundred pages of "English History" gives one a homely feeling of an unchanging social background'.[5] Virginia Woolf often uses the weather to give a kind of tone to a particular century. In *Jacob's Room* we are told that 'The bitter eighteenth-century rain rushed down the kennel.'[6] In *Orlando* each century has its appropriate weather. The nineteenth century, the hated Victorian period, is thus characterised by a general dampness: 'The great cloud which hung, not only over London, but over the whole of the British Isles on the first day of the nineteenth century. . .'[7] 'Weather' and 'climate' (one referring to change, the other to the unchanging) are part of that repetition and change which we are investigating in Virginia Woolf's work. This can be seen in *The Years*, in which each chapter has a prelude which describes the weather that will prevail throughout. There is no orderly progression of the seasons from section to section and no orderly historical cycle. We jump from season to season and from 1880 to 1891 to 1901 and so on in a quite random way. There is an aimless, arbitrary movement which is at the same time full of repetitions. All other order is a delusion, and repetition stands out in all its bareness. We must accept the weather or the climate, randomness without meaning or sickening repetition.

Philosophers of history differentiate between 'the facts' (chronicle) and 'the cause or pattern of the facts' (history), which parallels E. M. Forster's distinction between plot and story, or the difference between climate and weather. According to Forster the story is simply 'what happens next' whereas the plot tells us why something happened. Story simply changes, whereas plot needs some constant element, some underlying pattern. We can understand why Forster regretted the need for story – it is by definition shapeless; in Virginia Woolf's terms it is simply Tuesday following Monday. For plot some underlying principle is required, but Virginia Woolf is obsessed by the principle which underlies these principles, with repetition itself, and she wishes to dispense with both story and plot. In her diary she admits that 'I can make up situations, but I cannot make up plots.'[8] As I have indicated, *The Years* consists simply in a series of incidents which are repeated with slight variations throughout the novel. It is the history, the saga, of the Pargiter family, but these repetitions make it quite different from the traditional family saga. Her explicit concern with these repetitions can be seen in the diary, where she speaks of the composition of *The Years* in the following way: 'I must still condense and point: give pauses their effect, and repetitions, and the run on.'[9]

In her attempt to get away from the traditional idea of story and plot, Virginia Woolf came to dislike the use of the term 'novel' to describe her books.[10] Her own art is similar to that of Bernard in *The Waves*: 'Alone over my dead fire, I tend to see the thin places in my own stories. The real novelist, the perfectly simple human being, could go on, indefinitely, imagining. He would not integrate, as I do. He would not have this devastating sense of grey ashes in a burnt-out grate.'[11] The perception of the single moment makes the sequence of one thing following another, like story, seem false. This is a constant theme in Virginia Woolf's work. Orlando, who has been reincarnated in various forms since the sixteenth century feels the shock of the present moment:

It was the eleventh of October. It was 1928. It was the present moment.

No one need wonder that Orlando started, pressed her hand to her heart, and turned pale. For what more terrifying revelation can there be than that it is the present moment? That we survive the shock at all is only possible because the past shelters us on one side and the future on another.[12]

Neville in *The Waves* praises the individual moment in all its unique-ness, criticising Bernard's phrase-making and story-telling: 'They want a plot, do they? They want a reason? It is not enough for them, this ordinary scene.'[13] Bernard develops towards an under-standing of this 'ordinary scene', yet he does not accept it as totally separate and unique, as does Neville. Bernard recognises that the moment is itself made up of other moments, or repetitions which come together, which globe entire like a drop of water. He realises that if these elements are disentangled they will take the shape of a story, which is inevitably a falsification:

But in order to make you understand, to give you my life, I must tell you a story – and there are so many, and so many – stories of childhood, stories of school, love, marriage, death, and so on; and none of them are true...How tired I am of stories...[14]

The orderly progression of plot, the simple story of one thing following another is set against the special emotional moment:

I begin to seek some design more in accordance with those moments of humiliation and triumph that come now and then undeniably. Lying in a ditch on a stormy day, when it has been raining, then enormous clouds come marching over the sky, tattered clouds, wisps of cloud. What delights me then is the confusion, the height, the indifference and the fury. Great clouds always changing, and movement; something sulphur-ous and sinister, bowled up, helter-skelter; towering, trailing, broken off, lost, and I forgotten, minute, in a ditch. Of story, of design, I do not see a trace then.[15]

The clouds, like the weather, are unique and formless. The problem of trying to place them into a pattern without falsification is that problem of transmuting repetition into rhythm which we have seen as the basis of Virginia Woolf's art. Bernard's summing-up, being a refraction of what has gone before, is an attempt to give us motion and stillness, to represent the clouds which have trailed through the novel since the early childhood of each of the characters.

Memory clearly involves repetition in a similar way to history and plot. These come together, for example, in the 'biography' of Orlando, where the history of the Sackville family is seen as a kind of memory embodied in the hero-heroine, who lives through many centuries. Memory is important in reading Virginia Woolf's novels, especially the memory involved in re-reading them, for she wished the novel to be seen as a whole:

Then suddenly without our willing it, for it is thus that Nature undertakes these transitions, the book will return, but differently. It will float to the top of the mind as a whole. And the book as a whole is different from the book received currently in separate phrases. Details now fit themselves into their places. We see the shape from start to finish; it is a barn, a pigsty, or a cathedral.[16]

The use of memory in reading a novel is aided when a writer uses repetitive devices, but Virginia Woolf is too self-conscious in her art simply to use such devices without turning her attention to the explicit idea of repetition. Her interest in the repetitions of memory and history can be seen in *The Years*.

In the '1880' chapter Kitty visits the Robson family and hears Jo Robson making hencoops in the back garden: 'Hammer, hammer, hammer, he went, fixing a board to the rotten roof.'[17] The hammering continues while she meets the rest of the family (this is the three-fold verbal repetition which we discussed earlier): 'Hammer, hammer, hammer came from the shed in the garden.'[18] The reiteration ensures that the reader will not forget the incident. When Kitty meets Jo, he reminds her of someone she had met in the past: 'He reminded her of Alf, the farm hand up at Carter's, who had kissed her under the shadow of the haystack when she was fifteen, and old Carter loomed up leading a bull with a ring through its nose and said "Stop that!"'[19] A little later, she remembers her visit to the Robsons and 'the sound of hammer, hammer, hammer still rang in her ears'.[20] She marries Lord Lasswade and the love of her cousin for her is unrequited. He translates *Antigone*, in which the heroine, like his love, is buried alive. Sara paraphrases it as follows: 'The man in the loin-cloth gave three sharp taps with his mallet on the brick. She was buried alive.'[21] We can see here the way in which Virginia Woolf uses the triple repetition, for a little earlier the hammering is related to the action of vultures pecking at the body of Antigone's brother: 'Quick, quick, quick with repeated jerks they

struck the mouldy flesh.'[22] Later Edward and Kitty go together to
see a performance of *Siegfried*, in which Wagner's leitmotif coincides
with that of the novel:

Here the curtain went up. She leant forward and looked at the stage.
The dwarf was hammering at the sword. Hammer, hammer, hammer,
he went with little short, sharp strokes...Hammer, hammer, hammer,
he went. She leant back again. What did that make her think of? A
young man who came into a room with shavings in his hair...when
she was very young. In Oxford? She had gone to tea with them; had sat
on a hard chair; in a very light room; and there was a sound of hammering in the garden. And then a boy came in with shavings in his hair.
And she had wanted him to kiss her. Or was it the farm hand up at
Carter's, when old Carter had loomed up suddenly leading a bull with
a ring through its nose?[23]

In constructing this hammering device perhaps she remembered,
consciously or otherwise, the review she had written many years
before, of another family saga, *The Three Black Pennys*:

In their obdurate ways of impressing themselves upon other people
they more resembled the great hammer at Myrtle Forge, persistently
and relentlessly beating out iron, than the iron itself. 'If the hammer
stops,' Howat told his wife in the eighteenth century, 'all this, the
Pennys, stop, too.'...If, curiously enough, a certain type of character
occurs at intervals in the same family, it occurs as a blue or a green
might repeat itself beautifully in a pattern. The beat of the great
hammer recurs too; when it stops we know that something more
important has ceased; the racoon hunt repeats itself; for, as we began
by saying, Mr Hergesheimer has a strong sense of form, and these are
some of the more obvious devices used by him to hold his story together,
to secure continuity, to bind his gem in a circle of gold...[24]

The reader will perhaps recall here the hammering in *Time Regained*
which is one of the triggers for Marcel's memory. But what is
important for Virginia Woolf is not the emotional power of memory,
it is the fact that it is based on repetitions. The familiar mirror on
mirror effect is given here, for the self-conscious reference to the
leitmotif gives a much barer effect than similar memories in Proust,
where the emotional evocations and overtones are so important.
For Virginia Woolf, memory is not a means of regaining time, it is
not a means to salvation, for, like repetition, it is two-edged.

Memories can be 'so interesting; so safe; so unreal'[25] but they can also give a sense of desolate emptiness. Such aridity arising from the repetitive aspect of memory can be seen in the following passage, in which, once again, the tell-tale parrot lurks:

My life's been other people's lives, Eleanor thought – my father's; Morris's; my friends' lives; Nicholas's... Fragments of a conversation with him came back to her. Either I'd been lunching with him or dining with him, she thought. It was in a restaurant. There was a parrot with a pink feather in a cage on the counter...
'Just as I was thinking of you!' she repeated. Indeed it was like part of her, a sunk part of her, coming to the surface.[26]

The past can become like a scene in a play with oneself as an actor. There is a division of the self and an effect of simultaneity as memory co-exists with the present moment:

They talked, she thought, as if Abercorn Terrace were a scene in a play. They talked as if they were speaking of people who were real, but not real in the way in which she felt herself to be real. It puzzled her; it made her feel that she was two different people at the same time; that she was living at two different times at the same moment. She was a little girl wearing a pink frock; and here she was in this room, now.[27]

This memory, like the conversation surrounding it, is a repetition, for Rose makes the same remark twice over, and Maggie and Sara reply with the remarks which they had predicted. As the book develops a further repetition is added. Here, we are told 'The glasses jingled on the table. She started slightly, roused from her thoughts about her childhood, and separated the glasses.'[28] Many years later history repeats itself, only this time it is Sara, not Rose, who parts the glasses. 'Something rattled on the table. The walls and the floor seemed to tremble... She parted two glasses that were jingling to-gether.'[29] These two occasions on which a younger member of the family meets an older, are linked together, the repetition reinforcing our perception of the emptiness of their lives. Once again we are reminded of *Time Regained*, where the sound of a spoon on a plate is one of the narrator's special memories.

Street criers and barrel organs sound throughout *The Years*. Our easy acceptance of an accustomed tune is related specifically to the usual art of the story, as Virginia Woolf describes it in an early review called 'Philosophy in Fiction':

After one has heard the first few bars of a tune upon a barrel organ the further course of the tune is instinctively foretold by the mind and any deviation from that pattern is received with reluctance and discomfort. A thousand tunes of the same sort have grooved a road in our minds and we insist that the next tune we hear shall flow smoothly down the same channels; nor are we often disobeyed. That is also the case with the usual run of stories.[30]

Virginia Woolf brings to the surface the repetitions involved in the usual stories, and so we hear the barrel organ of *The Years*:

Against the dull background of traffic noises, of wheels turning and brakes squeaking, there rose near at hand the cry of a woman suddenly alarmed for her child; the monotonous cry of a man selling vegetables; and far away a barrel organ was playing. It stopped; it began again.[31]

Earlier, we compared this passage to Kierkegaard's *Repetition*, and now we can relate it, through Kierkegaard, to Sartre, whose Roquentin rejects the traditional 'portrait gallery' kind of history; he hears the jazz record again and again and so gains his burdensome freedom.[32]

13

Character

In that famous essay on character in fiction 'Mr Bennett and Mrs Brown', Virginia Woolf criticises the materialist writers who concentrate on aspects of character which she considers unimportant. An idea of general importance and one which will not drive us into a simple 'Woolf versus Bennett' argument, is her perception that character is basically a convention. (Thinking of character in this way has been reinforced by modern Shakespearian criticism, as W. J. Harvey points out in his excellent book, *Character and the Novel*.) A convention is an agreement between writer and reader, but an agreement which shifts and evolves if it is not to become an empty formula. The old skins must be cast, and the time for this seems to be when they are recognised to be conventions apart from 'reality' and not connected with it at every point. Such a change came when Lytton Strachey asked why the biographies of the famous were always so blandly respectable, so boring, and required no less than two fat volumes to contain them. His biographies are not simply a debunking of the Victorian heroes and heroines, they are a new convention in biography, a new way of looking at a life, and are therefore important in modifying the view we take of a character in fiction.

Virginia Woolf constantly mocked this worn-out convention of the biographic style. A human being is not a fixed thing, as the traditional biography assumes. The selection involved and the writer's point of view all affect the biography – the story of the Brownings is quite different when seen through the eyes of their dog in *Flush*. The mock genealogy and the tracing of the etymology of 'spaniel' lead us back to the tradition of the anti-biography which goes back to *Don Quixote*. This novel convention, of reacting against an established convention, involves the question of repetition. If we try to avoid repetition by the use of some device, the device itself is repeated and we are back again with repetition. Now this clearly holds for a convention. Once the slavish copying of external detail is rejected, as Virginia Woolf and Strachey rejected it, then the repetition is not that of 'reality' being reflected, but of a repetition which is contained within the work. So Strachey builds up leitmotifs made of repeated phrases, and the basis on which Virginia Woolf builds her novels and characters, is also that of repetition.

Virginia Woolf begins from the position that one person's idea of another is inevitably a distortion.[1] Clearly, the name of a person has no meaning, for we are much more complex than the name which we happen to bear. Virginia Woolf uses the familiar device of repetition in order to show this. In *The Voyage Out* this is simply stated rather than shown: 'Voices crying behind them never reached through the waters in which they were now sunk. The repetition of Hewet's name in short, dissevered syllables was to them the crack of a dry branch or the laughter of a bird.'[2] Proper names have reference, but no meaning, and in *Jacob's Room* Virginia Woolf exploits semantic satiation to indicate this. This question of identity is one of the novel's themes: we saw earlier how all the characters are depicted as either statues or ghosts, granite or rainbow. People can be robbed of all identity in trivial exchanges which are far from being real communication:

'Are you going away for Christmas?' said Mr Calthorp.
'If my brother gets his leaves,' said Miss Edwards.
'What regiment is he in?' said Mr Calthorp.
'The Twentieth Hussars,' said Miss Edwards.
'Perhaps he knows my brother?' said Mr Calthorp.
'I am afraid I did not catch your name,' said Miss Edwards.
'Calthorp', said Mr Calthorp.[3]

'Mr Salvin' is treated in a similar way in the previous paragraphs. This technique, in which the names are emptied of meaning, can be compared with Strachey's similar use of the device in his *Queen Victoria*:

One night Mr Greville, the Clerk of the Privy Council, was present; his turn soon came; the middle-aged, hard-faced *viveur* was addressed by his young hostess. 'Have you been riding to-day, Mr Greville?' asked the Queen. 'No, Madam, I have not,' replied Mr Greville. 'It was a fine day,' continued the Queen. 'Yes, Madam, a very fine day,' said Mr Greville. 'It was rather cold, though,' said the Queen. 'It *was* rather cold, Madam,' said Mr Greville. 'Your sister, Lady Francis Egerton, rides, I think, doesn't she?' said the Queen. 'She does ride sometimes, Madam,' said Mr Greville. There was a pause, after which Mr Greville ventured to take the lead, though he did not venture to change the subject. 'Has your Majesty been riding to-day?' asked Mr Greville. 'Oh yes, a very long ride,' answered the Queen with animation. 'Has your Majesty got a nice horse?' said Mr Greville... [4]

This satirical repetition of names has the effect of emptying them of meaning and makes the whole situation seem ludicrous.

At times characters are defined by repetition, if their lives are governed by habit. Such characters are often comic, like Mary Datchet's father in *Night and Day* who springs upon his guests his detailed concern with the size and times of railway trains.[5] The repetition and the specialist interest make him a good illustration of Bergson's theory of laughter. Human beings can become mechanical, repeating the same phrases over and over again. But the laughter which this might cause is, in the end, masked by the bitterness which Bergson senses behind all laughter. The flower-seller in *The Years* exemplifies this. He is not only repetitive himself, he is also reincarnated in a form which only slightly alters from generation to generation throughout the novel:

'Nice vilets, fresh vilets', he repeated automatically as the people passed. Most of them went by without looking. But he went on repeating his formula automatically. 'Nice vilets, fresh vilets', as if he scarcely expected anyone to buy. Then two ladies came; and he held out his violets, and he said once more 'Nice vilets, fresh vilets.'[6]

He has made himself into a gramophone by his dehumanised repetition. The repetitions involved in creating these minor characters are highly stylised. For example, there is the use of three parallel characters. In *Orlando* there are the three mistresses who exemplify various faults and graces;[7] also the schematic morality figures Ambition, Poetry, and Desire of Fame;[8] and Purity, Chastity and Modesty.[9] In *Jacob's Room* we have the three types of professor, Huxtable, Sopwith and Cowan.

We have been dealing so far with the creation of minor characters, but we must move on to consider the idea of character itself. We have seen that a proper name can be separated from the person to whom it refers, but it falsifies in another sense, for it is one name, whereas a person is no single thing. The characters in *The Waves*, for example, are bound up with each other and define each other, as Bernard points out: 'I am not one person; I am many people; I do not altogether know who I am – Jinny, Susan, Neville, Rhoda, or Louis; or how to distinguish my life from theirs.'[10] The idea of a persona, a mask, lies behind our notion of a person. Speaking to oneself is a division of the self, but to whom are we speaking? The process of character creation can be seen clearly in the case of Septimus Smith and Clarissa Dalloway. A 'double' is the secret sharer of our suppressed life, or he represents 'what we might have been', and this helps to explain the relationship between Clarissa and Septimus. We have a valuable insight into the process of character creation here, for in a preface Virginia Woolf tells us that a single character was divided in order to create these two: 'in the first version Septimus, who later is intended to be her double, had no existence; and that Mrs Dalloway was originally to kill herself at the end of the party'.[11] Clarissa is identified with Septimus in a much closer way than simply through feelings of sympathy or pity. He is truly part of herself, their pain is shared.

Virginia Woolf's artists, because they are open to all sorts of influences and possibilities, are like chameleons. They cannot be pinned down to certain fixed traits. This explains the androgeneity of Orlando, Miss La Trobe and Lily Briscoe. In the following passage, Bernard brings together many of the elements of character which we have been discussing:

But 'joined to the sensibility of a woman' (I am here quoting my own biographer) 'Bernard possessed the logical sobriety of a man.' Now people who make a single impression, and that, in the main, a good one (for there seems to be a virtue in simplicity), are those who keep their equilibrium in mid-stream. (I instantly see fish with their noses one way, the stream rushing past another.) Canon, Lycett, Peters, Hawkins, Larpent, Neville – all fish in mid-stream. But *you* understand, *you*, my self, who always comes at a call (that would be a harrowing experience to call and for no one to come; that would make the midnight hollow, and explains the expression of old men in clubs – they have given up calling for a self who does not come), you understand that I am only superficially represented by what I was saying to-night. Underneath, and at the moment when I am most disparate, I am also integrated.[12]

Here we have the androgeneity, and the division of the self which are the distinctive traits of Virginia Woolf's artists. Here also are Canon, Lycett, Peters and the others. Their names are repeated throughout the novel, but they remain simply names. The element of mock-biography reminds us that a person can never be summed up neatly.

Shortly after Virginia Woolf's essay on character in the novel, 'Mr Bennett and Mrs Brown' appeared in *The Nation and The Athenaeum*, Logan Pearsall Smith joined the subsequent discussion with an interesting article. He explains the lack of character-making ability in contemporary writers in the following way:

The impression of individual character is produced by an individual way of speech; each personage possesses an idiom, a diction, a rhythm, a sort of sing-song of his own...Dickens and the other Victorians no doubt abused this enchantment, this way of making their characters sing themselves into existence; they reiterated their little tunes and catch-phrases so monotonously that their successors became disgusted with this method, and adopted the method of description and analysis instead. Is this, perhaps, the cause of that loss of character-creating power which Mrs Woolf notes in them...?[13]

His remarks on the role of repetition in building up character are especially interesting:

Hamlet is made real to us very largely by his speech-rhythms and intonations – there is, for instance, as Mr Bradley has finely noted, nothing in the play more intensely characteristic, and more unmistakeably individual, than Hamlet's trick of verbal repetitions. 'Words, words, words' – 'very like, very like' – 'thrift, thrift, Horatio' – 'except my life, except my life' – is not the very essence of Hamlet embodied in these little phrases? Could any number of pages of analysis and description have made him more living to us?[14]

We can see in *The Waves* how Virginia Woolf developed the idea of building up character from repeated phrases and images. There are a number of repeated images which recur throughout her works, giving them a kind of integrity.

In an earlier chapter we looked at a recurrent image of repetition in the work of Virginia Woolf, the mirror. A recurrent image of any kind is a repetition showing the mind of the writer circling around a constant problem, or trying to connect disparate parts of his experience. With Virginia Woolf the repetition is more striking in that the mirror, and that other recurring image, the parrot, are themselves images of repetition. We can see from her diary that the parrot is a personal symbol for the mechanical and horrifying aspect of repetition. She speaks of the 'parrot prattle' of the gramophone at Shakespeare's birthplace – the gramophone, as we can see in *Between the Acts*, being a related image of the hateful mechanical aspect of repetition. The parrot simply imitates noises, there is no real communication. This also applies to art; in the first instance, to the mistaken idea that art should be a copy of 'reality', but also to the empty abstract nouns connected with such an art. Both criticisms are contained in the following passage from an essay which describes a visit to the Royal Academy:

Suddenly the great rooms rang like a parrot-house with the intolerable vociferations of gaudy and brainless birds. How they shrieked and gibbered! How they danced and sidled! Honour, patriotism, chastity, wealth, success, importance, position, patronage, power – their cries rang and echoed from all quarters.[15]

As a useless superfluous ornament, the parrot symbolises the meaningless social round of Clarissa's youth:

Devonshire House, Bath House, the house with the china cockatoo, she had seen them all lit up once; and remembered Sylvia, Fred, Sally Seton – such hosts of people; and dancing all night; and the wagons plodding past to market; and driving home across the Park.[16]

Once we have become sensitised to Virginia Woolf's use of the cockatoo image, the sense of emptiness and death follows naturally from these memories: 'Did it matter then, she asked herself, walking towards Bond Street, did it matter that she must inevitably cease completely; all this must go on without her; did she resent it; or did it not become consoling to believe that death ended absolutely?'[17] In *The Waves* the parrot gives us a sense of the jungle within, and with the repeated 'come' of our bodily needs:

For now my body, my companion, which is always sending its signals, the rough black 'No', the golden 'Come', in rapid running arrows of sensation, beckons. Someone moves. Did I raise my arm? Did I look? Did my yellow scarf with the strawberry spots float and signal? He has broken from the wall. He follows. I am pursued through the forest. All is rapt, all is nocturnal, and the parrots go screaming through the branches. All my senses stand erect. Now I feel the roughness of the fibre of the curtain through which I push; now I feel the cold iron railing and its blistered paint beneath my palm. Now the cool tide of darkness breaks its waters over me. We are out of doors. Night opens; night traversed by wandering moths; night hiding lovers roaming to adventure. I smell roses; I smell violets; I see red and blue just hidden. Now gravel is under my shoes; now grass. Up reel the tall backs of houses guilty with lights. All London is uneasy with flashing lights. Now let us sing our love song – Come, come, come. Now my gold signal is like a dragon-fly flying taut. Jug, jug, jug, I sing like the nightingale whose melody is crowded in the too narrow passage of her throat. Now I hear crash and rending of boughs and the crack of antlers as if the beasts of the forest were all hunting, all rearing high and plunging down among the thorns. One has pierced me. One is driven deep within me.[18]

In this passage Jinny feels the excitement of bodily sensations and fiercely accepts her sexual need, accepts the repetition which her body imposes. The same imagery of antlers, forest and parrot are given a completely different colouring by Rhoda – the tone here is not excitement and acceptance, but fear. Jinny, accepting the crushing emotion, moves inward, into the constricted throat of the nightingale, whereas Rhoda, fleeing from the emotion, turns outward, to 'history' and to a distant picture of the corners of the world:

Here in this dining-room you see the antlers and the tumblers; the salt-cellars; the yellow stains on the table-cloth. 'Waiter!' says Bernard. 'Bread!' says Susan. And the waiter comes; he brings bread. But I see the side of a cup like a mountain and only parts of antlers, and the brightness on the side of that jug like a crack in darkness with wonder and terror. Your voices sound like trees creaking in a forest. So with your faces and their prominences and hollows. How beautiful, standing at a distance immobile at midnight against the railings of some square! Behind you is a white crescent of foam, and fishermen on the verge of the world are drawing in nets and casting them. A wind ruffles the topmost leaves of primeval trees. (Yet here we sit at Hampton Court.) Parrots shrieking break the intense stillness of the jungle. (Here the trams start.) The swallow dips her wings in midnight pools. (Here we talk.) That is the circumference that I try to grasp as we sit together. Thus I must undergo the penance of Hampton Court at seven-thirty precisely.[19]

172

The repeated pattern of Neville's curtain is a parrot pecking fruit. Once again it is connected with sexual desire:

Now I have listened to them talking. They have gone now. I am alone. I could be content to watch the fire burn for ever, like a dome, like a furnace; now some spike of wood takes the look of a scaffold, or pit, or happy valley; now it is a serpent curled crimson with white scales. The fruit on the curtains swells beneath the parrot's beak. Cheep, cheep, creaks the fire, like the cheep of insects in the middle of a forest. Cheep, cheep, it clicks while out there the branches thrash the air, and now, like a volley of shot, a tree falls. These are the sounds of a London night. Then I hear the one sound I wait for. Up and up it comes, approaches, hesitates, stops at my door. I cry, 'Come in. Sit by me. Sit on the edge of the chair.' Swept away by the old hallucination, I cry, 'come closer, closer.'[20]

The repeated insistence of instinct is one of the ways in which we feel our own continuity. This insistence finds expression in certain constant personal symbols. For the artist, who works by analogies and repetitions, the universe really does seem to be, as Wallace Stevens suggests, the 'parakeet of parakeets'.[21]

Conclusion

14

'To the Lighthouse'

Many of the ideas which we have been discussing are crystallised in *To the Lighthouse*. The novel evolved partly from Virginia Woolf's desire to see her parents in a true perspective, and because of this autobiographical background to the novel, many critics have seen a greater 'solidity' in the portrayal of Mr and Mrs Ramsay than in most of Virginia Woolf's other characters. However, even here she does not seek for psychological realism, but for the establishment of a relation, and this involves a high degree of stylisation, even in these apparently solid characters.

We note first of all that their relationship is an antithetical one. Mrs Ramsay has an acute awareness of the double nature of repetition, as we can see in the following passage:

But here, as she turned the page, suddenly her search for the picture of a rake or a mowing-machine was interrupted. The gruff murmur, irregularly broken by the taking out of pipes and putting in of pipes which had kept on assuring her, though she could not hear what was said (as she sat in the window), that the men were happily talking; this sound, which had lasted now half an hour and had taken its place soothingly in the scale of sounds pressing on top of her, such as the tap of balls upon bats, the sharp, sudden bark now and then, 'How's that? How's that?' of the children playing cricket, had ceased; so that the monotonous fall of the waves on the beach, which for the most part beat a measured and soothing tattoo to her thoughts and seemed consolingly to repeat over and over again as she sat with the children the words of some old cradle song, murmured by nature, 'I am guarding you – I am your support,' but at other times suddenly and unexpectedly, especially when her mind raised itself slightly from the task actually in hand, had no such kindly meaning, but like a ghostly roll of drums remorselessly beat the measure of life, made one think of the destruction of the island and its engulfment in the sea, and warned her whose day had slipped past in one quick doing after another that it was all ephemeral as a rainbow --

this sound which had been obscured and concealed under the other sounds suddenly thundered hollow in her ears and made her look up with an impulse of terror.

They had ceased to talk; that was the explanation.[1]

There are soothing modified repetitions, the 'irregularly broken' murmur of conversation and the tap of bat and ball in the game of cricket. These human repetitions modify the 'monotonous fall of the waves'. When there is no human rhythm in counterpoint with this basic natural repetition then it becomes terrifying; we see only the remorseless repetition of death which makes life seem hollow. But this feeling comes only for a moment, because human repetitions can take our attention away from this fear. Mrs Ramsay finds comfort in domesticity, where 'custom crooned its soothing rhythm'.[2] She makes a positive effort to create these comforting social rhythms to save herself from drowning in the despair which an awareness of the deathly repetition can bring. This is what lies behind her deep feeling about an apparently trivial party:

Again she felt, as a fact without hostility, the sterility of men, for if she did not do it nobody would do it, and so, giving herself the little shake one gives a watch that has stopped, the old familiar pulse began beating, as the watch begins ticking – one, two, three, one, two, three. And so on and so on, she repeated, listening to it, sheltering and fostering the still feeble pulse as one might guard a weak flame with a newspaper...life being now strong enough to bear her on again, she began all this business, as a sailor not without weariness sees the wind fill his sail and yet hardly wants to be off again and thinks how, had the ship sunk, he would have whirled round and round and found rest on the floor of the sea.[3]

Mrs Ramsay sees importance in immediate things, in the close-up (we are told that she is short-sighted). This enables her to get 'inside' the repetition and thus transform it into a rhythm. She sees the 'first two quick strokes' of the lighthouse, but it is the long third stroke which modifies this repetition, and transforms it into a rhythm. This is Mrs Ramsay's rhythm, for she 'becomes' the third stroke:

and pausing there she looked out to meet that stroke of the Lighthouse, the long steady stroke, the last of the three, which was her stroke, for watching them in this mood always at this hour one could not help

178

attaching oneself to one thing especially of the things one saw; and this thing, the long steady stroke, was her stroke. Often she found herself sitting and looking, sitting and looking, with her work in her hands until she became the thing she looked at – that light for example.[4]

We saw earlier how Virginia Woolf translates into the terms of everyday life Roger Fry's thoughts about Impressionism. In *Jacob's Room* the natural scene becomes a kind of rudimentary impressionist painting when it is viewed through tears. In *To the Lighthouse* the equivalent everyday vision is the short-sightedness of Mrs Ramsay. Perhaps this indicates her intellectual limitations as well, for the visual and psychological cannot be disentangled here. The short-comings which Fry saw in the paintings of the Impressionists also apply to Mrs Ramsay's short-sighted vision of the world. Like them, she sees the full mosaic of her visual field, but it is insufficiently articulated. This is necessarily so, for articulation involves the rejection of some of the elements which make up our immediate experience. Mrs Ramsay does not want to relinquish any aspect of her immediate feelings and so she becomes absolutely identified with the thing she is looking at. Her all-embracing passivity can be seen in the following passage:

It was odd, she thought, how if one was alone, one leant to things, inanimate things; trees, streams, flowers; felt they expressed one; felt they became one; felt they knew one, in a sense were one; felt an irrational tenderness thus (she looked at that long steady light) as for oneself. There rose, and she looked and looked with her needles suspended, there curled up off the floor of the mind, rose from the lake of one's being, a mist, a bride to meet her lover.[5]

There is a lack of choice, of distance and of form in her vision. Her way of looking at things has a certain validity and truth, but she needs her husband to give her support, to complement her perspective.

Mr Ramsay is long-sighted and cannot become part of a rhythm. He sees things from the outside, where the hateful aspect of repetition is most in evidence. His relationship with William Bankes becomes repetitive because it cannot develop into a rhythm. William describes what has happened: 'After that, what with one thing and another, the pulp had gone out of their friendship. Whose fault it was he could not say, only, after a time, repetition had taken the place of newness. It was to repeat that they met.'[6] Mr Ramsay is working logically on the problem of the way in which we understand the world; Andrew sums up his father's work as dealing with 'subject and object and the nature of reality'.[7] But his academic work is a repetition of what he achieved when he was a young man: 'He had made a definite contribution to philosophy in one little book when he was only five and twenty; what came after was more or less amplification, repetition.'[8] Mr Ramsay is usually very distant from the object. We saw earlier that in her essay of Defoe, Virginia Woolf saw the plain earthenware pot standing in the foreground of *Robinson Crusoe*, giving a perspective from which the tale was told. The stone urn beside which Mr Ramsay conducts his philosophical speculations has a similar function. It is a fixed point from which he moves away into the world of abstract speculation, and at the same time, of self-dramatisation. He stops for a moment by the urn, and knocks his pipe on its handle. Momentarily he sees the truth when he involuntarily *sees* the urn for its own sake:

The lizard's eye flickered once more. The veins on his forehead bulged. The geranium in the urn became startlingly visible and, displayed among its leaves, he could see, without wishing it, that old, that obvious distinction between the two classes of men; on the one hand the steady goers of superhuman strength who, plodding and persevering, repeat the whole alphabet in order, twenty-six letters in all, from start to finish; on the other the gifted, the inspired who, miraculously, lump all the letters together in one flash – the way of genius. He had not genius; he laid no claim to that: but he had, or might have had, the power to repeat every letter of the alphabet from A to Z accurately in order. Meanwhile, he stuck at Q. On, then, on to R.[9]

He then moves out to his usual 'distant' view. From this distance, human fame is reduced to nothing:

His fame lasts perhaps two thousand years. And what are two thousand years? (asked Mr Ramsay ironically, staring at the hedge). What, indeed, if you look from a mountain-top down the long wastes of the ages? The very stone one kicks with one's boot will outlast Shakespeare. His own little light would shine, not very brightly, for a year or two, and would then be merged in some bigger light, and that in a bigger still. (He looked into the darkness, into the intricacy of the twigs.)[10]

Mr Ramsay cannot see objects which are close to him, for his gaze is set upon 'distant' things, such as abstract ideas and posthumous fame. Mrs Ramsay's Impressionist view is set against his over-theoretical, abstract vision. He does not see the hedge as a beautiful mass of shapes and colours, as does his wife (and, as we saw earlier, Proust's narrator), he sees its 'intricacy'. Mr Ramsay looks into the distance and into future time 'ironically', that is to say, critically, and this entails a neglect of the quality of the immediate scene. He translates this into a 'long-sighted' visual metaphor, but it is the abstract distance of the scene which is emphasised, not any intrinsic quality:

Who then could blame the leader of that forlorn party which after all has climbed high enough to see the waste of the years and the perishing of stars, if before death stiffens his limbs beyond the power of movement he does a little consciously raise his numbed fingers to his brow, and square his shoulders, so that when the search party comes they will find him dead at his post, the fine figure of a soldier? Mr Ramsay squared his shoulders and stood very upright by the urn.[11]

Here we see the advantage which Mrs Ramsay's vision has, for her undifferentiated view does prevent the egoistic self-dramatisation which is so typical of Mr Ramsay, and by extension, of the critical spirit in general. Although the visual metaphor is used, Mr Ramsay usually sees nothing. He stands beside the urn, which we have been told contains a geranium, but apart from a momentary coincidence of vision and insight he sees only abstract things: distance, intricacy, waste and perishing. But when he returns from his journey into distant speculation and his gaze rests on his wife he is able to appreciate the scene before him 'for its own sake', in other words, he actually sees it:

Who will not secretly rejoice when the hero puts his armour off, and halts by the window and gazes at his wife and son, who very distant at first, gradually come closer and closer, till lips and book and head are clearly before him, though still lovely and unfamiliar from the intensity of his isolation and the waste of ages and the perishing of the stars, and finally putting his pipe in his pocket and bending his magnificent head before her – who will blame him if he does homage to the beauty of the world?[12]

Because he is one of the men who repeat rather than seeing things in a flash of intuition, like Lily and Mrs Ramsay, he 'could not remember the whole shape' of the novel which he is reading. This 'whole shape' is precisely what Virginia Woolf wanted her readers to see when they read her novels and it is the pattern of repetitions and the insight into repetition and rhythm throughout her work which helps her to achieve this effect.

This ability to see things as a whole is not a denial of repetition, but an ability to plunge into its midst and so take on a rhythm:

And, what was even more exciting, she felt, too, as she saw Mr Ramsay bearing down and retreating, and Mrs Ramsay sitting with James in the window and the cloud moving and the tree bending, how life, from being made up of little separate incidents which one lived one by one, became curled and whole like a wave which bore one up with it and threw one down with it, there, with a dash on the beach.[13]

Here, Lily becomes one with the wave. As an artist, she tries to combine the short-sight of Mrs Ramsay and the long-sight of Mr Ramsay. She senses the rhythm of the wave in the passage above, but she can also see from a distance the formal pattern which the waves make: 'as the waves shape themselves symmetrically from the cliff top, but to the swimmer among them are divided by steep gulfs, and foaming crests'.[14] Lily sees the beauty and completeness of things close at hand, but can also look into the distance and see shape and form. She has a myriad of impressions, like Mrs Ramsay, but like Mr Ramsay can distance herself and see the form of things. Her impressions are apparently free but there is an underlying pattern given to them, they are controlled:

All of this danced up and down, like a company of gnats, each separate, but all marvellously controlled in an invisible elastic net – danced up and down in Lily's mind, in and about the branches of the pear tree, where still hung in effigy the scrubbed kitchen table, symbol of her profound respect for Mr Ramsay's mind, until her thought which had spun quicker and quicker exploded of its own intensity...[15]

The form is not an abstract one here, like that of Mr Ramsay's philosophical speculations; it does not move too far away from the given data of her visual impressions. We can see this in her literal approach to the philosophical problems and examples. Andrew had used the example of the kitchen table to illustrate the kind of abstract speculation upon which his father was engaged:

Whenever she 'thought of his work' she always saw clearly before her a large kitchen table. It was Andrew's doing. She asked him what his father's books were about. 'Subject and object and the nature of reality', Andrew had said. And when she said Heavens, she had no notion what that meant. 'Think of a kitchen table then', he told her, 'when you're not there.'[16]

This abstract discussion about the existence of an object when there is nobody to observe it, she relates to her 'own' object, the tree:

So she always saw, when she thought of Mr Ramsay's work, a scrubbed kitchen table. It lodged now in the fork of a pear tree, for they had reached the orchard. And with a painful effort of concentration, she focused her mind, not upon the silver-bossed bark of the tree, or upon its fish-shaped leaves, but upon a phantom kitchen table, one of those scrubbed board tables, grained and knotted, whose virtue seems to have been laid bare by years of muscular integrity, which stuck there, its four legs in air. Naturally, if one's days were passed in this seeing of angular essences, this reducing of lovely evenings, with all their flamingo clouds and blue and silver to a white deal four-legged table (and it was a mark of the finest minds so to do), naturally one could not be judged like an ordinary person.[17]

Lily's vision is here contrasted both with that of Mr Ramsay and of Mr Bankes. For the one, the table is an 'angular essence', for the other it is useful, it has 'muscular integrity'. Lily Briscoe contrasts the abstraction of Ramsay with the beauty of the evening, and that of Bankes with the beauty of the tree, from which the table has been painfully constructed (both tree and evening are silver). A further depth is given to the passage by the fish-shaped leaves, for these relate the silver tree to the fish which Macalister's boy mutilates later in the novel, which in turn is related to Lily's pain at the loss of Mrs Ramsay. The tree is to Lily's painting what the lighthouse is to the novel. The salt cellar on the table reminds her that she will move the tree to the middle, to the position which the lighthouse holds in the central section of the novel. Lily has an affection for the tree, but it is less than Mrs Ramsay's reverence for inanimate objects. It is a fixed point against which she can measure other things, it is a symbol, and a source of metaphor.

Virginia Woolf approaches the truth by indirections. There are innumerable points of view in the novel, none of which is quite simply the correct direction. Lily recognises this complexity, which she expresses as a need for 'fifty pairs of eyes' to see the complete picture of Mrs Ramsay. We can see from this that Lily shares with Mrs Ramsay the habit of exaggeration, which is seen as an indirect way of reaching the truth.

Many critics have championed Mrs Ramsay's vision, some have excused Mr Ramsay's, but few have seen that the two are complementary and that Lily achieves a successful *aesthetic* fusion of impressionism and logic in her Post-Impressionist vision: 'She saw the colour burning on a framework of steel; the light of a butterfly's wing lying upon the arches of a cathedral.'[18] The patterning and design in the relationships of the main characters in the novel indicate that it is not simply autobiographical. Nor is it merely 'impressionistic' for there is an underlying strength given by its architecture – its steel framework and cathedral arches. Lily's fusion of the two points of view is only aesthetically successful. It is achieved at the cost of loneliness and isolation; the loss of family life and the kind of joy which Mrs Ramsay finds in social creation. The science of William Bankes, the philosophy of Ramsay, and Lily's art, all require selection from the totality of experience, and this selection involves various kinds of loss; on the other, hand, Mrs Ramsay is criticised for her lack of selection. The problem is stated, and the tension remains – as it must do if the novel is to retain its value, for there can be no single 'correct' view. Impressionism has its valuable place, but it is only one of the many valuable visions in the novel, and it must constantly struggle with the logic of form or design.

Repetition is again one of the themes in this novel. Speech can be heard as the mere production of noises, as we sometimes realise when we hear a child speaking. Mrs Ramsay's youngest child, Cam, is asked to deliver a message to the cook and to bring back the reply:

What was she dreaming about, Mrs Ramsay wondered, seeing her engrossed, as she stood there, with some thought of her own, so that she had to repeat the message twice – ask Mildred if Andrew, Miss Doyle, and Mr Rayley have come back? – The words seemed to be dropped into a well, where, if the waters were clear, they were also so extraordinarily distorting that, even as they descended, one saw them twisting about to make Heaven knows what pattern on the floor of the child's mind. What message would Cam give the cook? Mrs

Ramsay wondered. And indeed it was only by waiting patiently, and hearing that there was an old woman in the kitchen with very red cheeks, drinking soup out of a basin, that Mrs Ramsay at last prompted that parrot-like instinct which had picked up Mildred's words quite accurately and could now produce them, if one waited, in a colourless singsong. Shifting from foot to foot, Cam repeated the words, 'No, they haven't, and I've told Ellen to clear away tea.'[19]

This parroting ability of children is carried over into adult life, where much social chatter is as meaningless as the message was to Cam; it is simply a series of noises. This is amusingly described when Mrs Ramsay remembers the empty social conversation which she had to keep up with Minta's mother. The subject of the conversation, the parrot, also symbolises the kind of conversation which it is:

How did she exist in that portentous atmosphere where the maid was always removing in a dust-pan the sand that the parrot had scattered, and conversation was almost entirely reduced to the exploits – interesting perhaps, but limited after all – of that bird? Naturally, one had asked her to lunch, tea, dinner, finally to stay with them up at Finlay, which had resulted in some friction with the Owl, her mother, and more calling, and more conversation, and more sand, and really at the end of it, she had told enough lies about parrots to last her a lifetime...[20]

Virginia Woolf employs triple repetition here to a much lesser extent than in her later works, *Three Guineas* and *Between the Acts*, where it becomes obsessive. It is used in *To the Lighthouse* to express Tansley's anger at his sense of the emptiness of the lives of 'these silly women', Mrs Ramsay and Lily, who 'did nothing but talk, talk, talk, eat, eat, eat'.[21] It is used more significantly to express Paul's thoughts after he had proposed to Minta Doyle. He is dazed by the lights of the house and by his emotions, and he seeks reassurance in child-like repetition:

The house was all lit up, and the lights after the darkness made his eyes feel full, and he said to himself, childishly, as he walked up the drive, Lights, lights, lights, and repeated in a dazed way, Lights, lights, lights, as they came into the house, staring about him with his face quite stiff.[22]

Of more interest is the use of repeated phrases or refrains. Tansley's mechanically repeated 'Women can't paint, women can't write'[23] echoes hollowly in Lily's thoughts. But the repetition of a phrase can be comforting. Lily finds relief from the complexity of life by the repeated thought that she would 'move the tree to the middle': 'She had been looking at the table-cloth, and it had flashed upon her that she would move the tree to the middle, and need never marry anybody, and she had felt an enormous exultation.'[24] The phrase is repeated throughout the novel, illustrating the way in which Lily finds comfort in her concern with form, which is itself a kind of repetition. The phrase stays with her from the conception of her painting in the first part of the book until it is completed in the last paragraph. Her final stroke is to 'move the tree to the middle': 'With a sudden intensity, as if she saw it clear for a second, she drew a line there, in the centre.'[25] Refrain is used, as it is throughout Virginia Woolf's works, to give a sense of the cycle of birth and death. 'We perished, each alone' echoes in this way throughout the final section of the novel. But refrain can become too glib, the adoption of a false attitude. Virginia Woolf conveys this in the mock-heroic compact between James and Cam to oppose their father: 'But they vowed, in silence, as they walked, to stand by each other and carry out the great compact – to resist tyranny to the death.'[26] The falsity of this adopted attitude ('to resist tyranny to the death') is shown gradually on the journey to the lighthouse, as first Cam, then James come to feel in some measure the respect which Mrs Ramsay had for her husband: 'Cam would never resist tyranny to the death, he thought grimly, watching her face, sad, sulky, yielding.'[27] But repeated phrases can come close to true communication which exact meaning prevents. In the following passage language becomes like music, having 'significance' but no meaning:

She could see the words echoing as she spoke them rhythmically in Cam's mind, and Cam was repeating after her how it was like a mountain, a bird's nest, a garden, and there were little antelopes, and her eyes were opening and shutting, and Mrs Ramsay went on saying still more monotonously, and more rhythmically and more nonsensically, how she must shut her eyes and go to sleep and dream of mountains and valleys and stars falling and parrots and antelopes and gardens, and everything lovely, she said, raising her head very slowly and speaking more and more mechanically, until she sat upright and saw that Cam was asleep.[28]

It is with nonsensical, rhythmical repetition that one comes closest to the movement of nature. Just as the old woman in *Mrs Dalloway* 'becomes' the tree as she sings a song 'with an absence of all human meaning',[29] so the housekeeper in *To the Lighthouse* is at one with nature:

but now, coming from the toothless, bonneted, care-taking woman, was robbed of meaning, was like the voice of witlessness, humour, persistency itself, trodden down but springing up again, so that she lurched, dusting, wiping, she seemed to say how it was one long sorrow and trouble, how it was getting up and going to bed again, and bringing things out and putting them away again.[30]

This repetition is boring and painful, and she asks 'how long shall it endure?' But when she looks in the mirror, and through imagination, and that other repetition, memory, she gains consolation:

looking sideways in the glass, as if, after all, she had her consolations, as if indeed there twined about her dirge some incorrigible hope. Visions of joy there must have been at the wash-tub, say with her children (yet two had been base-born and one had deserted her), at the public-house, drinking; turning over scraps in her drawers. Some cleavage of the dark there must have been, some channel in the depths of obscurity through which light enough issued to twist her face grinning in the glass and make her, turning to her job again, mumble out the old music hall song.[31]

Her face is twisted in the glass, just like that of the mystic in the pool which he stirs. Whilst Mrs MacNab is immersed in the routine and comforting repetition of memory, the mystic, has perhaps, a vision of 'repetition' itself:

Meanwhile the mystic, the visionary, walked the beach, stirred a puddle, looked at a stone, and asked themselves 'What am I?' 'What is this?' and suddenly an answer was vouchsafed them (what it was they could not say): so that they were warm in the frost and had comfort in the desert. But Mrs MacNab continued to drink and gossip as before.[32]

The repetition involved in memory is an important aspect of *To the Lighthouse*. The circling of memory is beautifully conveyed in the following passage, where the reiterated phrases convey the sense of meditation and also accord with the fact that the friendship between William and Mr Ramsay has failed to develop:

Looking at the far sand hills, William Bankes thought of Ramsay: thought of a road in Westmorland, thought of Ramsay striding along a road by himself hung round with that solitude which seemed to be his natural air. But this was suddenly interrupted, William Bankes remembered (and this must refer to some actual incident), by a hen, straddling her wings in protection of a covey of little chicks, upon which Ramsay, stopping, pointed his stick and said 'Pretty, – pretty,' an odd illumination into his heart, Bankes had thought it, which showed his simplicity, his sympathy with humble things; but it seemed to him as if their friendship had ceased, there, on that stretch of road. After that, Ramsay had married. After that, what with one thing and another, the pulp had gone out of their friendship. Whose fault it was he could not say, only, after a time, repetition had taken the place of newness. It was to repeat that they met. But in this dumb colloquy with the sand dunes he maintained that his affection for Ramsay had in no way diminished; but there, like the body of a young man laid up in peat for a century, with the red fresh on his lips was his friendship, in its acuteness and reality laid up across the bay among the sandhills.[33]

In the paragraphs following this, certain phrases are repeated with slight modifications, giving the sense of circling, of the lack of development. Their friendship is fresh in William's memory, but the freshness is of something dead but preserved, 'laid up in peat' like the young man in the image. William wonders whether he had 'dried and shrunk' and the phrase is repeated 'He must have dried and shrunk.'[34] In the last section of the novel the events of the first part are remembered, particularly by Lily Briscoe. She wonders whether she has 'dried and withered': 'But why repeat this over and over again? Why be always trying to bring up some feeling she had not got? There was a kind of blasphemy in it. It was all dry: all withered: all spent.'[35] But the remembered moment can be like a work of art: '. . .this moment of friendship and liking – which survived, after all these years, complete, so that she dipped into it to re-fashion her memory of him, and it stayed in the mind almost like a work of art'.[36] But underlying all this, the moment, memories, her painting, lies a sense of repetition. This is the 'buried feeling' which lies behind her art, as it does that of Virginia Woolf herself:

She was not inventing; she was only trying to smooth out something she had been given years ago folded up; something she had seen. For in the rough and tumble of daily life, with all those children about, all those visitors, one had constantly a sense of repetition – of one thing falling where another had fallen, and so setting up an echo which chimed in the air and made it full of vibrations.[37]

These 'vibrations' remind us of Butler's *Note-Books* and his interesting comments on the connection between language, art and sensation. As we have seen in the earlier discussion, language and art gain their value by their difference from sensation, by their escape from the tyranny of immediacy. Lily Briscoe's great desire, to convey the 'jar on the nerves', is one felt by many artists:

She must try to get hold of something that evaded her. It evaded her when she thought of Mrs Ramsay; it evaded her now when she thought of her picture. Phrases came. Visions came. Beautiful pictures. Beautiful phrases. But what she wished to get hold of was that very jar on the nerves, the thing itself before it has been made anything.[38]

Painting, we often feel, is nearer to 'sensation' than literature; it has an immediate, almost physiological impact. Literary interpretations of visual art often obstruct this non-verbal appreciation of form of colour. This accounts partly for Fry's wish to free painting from anecdotal criticism and his disparagement of such painting as was amenable to that approach. He felt that in the past, literature in England had been so dominant that it had pushed painting in a literary direction. The co-operation between himself and Virginia Woolf turns out to be, in a sense, an attempt to reverse the process, and this is particularly evident in *To the Lighthouse*. That 'jar on the nerves' which a painter can more adequately convey than an artist in words is what Virginia Woolf wishes to achieve, and the anecdotal aspect of the novel, as in most of her work, is neglected. The visual shock which Lily tries to put on to her canvas has its origin in the more general sensations of everyday life. Just as the Impressionist blur becomes Mrs Ramsay's short-sightedness, so the visual shock of a painting is related to all the other shocks which we suffer, not only visual, but to the other senses, and emotional shocks as well. The sound of a gun wakes Lily from her reverie, and echoes the 'explosion' of her thoughts. We are then given a picture of the scene as she comes round from her day-dream: 'until her thought which had spun quicker and quicker exploded of its own intensity; she felt released; a shot went off close at hand, and there came, flying from its fragments, frightened, effusive, tumultuous, a flock of starlings'.[39] There follows immediately afterwards another shock, and then the calming down is expressed in visual terms again, with the settling of the starlings on the trees:

Following the scatter of swift-flying birds in the sky they stepped through the gap in the high hedge straight into Mr Ramsay, who boomed tragically at them, 'Someone had blundered!'

His eyes, glazed with emotion, defiant with tragic intensity, met theirs for a second, and trembled on the verge of recognition; but then, raising his hand half-way to his face as if to avert, to brush off, in an agony of peevish shame, their normal gaze, as if he begged them to withhold for a moment what he knew to be inevitable, as if he impressed upon them his own child-like resentment of interruption, yet even in the moment of discovery was not to be routed utterly, but was determined to hold fast to something of this delicious emotion, this impure rhapsody of which he was ashamed, but in which he revelled – he turned abruptly, slammed his private door on them; and, Lily Briscoe and Mr Bankes, looking uneasily up into the sky, observed that the flock of starlings which Jasper had routed with his gun had settled on the tops of the elm trees.[40]

Later in the novel Lily is awakened from her private thoughts by the banging of a gate, and this is related to a blow in the face from a sprung bramble branch. The long sentence of reverie is brought to a sudden end by the two abrupt sentences at the end of the section. A new movement begins in the next section as Lily gets down to the problem of her painting, but the preceding shock is carried over in the image of a blow in the face:

And then, she recalled, there was that sudden revivification, that sudden flare (when she praised his boots), that sudden recovery of vitality and interest in ordinary human things, which too passed and changed (for he was always changing, and hid nothing) into that other final phase which was new to her and had, she owned, made herself ashamed of her own irritability, when it seemed as if he had shed worries and ambitions, and the hope of sympathy and the desire for praise, had entered some other region, was drawn on, as if by curiosity, in dumb colloquy, whether with himself or another, at the head of that little procession out of one's range. An extraordinary face! The gate banged.

3.

So they're gone, she thought, sighing with relief and disappointment. Her sympathy seemed to fly back in her face, like a bramble sprung.[41]

There are similar little shocks throughout the novel, which are an attempt to give that 'jar on the nerves' which Lily speaks of.

In view of the agreement between Roger Fry and Virginia Woolf in their attack on photographic representation in painting and literature, it follows that a thoughtful artist like Lily Briscoe would not be portrayed as a representational painter. Indeed in the novel she is contrasted with Mr Paunceforte and his disciples. Mrs Ramsay notices that 'Since Mr Paunceforte had been there, three years before, all the pictures were like that she said, green and grey, with lemon-coloured sailing-boats, and pink women on the beach.'[42] Like Roger Fry, Lily sees things in terms of 'form' and 'geometry'. Mrs Ramsay is seen as 'dome shaped'[43] and in the final painting she appears as a purple triangle. To some extent, then, Lily is an abstract artist. The act of selection inevitably involves some degree of abstraction, but there remains the moral problem of whether it is right to reduce a person to a triangle. The emotional importance of form as opposed to the obvious appeal of recognisable subject-matter, is seen in the following passage, in which Lily and William Bankes discuss the dehumanisation of art. It might be useful here to remember Roger Fry's discussion of this problem in *Vision and Design*:

In such circumstances the greatest object of art becomes of no more significance than any casual piece of matter; a man's head is no more and no less important than a pumpkin, or, rather, these things may be so or not according to the rhythm that obsesses the artist and crystallises his vision. Since it is the habitual practice of the artist to be on the look-out for these peculiar arrangements of objects that arouse the creative vision, and become material for creative contemplation, he is liable to look at all objects from this point of view...It is irrelevant to ask him, while he is looking with this generalised and all-embracing vision, about the nature of the objects which compose it.[44]

In the following discussion Lily speaks for precisely this habitual vision of the artist:

Nothing could be cooler and quieter. Taking out a penknife, Mr Bankes tapped the canvas with the bone handle. What did she wish to indicate by the triangular purple shape, 'just there?' he asked.

It was Mrs Ramsay reading to James, she said, She knew his objection – that no one could tell it for a human shape. But she had made no attempt at likeness, she said. For what reason had she introduced them then? he asked. Why indeed? – except that if there, in that corner, it was bright, here, in this, she felt the need of darkness. Simple, obvious,

191

commonplace, as it was, Mr Bankes was interested. Mother and child then – objects of universal veneration, and in this case the mother was famous for her beauty – might be reduced, he pondered, to a purple shadow without irreverence.[45]

William Bankes is one of those people who, in Fry's terms, would say of a landscape 'What a nice place' instead of 'What a good picture'. William's other criteria, the unaesthetic ones of size and monetary value, are also very much those which Roger Fry constantly rejected: 'The truth was that all his prejudices were on the other side, he explained. The largest picture in his drawing-room, which painters had praised, and valued at a higher price than he had given for it, was of the cherry trees in blossom on the banks of the Kennet.'[46] William also brings into the discussion irrelevant private emotional associations: 'He had spent his honeymoon on the banks of the Kennet, he said. Lily must come and see that picture, he said.'[47] The kind of abstraction that Lily is concerned with is very different from the scientific examination which he is used to. Her abstraction can only be conveyed in paint, it can only be expressed with her paint-brush:

But now – he turned, with his glasses raised to the scientific examination of her canvas. The question being one of the relations of masses, of lights and shadows, which, to be honest, he had never considered before, he would like to have it explained – what then did she wish to make of it? And he indicated the scene before them. She looked. She could not show him what she wished to make of it, could not see it even herself, without a brush in her hand.[48]

It is only in the actual making of the work of art that she realises what she wants to 'say'. Mrs Ramsay's distinguished presence and Lily's affection for her are very important in the novel, but Lily as painter must select only the formal, visual aspects of her experience, and so Mrs Ramsay becomes a purple triangle. The equivalent problem for Virginia Woolf herself was the transmutation of her knowledge of her mother and father into the characters of Mr and Mrs Ramsay. The careful balancing which we can see in their portrayal gives them a formal significance which is more generally valid than a straight autobiography or biography would be. There is a careful selection and abstraction here which is emotionally significant.

As we saw in the earlier chapter, colour as a physiological effect cannot be captured in literature; but we also saw that this aspect of colour is only a small part of its significance even in visual art. Only by moving away from sensation, only by the establishment of a relation or by the use of a colour word can there be any meaning. We saw earlier the way in which Virginia Woolf investigates the use of colour in literature in 'An Unwritten Novel'. In *To the Lighthouse*, as we might expect in a novel concerned with painting, the use of colour is quite distinctive. I think it can be shown that there is a range of colour in a kind of scale here, similar to the 'keyboard' of metaphor in *Mrs Dalloway*.

In *To the Lighthouse*, 'white', the absence of colour, symbolises just that – the uncolourful, definite meaning of science and abstract thought. William Bankes seems to be clothed in a white scientific coat[49] and Lily Briscoe thinks of his work in terms of sections of potatoes.[50] Mr Ramsay's work on 'subject and object' she sees as a white scrubbed table.[51]

The next colour group as we move along the scale is that of red and brown. David Daiches rightly points out that there is 'colour symbolism running right through the book'. He goes on to say that:

Red and brown appear to be the colours of individuality and egotism, while blue and green are the colours of impersonality. Mr Ramsay, until the very end of the book, is represented as an egotist, and his colour is red or brown; Lily is the impersonal artist, and her colour is blue; Mrs Ramsay stands somewhere between, and her colour is purple.[52]

This is to some extent valid, and might be supported by the passage in which Mrs Ramsay imagines James dressed in a judge's red gown.[53] Here, red is connected with the public world of men and the professions. The red-brown stocking which Mrs Ramsay is knitting for the lighthouse-keeper's son puts her philanthropic gesture into the same general area of meaning. But this is already something much vaguer than Daiches suggests – we are drifting away from his 'individuality and egotism'. The use of red-brown, in contrast to the use of white, is deliberately blurred, it covers a wider area of half-meaning.

As we move along the scale, the use of colour becomes less 'literary' in the traditional way. Colour is used to convey something which can be described vaguely as an emotional equivalence, a subtle relation which is not logical. As we pointed out earlier, Roger Fry describes the physiological effect of colour as being less important in painting than the establishment of a relation. We can see this sort of emotional relation established in the equivalence which is made between the ashen ship which leaves behind a purple patch of oil[54] and Mrs Ramsay, whose grey clothes are mentioned[55] and who becomes a purple triangle in Lily's painting.

In her use of yellow in the novel, Virginia Woolf is trying to come close to the 'pure' colour of a painting – colour without any literary meaning. This is very much Carmichael's colour. His beard is white with a streak of yellow. There is again a relation established, like that between Mrs Ramsay and the ship, for earlier in the novel James colours a white shirt yellow.[56] Yellow is a positive avoidance of logical meaning, in contrast with white, which is a negative lack of colour. In the scale we have been constructing then, yellow and white are the extreme terms. Carmichael is a poet and an opium addict, the embodiment of 'things in themselves', of autonomy, and this rubs off on to the colour with which he is associated. Yellow means simply yellow, it represents the quality of colour which cannot be translated into other terms. G. E. Moore makes this point in *Principia Ethica*, and by coincidence his example is the same:

Consider yellow, for example. We may try to define it, by describing its physical equivalent; we may state what kind of light-vibrations must stimulate the normal eye, in order that we may perceive it. But a moment's reflection is sufficient to shew that those light-vibrations are not themselves what we mean by yellow. *They* are not what we perceive. Indeed we should never have been able to discover their existence, unless we had first been struck by the patent difference of quality between the different colours. The most we can be entitled to say of those vibrations is that they are what corresponds in space to the yellow which we actually perceive.[57]

Blue, Daiches sees as 'impersonality'. Once again, as with his discussion of 'red', his definition is too limiting. Certainly, impersonality might be included in the meaning, but blue also indicates 'distance' and 'space', which are more general than the purely literary idea of impersonality. As we shall see in the subsequent discussion, Virginia Woolf is trying to create spatial effects in the novel. In its formal sense, the blue is that which we see on the distant horizon. This is impersonal, but it does not *mean* impersonal. Blue is used in the novel to give the spatial, pictorial effect, in conjunction with the literary spaces of the sea, history, the eyes of another person, and so on. The people in the novel have blue eyes, except Carmichael, whose eyes are green, that is, a mixture of autonomous yellow and 'distant' blue.

As we saw earlier, the idea of the frame is of some importance in the aesthetics of Roger Fry and Virginia Woolf. It can convert the everyday scene into a rudimentary work of art. Mrs Ramsay's head is framed in this way by a picture frame hanging behind her and so becomes something to contemplate, like a picture:

> Knitting her reddish-brown hairy stocking, with her head outlined absurdly by the gilt frame, the green shawl which she had tossed over the edge of the frame, and the authenticated masterpiece by Michael Angelo, Mrs Ramsay smoothed out what had been harsh in her manner a moment before, raised his head, and kissed her little boy on the forehead. 'Let's find another picture to cut out,' she said.[58]

This frame, or any work of art, no matter how exalted, helps us to recapture the imaginative power which many children possess. Mrs Ramsay, who is outlined here by the picture frame, is also, for Lily painting her garden, framed by the window. She is no longer simply Mrs Ramsay, she is cut off from the practical world and transfigured into something like a painting of the Mother and Child. This process of framing, of taking objects out of the stream of everyday 'practical' life, is described earlier in the novel from a child's point of view. As with the 'impressionism' in the novel the artistic imagination is seen in its 'everyday' form: James cuts out pictures of commonplace objects and invests them with an emotional significance:

> Since he belonged, even at the age of six, to that great clan which cannot keep this feeling separate from that, but must let future prospects, with their joys and sorrows, cloud what is actually at hand, since to such people even in earliest childhood any turn in the wheel of sensation has the power to crystallise and transfix the moment upon which its gloom or radiance rests, James Ramsay, sitting on the floor cutting out pictures from the illustrated catalogue of the Army and Navy Stores, endowed the picture of a refrigerator as his mother spoke with heavenly bliss. It was fringed with joy. The wheelbarrow, the lawn-mower, the sound of poplar trees, leaves whitening before rain, rooks cawing,

brooms knocking, dresses rustling – all these were so coloured and distinguished in his mind that he had already his private code, his secret language, though he appeared the image of stark and uncompromising severity, with his high forehead and his fierce blue eyes, impeccably candid and pure, frowning slightly at the sight of human frailty...[59]

James' cutting out and the act of framing are seen as similar acts of imagination.

The familiar image of mimesis, of holding a mirror up to nature, is again used in this novel, as it is throughout Virginia Woolf's works. The image of a mirror or reflecting pool is used to illustrate the complex relationship between art and external reality, which is bound up with the problem of the relationship between human nature and 'Nature'. We saw in *Mrs Dalloway* how this took the Wordsworthian form of a fusion between an old lady and a stream and water pump. Here again the terms are those of the Romantic poets. The most important passage in this connection is part 6 of the central section of the novel. Spring is seen here as the time of growth, of hope and marriage: '[Prue Ramsay, leaning on her father's arm, was given in marriage that May. What, people said, could have been more fitting? And, they added, how beautiful she looked!]'[60] It is fitting, for the human is here in tune with the natural world, as the next paragraph indicates, with its Shelleyan images:

As summer neared, as the evenings lengthened, there came to the wakeful, the hopeful, walking the beach, stirring the pool, imaginations of the strangest kind – of flesh turned to atoms which drove before the wind, of stars flashing in their hearts, of cliff, sea, cloud, and sky brought purposely together to assemble outwardly the scattered parts of the vision within. In those mirrors, the minds of men, in those pools of uneasy water, in which clouds forever turn and shadows form, dreams persisted, and it was impossible to resist the strange intimation which every gull, flower, tree, man and woman, and the white earth itself seemed to declare (but if questioned at once to withdraw) that good triumphs, happiness prevails, order rules; or to resist the extraordinary stimulus to range hither and thither in search of some absolute good, some crystal of intensity, remote from the known pleasures and familiar virtues, something alien to the processes of domestic life, single, hard, bright, like a diamond in the sand, which would render the possessor secure.[61]

Blake's comment on the Wordsworthian consonance between mind and nature is perhaps relevant here: 'You shall not bring me down to believe such fitting & fitted. I know better & please your Lordship.'[62] Prue's death in childbirth bears out Blake's reservation. Things are even more out of joint than this, however, for the Great War kills Andrew Ramsay. What can we make of the supposed harmony of inner and outer in the face of this? Many such unpleasant facts must be excluded if we are to maintain a belief in the harmony between Nature and the mind of man:

It was difficult blandly to overlook them, to abolish their significance in the landscape; to continue, as one walked by the sea, to marvel how beauty outside mirrored beauty within.

Did Nature supplement what man advanced? Did she complete what he began? With equal complacence she saw his misery, condoned his meanness, and acquiesced in his torture. That dream, then, of sharing, completing, finding in solitude on the beach an answer, was but a reflection in a mirror, and the mirror itself was but the surface glassiness which forms in quiescence when the nobler powers sleep beneath? Impatient, despairing yet loth to go (for beauty offers her lures, has her consolations), to pace the beach was impossible; contemplation was unendurable; the mirror was broken.[63]

In *To the Lighthouse* only the simple unthinking person can be in a kind of accord with nature, only such an uncritical creature as Mrs McNab. In *Between the Acts* we see that it is only reflecting fragments which give us a true picture of 'reality'.

The analogy between brushstrokes and sentences was a common one for Virginia Woolf. Long sentences in the novel might indeed be seen as sweeping strokes with a full brush, but this is simply a metaphor that might be applied to many writers in a vague general way. In *Contemporary Writers*, Virginia Woolf speaks of the 'accustomed curve' of a writer's sentences and the danger of falling into a set pattern. The precise danger is not specified, but it can be illustrated from this novel. There are a great many sentences beginning 'Never was...' and 'Never did...', giving an exaggerated, emphatic effect. This is in keeping with one of the themes of the novel, the exaggeration to which both Mr and Mrs Ramsay are prone. The danger of Mrs Ramsay falling into the 'accustomed curve' of this attitude can be illustrated in the following passage:

And it would lift up on it some little phrase or other which had been lying in her mind like that – 'Children don't forget, children don't forget' – which she would repeat and begin adding to it, It will end, It will end she said. It will come, it will come, when suddenly she added, We are in the hands of the Lord.[64]

Here we have the curve of a set of sentences which consist of short repeated phrases culminating in a climax. The need for a final ending betrays Mrs Ramsay into a falsity, as she is quick to realise: 'But instantly she was annoyed with herself for saying that. Who had said it? not she; she had been trapped into saying something she did not mean.'[65] Later, she finds the true ending to her set of phrases, which is an ending, but not a falsely sentimental climax: 'It is enough! It is enough!'[66] This is a true conclusion, one not dictated by the need to complete the 'accustomed curve'.

But these are very general parallels between curves and sentences. Virginia Woolf attempts more specifically in the novel to simulate certain spatial aspects of visual art. This has sometimes been attempted in the past by the use of typographical devices, but it is difficult to fuse the two arts in this way. In *To the Lighthouse* the use of square and round brackets cannot be described simply as a typographical device, although this is certainly part of it. Virginia Woolf uses parentheses as something more than a mere device in the novel, for the whole form can be seen as a parenthesis. The first and last sections, being parallel, form brackets around the central section, 'Time Passes'. Throughout the novel smaller parentheses mirror this overall pattern; the book is made up of 'curves and arabesques flourishing round a centre of complete emptiness'.[67] Within the 'emptiness' of the central section, there are various parentheses which give a sense of the mere contingency of human life. The death of Andrew Ramsay is given in this way: '[A shell exploded. Twenty or thirty young men were blown up in France, among them Andrew Ramsay, whose death, mercifully, was instantaneous.]'[68] Even the fact of Mrs Ramsay's death is conveyed in a parenthesis, quite casually, as if she were only a very minor character in whom we had little interest: '[Mr Ramsay stumbling along a passage stretched his arms out one dark morning, but, Mrs Ramsay having died rather suddenly the night before, he stretched his arms out. They remained empty.]'[69] The effect is partly one of irony, which is intensified by the fact that the parenthesis equates these deaths with a candle blown out: '[Here Mr Carmichael, who was reading Virgil, blew out his candle. It was past midnight.]'[70] The square brackets are essentially vertical, like the lighthouse itself, or the tree which Lily would move to the middle of the painting. Seeing the novel as a whole shape, the thin central section is like a vertical line, as well as being an empty space bracketed by the first and last sections.

The other dominant shape in *To the Lighthouse* is the arabesque, which is described by the rounded brackets. The word 'arabesque' appears frequently throughout the novel, as it does in Roger Fry's criticism. Much of the movement of the novel is curved. The boat slices a curve in the bay, and the ball describes an arc when the children are playing catches. There is recurrent mention of beak and scimitar shapes.[71] The curve is linked with the scythe of Father Time and also with the indirect method of achieving the truth, but a further intention is to make the novel approximate as nearly as possible to the visual effect of a painting.

We have suggested that space is indicated by the use of blue, and that parenthesis, the picture frame, and the looking-glass hold a 'world hollowed out'. Lily's method of working is described as 'tunnelling her way into her picture, into the past'.[72] This is close to the 'tunnelling' which Virginia Woolf describes in her own diary, and is strikingly similar to that phrase of Seurat's which Fry was fond of quoting: 'hollowing out a canvas'. This creation of space, this 'framing' in order to cut off the picture space from ordinary space, is the basis of all painting. Lily Briscoe sees her painting as enclosing a space, and compares it to the trough between waves; it is a rhythmical space, and to capture it, she herself takes on a wave-like motion:

And so pausing and so flickering, she attained a dancing rhythmical movement, as if the pauses were one part of the rhythm and the strokes another, and all were related; and so, lightly and swiftly pausing, striking, she scored her canvas with brown running nervous lines which had no sooner settled there than they enclosed (she felt it looming out at her) a space. Down in the hollow of one wave she saw the next wave towering higher and higher above her. For what could be more formidable than that space?[73]

Here the sense of space is indeed conveyed by that parenthesis coming out from the page: '(she felt it looming out at her) a space'.[74] This space is formidable as an artistic problem – but it is a relief to have such formal problems, which both drown, and give expression to, simultaneous problems of emotion and memory:

'Is it a boat? Is it a cork?' she would say, Lily repeated, turning back, reluctantly again, to her canvas. Heaven be praised for it, the problem of space remained, she thought, taking up her brush again. It glared at her. The whole mass of the picture was poised upon that weight... And she began to lay on a red, a grey, and she began to model her way into the hollow there. At the same time, she seemed to be sitting beside Mrs Ramsay on the beach.[75]

Space is formidable, because it is 'empty', like the middle section of the novel. There, we hear the repeated shock of guns[76] and remember perhaps the artilleryman's sense of 'bracketing'. Silence, space, 'emptiness', give us a sense of freedom. They are full of every possibility, as Mrs Ramsay realises when she becomes a 'wedge-shaped core of darkness' (the purple triangle of Lily's picture):

For now she need not think about anybody. She could be herself, by herself. And that was what now she often felt the need of – to think; well not even to think, To be silent; to be alone. All the being and the doing, expansive glittering, vocal, evaporated; and one shrunk, with a sense of solemnity, to being oneself, a wedge-shaped core of darkness, something invisible to others. Although she continued to knit, and sat upright, it was thus that she felt herself; and this self having shed its attachments was free for the strangest adventures. When life sank down for a moment, the range of experience seemed limitless. And to everybody there was always this sense of unlimited resources, she supposed; one after another, she, Lily, Augustus Carmichael, must feel, our apparitions, the things you know us by, are simply childish.[77]

The 'free circulation of air' which Roger Fry often admired in paintings gives us a sense of space and freedom and Virginia Woolf tries to achieve a similar effect in the novel. We cannot simply see 'space', for it is defined by the objects which it 'holds'. In the following passage, Mrs Ramsay looks into the distance and the sense of space is given by the lights of the town which seem freely suspended there:

So she looked over her shoulder, at the town. The lights were rippling and running as if they were drops of silver water held firm in a wind. And all the poverty, all the suffering had turned to that, Mrs Ramsay thought. The lights of the town and of the harbour and of the boats seemed like a phantom net floating there to mark something which had sunk.[78]

In daytime the space is defined by the free drifting of smoke: 'A steamer far out at sea had drawn in the air a great scroll of smoke which stayed there curving and circling decoratively, as if the air were a fine gauze which held things and kept them softly in its mesh, only gently swaying them this way and that.'[79] Here, in both passages, there is an underlying form given to this space – there is a net and a gauze. If space is not given this underlying form, then it becomes a void, a negation. It is like a painful emotion which has not yet been transmuted into art. In this way, Lily sees the death of Mrs Ramsay as a space which must be filled if her pain is to be eased:

For one moment she felt that if they both got up, here, now on the lawn, and demanded an explanation, why was it so short, why was it so inexplicable, said it with violence, as two fully equipped human beings from whom nothing should be hid might speak, then, beauty would roll itself up; the space would fill; those empty flourishes would form into a shape; if they shouted loud enough Mrs Ramsay would return. 'Mrs Ramsay!' she said aloud, 'Mrs Ramsay!' The tears ran down her face.[80]

This is a vacancy which she will fill later by 'moving the tree to the middle', just as Virginia Woolf moves the lighthouse to the central position in her novel. Lily sees her formal problem in the following way:

It was a question, she remembered, how to connect this mass on the right hand with that on the left. She might do it by bringing the line of the branch across so; or break the vacancy in the foreground by an object (James perhaps) so. But the danger was that by doing that the unity of the whole might be broken. She stopped; she did not want to bore him; she took the canvas lightly off the easel.[81]

This is precisely Virginia Woolf's problem – how to connect the first and last sections of the novel without breaking the unity, and this she accomplishes in the brief central section.

This concern with 'distance' and 'space' also involves the idea of perspective and point of view. To see the full picture, especially of something as complex as a person, one needs to see them from many points of view. In the passage above, Lily sees James as an 'object' which might 'break the vacancy in the foreground', and Mrs Ramsay becomes a purple triangle in the painting. These are examples of the aesthetic or formal point of view, but others are possible, as Lily realises:

One wanted fifty pairs of eyes to see with, she reflected. Fifty pairs of eyes were not enough to get round that one woman with, she thought. Among them, must be one that was stone blind to her beauty. One wanted most some secret sense, fine as air, with which to steal through keyholes and surround her where she sat knitting, talking, sitting silent in the window alone; which took to itself and treasured up like the air which held the smoke of the steamer, her thoughts, her imaginations, her desires. What did the hedge mean to her, what did the garden mean to her, what did it mean to her when a wave broke?[82]

One needs the absolute 'ideal' freedom of the air, of space, to see all round a person. This is the sense of spatial freedom which Fry evokes in the following passage from *Flemish Art*, published in the same year as *To the Lighthouse*:

In this portrait of Egidius we are able to see something of those qualities of Metsys's art. There is still a certain meagreness and angularity about the forms – in comparison, for instance, with Lorenzo di Credi's portrait – but there is an approach to Italian art in the realisation of the volume of the whole figure and its relation to space. There is a free circulation of air about it which is new in Northern art.[83]

Lily feels the importance of 'distance' – it has, she says, 'an extraordinary power'. This is the distant past, the distance between people, and the blue distance of space, of the far horizon:

Lily stepped back to get her canvas – so – into perspective. It was an odd road to be walking, this of painting. Out and out one went, further and further, until at last one seemed to be on a narrow plank, perfectly alone, over the sea. And as she dipped into the blue paint, she dipped into the past there.[84]

The near and far are connected with the large and small. In the novel, as in Blake's 'Crystal Cabinet' there are smaller versions of Nature. The imagination of a child can make a pool into a seascape in this way. Once again the smoke of the steamer embodies and symbolises the spatial freedom of this activity:

Brooding, she changed the pool into the sea, and made the minnows into sharks and whales, and cast vast clouds over this tiny world by holding her hand against the sun, and so brought darkness and desolation, like God himself, to millions of ignorant and innocent creatures, and then took her hand away suddenly and let the sun stream down. Out on the pale criss-crossed sand, high-stepping, fringed, gauntletted, stalked some fantastic leviathan (she was still enlarging the pool), and slipped into the vast fissures of the mountain-side. And then, letting her eyes slide imperceptibly above the pool and rest on that wavering line of sea and sky, on the tree trunks which the smoke of steamers made waver upon the horizon, she became with all that dower sweeping savagely in and inevitably withdrawing, hypnotised, and the two senses of that vastness and this tininess (the pool had diminished again) flowering within it made her feel that she was bound hand and foot and unable to move by the intensity of feelings which reduced her own body, her own life, and the lives of all the people in the world, for ever, to nothingness. So listening to the waves, crouched over the pool, she brooded.[85]

Later in the novel this image of the rock-pool is taken up again to indicate quite explicitly that Virginia Woolf is concerned here with the way in which we perceive, or in Wordsworth's terms, 'half create' the external world. In that passage which we quoted earlier in the discussion, the problem of the interaction of the human and natural worlds is raised. The importance of the imagination in this transaction is stressed:

...imaginations of the strangest kind – of flesh turned to atoms which drove before the wind, of stars flashing in their hearts, of cliff, sea, cloud and sky brought purposely together to assemble outwardly the scattered parts of the vision within. In those mirrors, the minds of men, in those pools of uneasy water, in which clouds for ever turn and shadows form, dreams persisted...[86]

This free play of the imagination is the first step towards artistic creation. Mrs Ramsay transforms the skull hanging in Cam's bedroom into a landscape[87] just as she had done earlier with the dish of fruit, giving a wonderful evocation of space which is related to that of a painting:

Now eight candles were stood down the table, and after the first stoop the flames stood upright and drew with them into visibility the long table entire, and in the middle a yellow and purple dish of fruit. What had she done with it, Mrs Ramsay wondered, for Rose's arrangement of the grapes and pears, of the horny pink-lined shell, of the bananas, made her think of a trophy fetched from the bottom of the sea, of Neptune's banquet, of the bunch that hangs with vine leaves over the shoulder of Bacchus (in some picture), among the leopard skins and the torches lolloping red and gold...Thus brought up suddenly into the light it seemed possessed of great size and depth, was like a world in which one could take one's staff and climb up hills, she thought, and go down into valleys, and to her pleasure (for it brought them into sympathy momentarily) she saw that Augustus too feasted his eyes on the same plate of fruit, plunged in, broke off a bloom there, a tassel here, and returned, after feasting, to his hive. That was his way of looking, different from hers. But looking together united them.[88]

These large and small worlds are only relatively large or small – like Scott's 'mountains' or Jane Austen's 'roses on teacups', it all depends upon our imaginative point of view.[89]

It follows from the attack on 'proportion' which we saw in *Mrs Dalloway*, that exaggeration might be a valuable quality. It is part of the play with large and small, the shifting perspectives which are seen in the imaginative life of a child or an artist. James sees his mother as 'ten thousand times better' than Mr Ramsay. Mrs Ramsay's own habit of exaggeration is commented on by Mr Ramsay: '"You're teaching your daughters to exaggerate," said Mr Ramsay reproving her.'[90] Yet it is surely a saving grace in Mr Ramsay himself that he is prone to the same vice, or virtue:

They had laughed and laughed, like a couple of children, all because Mr Ramsay, finding an earwig in his milk at breakfast had sent the whole thing flying through the air on to the terrace outside. 'An earwig', Prue murmured, awestruck, 'in his milk.' Other people might find centipedes. But he had built round him such a fence of sanctity, and occupied the space with such a demeanour of majesty that an earwig in his milk was a monster.[91]

Exaggeration is set against over-careful exactitude and 'proportion', which are satirised in Charles Tansley's conversation and attitude to life:

She could not help laughing herself sometimes. She said, the other day, something about 'waves mountains high'. Yes, said Charles Tansley, it was a little rough. 'Aren't you drenched to the skin?' she had said.

'Damp, not wet through,' said Mr Tansley, pinching his sleeve, feeling his socks.[92]

Linked to this proportion is the carefulness, the lack of imagination, of all 'professionalism', which is mocked in Tansley's jargon:

his subject was now the influence of something upon somebody – they were walking on and Mrs Ramsay did not quite catch the meaning, only the words, here and there...dissertation...fellowship...readership...lectureship. She could not follow the ugly academic jargon, that rattled itself off so glibly...[93]

This is a typical novelist's stance in the face of restriction of any sort. Roger Fry's dislike of 'craftsmanship' in art stems from the same feeling that any specialisation is a barrier to the free play of the artist's imagination. Mr Paunceforte is the typical producer of 'well-made' paintings (what Fry would call 'opifacts'). Painting is a craft to him, and so he does not lack imitators:

She paused a moment. But now, she said, artists had come here. There indeed, only a few paces off, stood one of them, in Panama hat and yellow boots, seriously, softly, absorbedly, for all that he was watched by ten little boys, with an air of profound contentment on his round red face, gazing, and then, when he had gazed, dipping; imbuing the tip of his brush in some soft mound of green or pink. Since Mr Paunceforte had been there, three years before, all the pictures were like that she said, green and grey, with lemon-coloured sailing boats, and pink women on the beach.[94]

This artist's lack of any pain, his enjoyment of an audience, and his second-hand vision are all in direct contrast with Lily Briscoe's genuine artistic sense:

The jacmanna was bright violet; the wall staring white. She would not have considered it honest to tamper with the bright violet and the staring white, since she saw them like that, fashionable though it was, since Mr Paunceforte's visit, to see everything pale, elegant, semi-transparent.[95]

In spite of this dislike of professional artistry, there must be some 'design' as well as 'vision'. Lily struggles with formal problems which parallel Virginia Woolf's problems in writing the novel. It must not be 'well made' in the traditional sense, but it must have some underlying structure, some discernible shape. Science, abstract thought, and symmetry in art, as Fry points out in *Last Lectures*, work as a series of one plus one and so on – just as Mr Ramsay sees the letters of the alphabet one by one (he reaches Q but cannot go on to R). Similarly, he cannot see the 'whole shape' of the novel which he is reading. Lily can see the whole of the alphabet in a flash, just as one can take in the whole of a painting almost simultaneously. Virginia Woolf wishes her reader to feel something of the same quality when we reach the end of the novel. There are certain isolated 'moments of vision' throughout, such as that which Mrs Ramsay experiences at the dinner-party, but we are also meant to see the whole of the novel in a flash when we have read the last word. The reader is meant to share Lily's vision at the end:

Quickly, as if she were recalled by something over there, she turned to her canvas. There it was – her picture. Yes, with all its green and blues, its lines running up and across, its attempt at something. It would be hung in attics, she thought: it would be destroyed. But what did that matter? she asked herself, taking up her brush again. She looked at the steps; they were empty; she looked at her canvas; it was blurred. With a sudden intensity, as if she saw it clear for a second, she drew a line there, in the centre. It was done; it was finished. Yes, she thought, laying down her brush in extreme fatigue, I have had my vision.[96]

Appendix A

Roger Fry wrote many interesting articles and reviews, most of which have not been collected. The following is an extract from one of these. It is particularly interesting in that he makes a direct comparison at this early date (1919), between Virginia Woolf's writing and visual art.

I find that the artists I have mentioned are all more or less naturalistic. It is clear now that the modern movement is dividing into two main streams of influence – one which may be called Cubist, using the word in the vaguest and most generalized way; and the other Naturalist, though not of course the Naturalism of the nineteenth century. However much the Naturalists distort their vision, falsify perspective and change the proportions of objects, the general structure of their design is built on the appearances of our familiar three-dimensional space. The Cubists tend, on the other hand, to introduce at some point a complete break of connection between ordinary vision and the constructed pictorial vision. They may be highly realistic in detail, but internal necessities of design dictate the relations of the parts *de novo*, and not, as with the Naturalists, by a continued gradual distorting pressure upon the relations presented by ordinary vision. It is particularly interesting in the present exhibition to see two rather early works of Picasso in which the naturalistic origin of the vision is still clearly present, but in which the process of distortion and re-adjustment has gone so far that the next step (which Picasso was himself the first to take) is already indicated. The break having been once made and the idea of the construction of picture vision *de novo* having been once realized, a curious thing happened. It was seen that the complete break allowed the possibility of a new kind of literary painting. Ideas, symbolised by forms, could be juxtaposed, contrasted and combined almost as they can be by words on a page, and Futurism came into being. That this idea was seized on, perhaps originated, by a group of rather crude Italian journalists, and in all countries appealed to painters of a journalistic turn, has stigmatized this offshoot of Cubism. But now it would seem that it is returning to France to be taken up and explored by a very different type of mind. A number of pictures by Survage in the Mansard Gallery give one an idea of its possibilities in the hands of a man of refined and cultivated sensibility, a man who is not a journalist but a very up-to-date poet – and how much of modern literature is approximating to the same kind of relationship of ideas as Survage's pictures give us!

Just for the fun of testing my theory of these pictures, I will translate one of them into words; however clumsy a parody it may be, it will illustrate the point:

The Town

Houses, always houses, yellow fronts and pink fronts jostle one another, push one another this way and that way, crowd into every corner and climb into the sky; but however close they get together the leaves of trees push into their interstices, and mar the drilled decorum of their ranks; hard green leaves, delicate green leaves, veined all over with black lines, touched with rust between the veins, always more and more minutely articulated, more fragile and more irresistible. But the houses do not despair, they continue to line up, precise and prim, flat and textureless; always they have windows all over them and insides, bannisters, cornices, friezes; always in their proper places; they try to deny the leaves, but the leaves are harder than the houses and more persistent. Between houses and leaves there move the shapes of men; more transient than either, they scarcely leave a mark; their shadows stain the walls for a moment; they do not even rustle the leaves.

I see, now that I have done it, that it was meant for Mrs Virginia Woolf – that Survage is almost precisely the same thing in paint that Mrs Virginia Woolf is in prose. Only I like intensely such sequences of ideas presented to me in Mrs Virginia Woolf's prose, and as yet I have a rather strong distaste for Survage's visual statements. For all that, I feel the immense difference between this and the Italian use of a similar idea. It is possible that a place may be found, perhaps in illustration, for such a kind of literary picture. Of course Picasso himself has never become literary; indeed, in his Cubist work he is more purely plastic and less literary than he was in his early naturalistic days, and the main tradition of French Cubism remains severely formal. Braque, Juan Gris, Severini (who has returned from his Futurist venture to the classic fold), Maria Blanchard and all the rest, create forms which have no direct associations with ideas. Of this group the present exhibition hardly gives any idea. There are some charming and very accomplished essays by Marcussis, who follows Picasso's with little change, but with a personal taste of his own, and a Dutch artist who shows how rapidly the most revolutionary movements may be attacked by the parasite of academism.

From 'Modern French Art at the Mansard Gallery', I, *The Athenaeum* (8 August, 1919), pp. 723-4

Appendix B

Roger Fry's idea of 'craftsmanship' is similar to, and perhaps derives from, that of Veblen in *The Theory of the Leisure Class*. The following is close to Fry's comments on Japanese workmanship (see p. 63):

A display of efficient workmanship is pleasing simply as such, even where its remoter, for the time unconsidered, outcome is futile. There is a gratification of the artistic sense in the contemplation of skillful work. But it is also to be added that no such evidence of skillful workmanship, or of ingenious and effective adaptation of means to an end, will, in the long run, enjoy the approbation of the modern civilized consumer unless it has the sanction of the canon of conspicuous waste.

The position here taken is enforced in a felicitous manner by the place assigned in the economy of consumption to machine products. The point of material difference between machine-made goods and the hand-wrought goods which serve the same purposes is, ordinarily, that the former serve their primary purpose more adequately. They are a more perfect product – show a more perfect adaptation of means to end. This does not save them from disesteem and deprecation, for they fall short under the test of honorific waste. Hand labor is a more wasteful method of production; hence the goods turned out by this method are more serviceable for the purpose of pecuniary reputability; hence the marks of hand labor come to be honorific, and the goods which exhibit these marks take rank as of higher grade than the corresponding machine product. Commonly if not invariably, the honorific marks of hand labor are certain imperfections and irregularities in the lines of the hand-wrought article, showing where the workman has fallen short in the execution of the design. The ground of the superiority of hand-wrought goods, therefore, is a certain margin of crudeness. This margin must never be so wide as to show bungling workmanship, since that would be evidence of low cost, nor so narrow as to suggest the ideal precision attained only by the machine, for that would be evidence of low cost.

The appreciation of those evidences of honorific crudeness to which hand-wrought goods owe their superior worth and charm in the eyes of well-bred people is a matter of nice discrimination. It requires training and the formation of right habits of thought with respect to what may be called the physiognomy of goods. Machine-made goods of daily use are often admired and preferred precisely on account of their excessive perfection by the vulgar and the underbred who have not given due thought to the punctilios of elegant consumption. The ceremonial inferiority of machine products goes to show that the perfection of skill and workmanship embodied in any costly innovations in the finish of goods is not sufficient of itself to secure them acceptance and permanent favour. The innovation must have the support of the canon of conspicuous waste. Any feature in the physiognomy of goods, however pleasing in itself, and however well it may approve itself to the taste for effective work, will not be tolerated if it proves obnoxious to this norm of pecuniary reputability.

Thorstein Veblen, *The Theory of the Leisure Class* (1899; Allen and Unwin, 1970), pp. 113–14

Notes

Virginia Woolf citations. Where there has been more than one edition, the first of the two publication dates given in parentheses is that of the first edition (published by Hogarth Press unless stated to the contrary); the second that of the Hogarth Press Uniform Edition to which all references are made.

1 : *Samuel Butler on convention and repetition*

1 Virginia Woolf, *Contemporary Writers* (1965), p. 7.
2 See L. E. Holt, 'E. M. Forster and Samuel Butler', *P.M.L.A.*, LXI (1946), 804–19.
3 *Contemporary Writers*, p. 35.
4 David Lodge describes the similar way in which Virginia Woolf picks up the fire imagery of *Jane Eyre* (*Language of Fiction* (Routledge and Kegan Paul, 1966), p. 84).
5 Samuel Butler, *The Note-Books of Samuel Butler*, selections arranged and edited by H. F. Jones (1912; Cape, 1921), p. 272. (Subsequently, *Note-Books.*)
6 *Letters of Virginia Woolf and Lytton Strachey* (1956), p. 47.
7 *Note-Books*, pp. 58–9.
8 Ibid., p. 21.
9 *Note-Books*, p. 15.
10 *Contemporary Writers*, p. 33.
11 Ibid., p. 29.
12 *Note-Books*, p. 85.
13 Virginia Woolf, *Collected Essays* (2 vols., 1966), I, 183.
14 *Note-Books*, p. 85.
15 *Jacob's Room* (1922; 1945), p. 91.
16 Ibid., p. 92.
17 Ibid., p. 176.
18 *Note-Books*, p. 93.
19 *Essays*, I, 330–1.
20 Ibid., p. 331.
21 *Note-Books*, p. 93.
22 *Essays*, I, 331–2.
23 *Note-Books*, p. 9.
24 Ibid., p. 230.
25 Ibid., p. 66.
26 Ibid., p. 58.
27 *Essays*, II, 107.
28 *To the Lighthouse* (1927; 1930), p. 297.
29 *Mrs Dalloway* (1925; 1947), p. 21.
30 *Note-Books*, p. 60.
31 *Mrs Dalloway*, p. 16.
32 Ibid., pp. 44–5.
33 *Note-Books*, pp. 96–7.
34 Ibid., p. 16.
35 Leslie Stephen, *English Literature and Society in the Eighteenth Century* (Duckworth, 1904), p. 20. (See also p. 94.)
36 *Note-Books*, p. 312.
37 Ibid., p. 94.

2 : *Fry and the problem of representation*

1 Notably, J. K. Johnstone, J. H. Roberts, J. Guiguet, J. A. Schaeffer, and S. L. W. Proudfit.
2 Roger Fry, *Vision and Design* (1920; rev. ed., 1925, Chatto and Windus, 1928), p. 131n.
3 Q. Bell, *Roger Fry* (Leeds University, 1964).

4 Desmond MacCarthy, 'Roger Fry as a Critic', *The New Statesman and Nation* (15 Sept. 1934), pp. 324–5.
5 Quentin Bell in *Vision and Design. The Life, Work and Influence of Roger Fry (1866–1934)*, catalogue of an exhibition held by the Arts Council and the University of Nottingham, 1966.
6 Roger Fry, 'Chinese Bronzes at Messrs. Yamanaka's', *The Nation and The Athenaeum* (2 Jan. 1926), pp. 494–5.
7 William Gaunt, *The Aesthetic Adventure* (1945; Penguin, 1957), p. 242.
8 Ibid., p. 258.
9 Roger Fry, 'The French Gallery', *The Nation and The Athenaeum* (6 March, 1926), pp. 775–7.
10 Angus Wilson, *The Wild Garden, or Speaking of Writing* (Secker and Warburg, 1963), p. 9
11 Roger Fry, 'The Garden of Eden', *The Nation and The Athenaeum* (30 June 1928), p. 422.

12 Solomon Fishman, *The Interpretation of Art* (Univ. of Calif. Press, Berkeley and Los Angeles, 1963), p. 131.
13 L. H. Myers' character Rajah Amar criticises trivial aestheticism by asking the same question in *The Near and the Far* (collected edition, Cape, 1940), p. 457.
14 See for example his article 'De Gustibus', *The New Statesman and Nation* (21 Jan. 1933), pp. 67–8.
15 Evelyn Waugh, *Brideshead Revisited* (1945; rev. ed., 1960, Penguin, 1962), p. 79.
16 'Roger Fry as a Critic'.
17 *Brideshead Revisited*, p. 30.
18 Roger Fry, 'Mr MacColl and Drawing', *The Burlington Magazine*, XXXV (1919), 84–5.
19 Roger Fry, 'Sandro Botticelli', *The Burlington Magazine*, XLVIII (1926), 196ff.
20 Roger Fry, 'The Baroque', *The Burlington Magazine*, XXXIX (1921), 145.

3: *'The Voyage Out'* and *'Night and Day'*

1 *Vision and Design*, pp. 16–17.
2 Virginia Woolf, *Roger Fry* (1940), p. 108.
3 Ibid., p. 110.
4 Virginia Woolf, *Collected Essays* (2 vols., 1967), IV, 211.
5 E. M. Forster, 'Me, Them, and You' (1925), repr. in *Abinger Harvest* (1936; Penguin, 1967), pp. 39–40.
6 *Essays*, IV, 211.
7 Letter from Harry G. Sparks, *The Athenaeum* (12 Sept. 1919).
8 *Roger Fry*, p. 172.
9 J. K. Johnstone, *The Bloomsbury Group* (Secker and Warburg, 1954), p. 95.
10 *Roger Fry*, p. 240.
11 *The Voyage Out* (Duckworth, 1915; 1929), p. 102.
12 Ibid., p. 103.
13 Virginia Woolf, *A Writer's Diary* (1953), p. 24.

14 Ibid., pp. 3, 13.
15 She did use her reading in this way, to check and balance her own writing. We can see this process at work in her diary; here, for example, she feels that there are too many images in her writing: 'By God! What stuff I'm writing! Always these images. I write *Jacob* every morning now, feeling each day's work like a fence which I have to ride at, my heart in my mouth till it's over, and I've cleared, or knocked the bar out. (Another image, unthinking it was one. I must somehow get Hume's Essays and purge myself.)' (*Diary*, p. 28.)
16 *The Voyage Out*, p. 35.
17 Ibid., p. 398.
18 Ibid., p. 262.
19 Ibid., p. 332.
20 Ibid., p. 144.

3: *'The Voyage Out'* and *'Night and Day'*—continued

21 Ibid., p. 346.
22 Ibid., p. 144.
23 Ibid., p. 265.
24 Ibid., p. 145.
25 Ibid., p. 358.
26 See Appendix A.
27 *The Voyage Out*, p. 6.
28 *Night and Day* (Duckworth, 1919; 1930), p. 529.
29 *Diary*, p. 23.
30 *Essays*, I, 305.
31 Ibid., p. 307.
32 *Essays*, I, 305.

33 Ibid., pp. 311–12.
34 Joseph Conrad, *Victory* (1915; Penguin, 1963), p. 45.
35 Ibid., p. 278.
36 Ibid., p. 143.
37 Ibid., p. 208.
38 *Night and Day*, p. 92.
39 Ibid., p. 163.
40 Ibid., pp. 163–4.
41 *Victory*, pp. 19–20.
42 *Night and Day*, p. 123.
43 Ibid., p. 370.
44 Ibid., p. 151.

4: *'Mrs Dalloway'* and *'Flush'*

1 Ernst Cassirer, *The Philosophy of Symbolic Forms*, trans. Ralph Manheim (3 vols., Yale Univ. Press, 1953, 1955, 1957), I, 107. (Subsequently cited as *Symbolic Forms*.)
2 Ibid., pp. 107–8.
3 *Note-Books*, p. 211.
4 W. K. Wimsatt, Jr, *The Verbal Icon* (1954; Methuen, 1970), p. 217. (The quotation is from E. Cassirer, *Language and Myth*, tr. S. Langer (N.Y., 1946).)
5 *Note-Books*, p. 230.
6 Roger Fry, *A Sampler of Castile* (Leonard and Virginia Woolf, 1923), p. vi.
7 For example in his essay 'Thought and Language', given as a lecture in 1894 and reprinted in *The Humour of Homer* (1913).
8 *Diary*, pp. 54, 77.
9 Leonard Woolf, 'Words', *The Nation and The Athenaeum* (26 July 1924), p. 538.
10 *Essays*, II, 54.
11 Owen Barfield, *Poetic Diction, A Study in Meaning* (Faber and Gwyer, 1928), pp. 61–2.
12 Ibid., pp. 67–8.
13 *Mrs Dalloway*, p. 112.
14 Ibid., p. 5.
15 Ibid., p. 34.

16 Ibid., pp. 10–11.
17 Ibid., p. 51.
18 Ibid., p. 17.
19 Ibid., p. 16.
20 Ibid., p. 45.
21 Ibid., p. 15.
22 Ibid., p. 25.
23 Ibid., p. 21.
24 Ibid., p. 34.
25 Ibid., p. 177.
26 *Vision and Design*, p. 48.
27 Roger Fry, *Transformations* (Chatto and Windus, 1926), p. 3.
28 *Symbolic Forms*, III, 232.
29 See, for example, her *Diary*, p. 268.
30 E. Cassirer, *The Logic of the Humanities*, trans. C. S. Howe (Yale Univ. Press, 1960), p. 115.
31 *Transformations*, pp. 3–4.
32 *Essays*, I, 98.
33 *Transformations*, p. 4.
34 *Flush* (1933; 1933), p. 16.
35 Ibid., p. 22.
36 Ibid., p. 122.
37 Ibid., pp. 122–3.
38 *Symbolic Forms*, III, 120.
39 *Flush*, p. 125.
40 Ibid., p. 39.
41 Ibid., p. 125.
42 Ibid., p. 24.
43 *Transformations*, pp. 4–5.
44 *Flush*, p. 29.
45 Ibid., p. 124.

5: *Autonomy: 'Between the Acts'*

1 J. Isaacs, *An Assessment of Twen-tieth Century Literature* (Secker and Warburg, 1951), p. 15.

2 *Victory*, p. 12.

3 *Note-Books*, p. 93.

4 *Roger Fry*, p. 183.

5 Anton Ehrenzweig, *The Hidden Order of Art* (1967; Paladin, 1970).

6 *Giovanni Bellini*, Artists Library no. 2 (At the sign of the Unicorn, 1899), pp. 29–30.

7 *Essays*, II, 102.

8 *Giovanni Bellini*, p. 29.

9 *Vision and Design*, pp. 19–20.

10 *Roger Fry*, p. 239.

11 S. Mallarmé, *Poems*, trans. Roger Fry (Chatto and Windus, 1936), p. 295.

12 G. M. Turnell, 'Mallarmé', *Scrutiny*, V (March 1937), 425–38.

13 Lawrence uses the image of the mirror to explore the problem of self-consciousness and solipsism. It is the 'Lady of Shalott' theme in *The Virgin and the Gypsy*, and in *Women in Love* it is connected with the idea of repetition and is thus close to one of Virginia Woolf's continuing obsessions. (This will be discussed later, in Chapter 9.)

14 *Diary*, p. 315.

15 Ibid., p. 326.

16 *Essays*, II, 177–8.

17 J. M. Murry, 'The Future of English Fiction', *The Nation and The Athenaeum* (1 April 1922), pp. 24–5.

18 *Between the Acts* (1941; 1953), p. 67.

19 Ibid., p. 46.

20 Ibid., p. 47.

21 *Essays*, III, 218.

22 Ibid., p. 220.

23 Ibid., p. 219.

24 *Between the Acts*, p. 214.

25 Roger Fry, *Henri Matisse* (Zwemmer, 1930), pp. 33–4.

26 *Between the Acts*, p. 18.

27 Ibid., pp. 209–10.

28 Anton Chekhov, *Plays*, trans. Elisaveta Fen (Penguin, 1959), p. 121.

29 *Between the Acts*, p. 22.

30 Ibid., p. 26.

31 Ibid., pp. 19–20.

32 Quoted by Roger Fry in *Vision and Design*, p. 218.

33 Lytton Strachey, *Literary Essays* (1948; Chatto and Windus, 1961), p. 147.

34 William Blake, *Poetry and Prose*, ed. G. Keynes (1927; 4th ed., 1939,'Nonesuch, 1961), pp. 116–17.

35 *A Haunted House* (1943 i.e. 1944; 1953 i.e. 1954), pp. 86, 92.

6: *Craftsmanship*

1 Roger Fry, 'Exhibition of Old Masters at the Grafton Galleries', I, *The Burlington Magazine*, XX (1911–12), 66ff.

2 *Transformations*, p. 154.

3 Roger Fry (ed.), *Discourses Delivered to the Students of the Royal Academy by Sir Joshua Reynolds* (Seeley, 1905).

4 Roger Fry, 'Some Chinese Antiquities', *The Burlington Magazine*, XLIII (1923), pp. 276 ff.

5 Roger Fry, 'The Arts of Painting and Sculpture', in *An Outline of Modern Knowledge*, ed. W. Rose (Gollancz, 1931), pp. 937–8. (This notion of craftsmanship comes very close to that of T. Veblen in *The Theory of the Leisure Class*. See Appendix B.)

6 *A Sampler of Castile*, p. 50.

7 D. H. Lawrence, *Women in Love* (1921; Penguin, 1960), p. 103.

8 Ibid., p. 403.

9 Ibid., p. 536.

10 K. Alldritt has an interesting dis-cussion of Loerke's art in *The Visual Imagination of D. H. Law-rence* (Arnold, 1971).

11 *Contemporary Writers*, p. 117.

6: *Craftsmanship*—continued

12 *Essays*, II, 250–1.
13 *Essays*, II, 251.
14 Lytton Strachey, *Eminent Victorians* (1918; Chatto and Windus, 1948), p. 7.
15 Ibid., p. 8.
16 *Orlando* (Crosby, Gaige, N.Y., 1928; 1933), p. 62.
17 *Flush*, p. 12.
18 Miguel de Cervantes Saavedra, *Don Quixote of La Mancha*, trans.

Walter Starkie (New American Library, New York, 1964), p. 172.
19 *Flush*, p. 20.
20 Ibid., p. 162.
21 *A Haunted House*, p. 46.
22 *Mrs Dalloway*, p. 110.
23 *Mrs Dalloway*, pp. 110–11.
24 Ibid., p. 17.
25 Ibid., pp. 25–6.
26 Ibid., p. 76.
27 Ibid., pp. 103–4.

7: *Colour*

1 *Vision and Design*, p. 35.
2 Maurice Denis, 'Cézanne', II, trans. R. Fry, *The Burlington Magazine*, XVI (1909–10), 275ff.
3 Ibid.
4 Ibid., I, 207ff.
5 Ibid., II.
6 *Orlando*, p. 18.
7 Ibid., p. 94–5.
8 *A Haunted House*, p. 119.
9 *Between the Acts*, p. 83.
10 *Last Lectures*, p. 31.
11 Roger Fry, 'The Courtauld Fund', *The Nation and The Athenaeum* (30 Jan. 1926), pp. 613–14.
12 *Between the Acts*, p. 15.
13 *Symbolic Forms*, III, 129.
14 *Essays*, II, 233.
15 Sergei M. Eisenstein, *The Film Sense*, trans. Jay Leyda (1943; Faber, 1968), pp. 100–1.
16 Ibid., p. 120.
17 *A Haunted House*, pp. 21–2.
18 Ibid., p. 19.
19 Roger Fry, '*Horseman in a Wood*, by Corot', *The Burlington Magazine*, XLIV (1924), 157–8.
20 *A Haunted House*, p. 25.
21 Ibid., p. 26.
22 *Essays*, II, 241.
23 Ibid., 241–2.
24 *Transformations*, p. 213.
25 Ibid., p. 214.
26 Ibid.
27 Ibid., p. 216.
28 Ibid., p. 218.

29 Ibid.
30 Charles Mauron, *The Nature of Beauty in Art and Literature*, trans. R. Fry (Leonard and Virginia Woolf, 1927), p. 66.
31 *Vision and Design*, p. 10.
32 Roger Fry, *Characteristics of French Art* (Chatto and Windus, 1932).
33 *The Waves* (1931; 1943), p. 96.
34 Ibid., p. 148.
35 Ibid., p. 85.
36 Roger Fry, *Cézanne, A Study of His Development* (Hogarth Press, 1927), p. 40.
37 *The Waves*, p. 204.
38 Ibid., p. 6.
39 Ibid.
40 *Between the Acts*, p. 83.
41 *The Waves*, p. 11.
42 Ibid., p. 10.
43 Ibid., p. 44.
44 Ibid., p. 90.
45 Ibid., p. 18.
46 Ibid., p. 30.
47 Ibid., p. 73.
48 Ibid., p. 124.
49 Ibid., p. 156.
50 Ibid., p. 178.
51 Ibid., p. 145.
52 Ibid., p. 50.
53 Ibid., p. 46.
54 Ibid., p. 16.
55 Ibid., p. 17.
56 Ibid., p. 16.
57 Mallarmé, *Poems*, trans. Fry, p. 36.

58 *The Waves*, p. 13.
59 Ibid., p. 77.
60 Mallarmé, *Poems*, trans. Fry pp. 282–5.

61 Ibid., p. 286.
62 *The Waves*, p. 167.
63 Ibid., pp. 167–8.
64 Ibid., p. 168.

8: *Space: 'Hollowing out a canvas'*

1 William Troy, 'Virginia Woolf: The Novel of Sensibility' (1932), reprinted in *Literary Opinion in America*, ed. M.D. Zabel (3rd ed., revised, Harper and Row, New York, 1962), p. 328.
2 *The Voyage Out*, p. 29.
3 Ibid., p. 99.
4 Ibid., p. 100.
5 Ibid., p. 110.
6 Ibid., p. 150.
7 'The Novel of Sensibility', p. 332.
8 *Transformations*, p. 189.
9 Ibid., p. 195.
10 Susanne K. Langer, *Feeling and Form* (Routledge and Kegan Paul, 1953), p. 72.
11 *Orlando*, p. 228.
12 *Contemporary Writers*, p. 58.
13 Shiv Kumar, *Bergson and the Stream of Consciousness Novel* (Blackie, 1962).
14 *Contemporary Writers*, p. 42.
15 *Jacob's Room*, pp. 97–8.
16 *A Haunted House*, p. 119.
17 *Transformations*, p. 88.
18 *Flemish Art* (Chatto and Windus, 1927), pp. 24–5.
19 *Transformations*, p. 189.
20 See especially the description of the painting on p. 47.
21 *Mrs Dalloway*, p. 5.
22 *Diary*, p. 131.
23 *Transformations*, p. 41.
24 *Diary*, p. 96.
25 *Diary*, p. 83
26 *Essays*, I, 352–5.
27 M. Proust, *Remembrance of Things Past*: 1, *Swann's Way*, trans. C. K. Scott Moncrieff (1922; Chatto and Windus, 1966), 189–90.
28 *Essays*, I, 70.
29 Ibid.
30 The passage reminds one of Wallace Stevens' 'Anecdote of of the Jar'. His attitude towards visual art, specially to colour and to images is often similar to Virginia Woolf's.
31 *Essays*, I, 74–5.
32 *The Waves*, pp. 13, 53.

9: *An introduction to the problem*

1 *Note-Books*, pp. 54–5.
2 Ibid., p. 62.
3 Ibid., p. 312.
4 E. K. Brown, *Rhythm in the Novel* (1950; Univ of Toronto Press, 1963), p. 8.
5 Ibid., p. 115.
6 *Language of Fiction*, p. 82.
7 F. J. Hoffman, *Gertrude Stein* (Univ. of Minnesota Press, 1961), p. 20.
8 D. Sutherland, *Gertrude Stein, A Biography of Her Work* (Yale Univ. Press, New Haven, 1951), p. 11.
9 Elizabeth Sprigge, *Gertrude Stein, Her Life and Work* (Hamilton, 1957), p. 30.
10 Ibid., p. 99.
11 Clive Hart, *Structure and Motif in Finnegan's Wake* (Faber, 1962), pp. 164–5.
12 Ibid., p. 182.
13 Dorothy Richardson, *Pilgrimage* (4 vols., collected ed., 1938; re-issued, with previously unpublished section, *March Moonlight*, Dent, 1967), III, 129.
14 Lawrence, *Women in Love*, p. 45.
15 Ibid., p. 61.

9: *An Introduction to the problem*—continued

16 Ibid., p. 68.

17 Ibid., p. 216.

18 D. H. Lawrence, *Phoenix II*, ed. W. Roberts and H. T. Moore (Heinemann, 1968), p. 276.

19 *Women in Love*, p. 522.

20 Ibid., pp. 524–5.

21 Ibid., p. 28.

22 Ibid., p. 36.

23 Soren Kierkegaard, *Repetition*, trans. with an introduction and notes by Walter Lowrie (1941; Harper and Row, 1964), p. 13.

24 *The Years* (1937; 1940), p. 341.

25 H. Waley, *The Revival of Aesthetics* (Leonard and Virginia Woolf, 1926), p. 24.

26 Ibid., p. 26.

27 Ibid., p. 37.

28 J. B. Priestley, *Three Time-Plays* (Pan, 1947).

29 *The Years*, p. 398.

30 Joseph Heller employs this idea of *déjà vu* in his novel *Catch 22* (1962; Corgi, 1968) in which the form of the novel, with its repeated paragraphs, gives a sense of *déjà vu* hysteria, here caused by the stress of war.

31 I. M. L. Hunter, *Memory* (rev. ed., Penguin, 1964), p. 40.

32 *The Years*, p. 403.

33 Hunter, *Memory*, p. 109.

34 *The Years*, pp. 428–9.

35 *Between the Acts*, p. 47.

36 Hunter, *Memory*, p. 110.

37 *The Years*, p. 175.

38 Ibid., p. 424.

39 Ibid., p. 463.

40 *Pilgrimage*, I, 365.

41 *Feeling and Form*, p. 129.

42 *Mrs Dalloway*, p. 90.

43 Karin Stephen, *The Misuse of Mind* (Kegan, Paul, Trench, Trubner), 1922, p. 64.

44 Ibid., p. 13.

45 Ibid., p. 65.

46 Ibid., p. 88.

47 Ibid., pp. 103–4.

48 Ibid., p. 18.

49 *Vision and Design*, pp. 24–5.

50 *Roger Fry*, p. 214.

51 Roger Fry, 'The Exhibition of French Primitives', II, *The Burlington Magazine*, V (1904), 279ff.

52 D. S. MacColl, 'Mr Fry and Drawing', *The Burlington Magazine*, XXXIV (1919), 203ff.

53 Ibid.

54 Ibid.

55 'Mr MacColl and Drawing', pp. 84–5.

56 *Transformations*, p. 203.

57 Ibid., pp. 201–2.

58 Ibid., p. 206.

59 Fry (ed.), *Discourses, Sir Joshua Reynolds*, p. 69.

60 *Cézanne*, pp. 39–40.

61 Roger Shattuck, *The Banquet Years* (rev. ed., Cape, 1969), p. 104.

62 *Cézanne*, p. 48.

63 Ibid., p. 75.

64 Ibid., p. 57.

65 *Henri Matisse*, p. 36.

66 Ibid., p. 42.

67 *Last Lectures*, p. 27.

68 Roger Fry, 'La Parade', *The Burlington Magazine*, LV (1929), 289ff. Partially repr. in *Seurat*, ed. A. Blunt (Phaidon, 1965), p. 84.

69 *Banquet Years*, p. 352.

70 Ibid., p. 160.

71 Ibid., pp. 141–2.

72 Edmund Wilson, *To the Finland Station* (1940; Collins, 1960), p. 195.

73 *Pilgrimage*, III, 97–8.

74 Ibid., p. 60.

75 Ibid., p. 142.

76 Ibid., pp. 143–4.

77 *Diary*, p. 295.

78 *Three Guineas* (1938; 1943), pp. 107–8.

79 *Banquet Years*, pp. 184–5.

80 *The Bloomsbury Group*, p. 336.

81 Ibid., pp. 332–3.

82 Ibid., p. 334.

83. Ibid.
84. *Jacob's Room*, p. 37.
85 Ibid., p. 45.
86 Ibid., p. 81.
87 Ibid., p. 37.

88 Ibid., pp. 136–7.
89 Ibid., pp. 76–7.
90 Ibid., p. 11.
91 Ibid., p. 30.
92 Ibid., p. 176.

10: *The double nature of repetition: 'The Waves'*

1 David Jones, *In Parenthesis* (1937; Faber, 1963), p. 36.
2 C. Campos, *The View of France* (Oxford Univ. Press, 1965), p. 209.
3 It was observations of war neuroses which reinforced Freud's idea of the 'compulsion to repeat'. See *Beyond the Pleasure Principle* (1920), trans. James Strachey (rev. ed., Hogarth Press and The Institute of Psycho-Analysis, 1961).
4 *Mrs Dalloway*, p. 100.
5 *In Parenthesis*, p. 50.
6 *The Waves*, p. 174.
7 *Feeling and Form*, pp. 128–9.
8 *The Waves*, p. 49.
9 Ibid., p. 5.
10 Ibid., p. 78.
11 *Pilgrimage*, ii, 394.
12 *The Waves*, p. 67.
13 Ibid., p. 68.
14 Ibid., p. 8.
15 Ibid., p. 14.
16 Ibid., p. 28.
17 Ibid.
18 J. Schaefer, *The Three-Fold Nature of Reality in the Novels of Virginia Woolf*, (Mouton, The Hague, 1965), pp. 140–1.
19 Ibid., p. 141n.
20 *The Waves*, p. 121.
21 Ibid., p. 69. (We are reminded perhaps of that passage in *The Waste Land*:
Above the antique mantel was displayed
As though a window gave upon the sylvan scene
The change of Philomel, by the barbarous king
So rudely forced; yet there the nightingale

Filled all the desert with inviolable voice
And still she cried, and still the world pursues,
'Jug Jug' to dirty ears.
The Waste Land, ll. 97–103.)
22 *The Waves*, p. 155.
23 Ibid., p. 126.
24 *Diary*, p. 47.
25 *The Waves*, p. 140.
26 Ibid., p. 118.
27 Ibid., pp. 155–6. (We are reminded perhaps of Eliot's:
I am moved by fancies that are curled
Around these images, and cling:
The notion of some infinitely gentle
Infinitely suffering thing.
'Preludes', iv)
28 Ibid., p. 137.
29 Ibid., p. 146.
30 Ibid., pp. 113–14.
31 Ibid., p. 76.
32 Ibid., p. 164.
33 Ibid., pp. 164–5.
34 Ibid., p. 158.
35 Ibid., p. 116.
36 Ibid., p. 158.
37 Ibid., pp. 150–1.
38 Ibid., p. 151.
39 Ibid.
40 Ibid., p. 26.
41 Ibid., p. 93.
42 Ibid., p. 128.
43 Ibid., p. 129.
44 Ibid., p. 140.
45 Ibid., p. 37.
46 Ibid.
47 Ibid., p. 162.
48 Ibid., p. 124.
49 Ibid., p. 125.
50 Ibid., p. 139.
51 Ibid., p. 94.
52 Ibid., pp. 121–2.

10: *The double nature of repetition: 'The Waves'*—continued

53 Ibid., p. 122.
54 Ibid., p. 136.
55 Ibid., p. 165.
56 Ibid., p. 176.
57 Ibid., pp. 190–1.
58 Ibid., p. 202.
59 Ibid., pp. 21–2.
60 *Pilgrimage*, I, 349.
61 Ibid., p. 83.
62 Ibid., p. 109.
63 Ibid., p. 110.
64 Ibid., p. 112.

65 Ibid., pp. 132–3.
66 Ibid., p. 134.
67 Ibid., p. 166.
68 Ibid., p. 173.
69 Ibid., p. 172.
70 Ibid., p. 178.
71 Ibid., p. 190.
72 Ibid., p. 200.
73 Ibid.
74 Ibid., p. 185.
75 Ibid., p. 194.
76 Ibid., pp. 210–11.

11: *The symbolic keyboard: 'Mrs Dalloway'*

1 Mallarmé, *Poems*, trans. Fry, pp. 36–7.
2 R. Brower, *The Fields of Light* (1951; Oxford Univ. Press, N.Y., 1962), pp. 133–4.
3 B. Blackstone, *Virginia Woolf, a Commentary* (Hogarth Press, 1949), p. 243.
4 *Mrs Dalloway*, p. 124.
5 *Fields of Light*, p. 128.
6 Ibid., p. 135.
7 Ibid.
8 *Mrs Dalloway*, p. 90.
9 Ibid.
10 Ibid., p. 63.
11 Ibid., p. 64.
12 Ibid., p. 148.

13 Ibid., p. 26.
14 Ibid., p. 18.
15 Ibid., p. 51.
16 Ibid., p. 106.
17 Ibid., p. 32.
18 Ibid., pp. 32–3.
19 Ibid., p. 33.
20 Ibid., p. 133.
21 Ibid., p. 12.
22 Ibid., p. 64.
23 Ibid., p. 95.
24 Ibid., p. 189.
25 Ibid., p. 189.
26 Ibid., p. 34.
27 Ibid., p. 128.
28 Ibid., p. 129.
29 Ibid., p. 201.

12: *Plot, history and memory: 'The Years'*

1 *Essays*, I, 120.
2 J. B. Bury, *The Idea of Progress* (1920; Dover, N.Y., 1955), p. 12.
3 *The Years*, p. 120.
4 Ibid., p. 205.
5 Leonard Woolf, 'The Pageant of History', *The Nation and The Athenaeum* (19 Jan., 1924).
6 *Jacob's Room*, p. 63.
7 *Orlando*, p. 205.
8 *Diary*, p. 116.
9 Ibid., p. 261.
10 Ibid., p. 80.

11 *The Waves*, p. 58.
12 *Orlando*, p. 268.
13 *The Waves*, p. 140.
14 Ibid., p. 169.
15 Ibid., p. 169.
16 *Essays*, II, 8.
17 *The Years*, p. 70.
18 Ibid., p. 73.
19 *The Years*, p. 75.
20 Ibid., p. 81.
21 Ibid., p. 146.
22 Ibid., p. 145.
23 Ibid., pp. 197–8.
24 *Contemporary Writers*, pp. 105–6.

25 *The Years*, p. 358.
26 Ibid., p. 396.
27 Ibid., pp. 179–80.
28 Ibid., p. 180.
29 Ibid., p. 343.
30 *Contemporary Writers*, p. 67.

31 *The Years*, p. 341.
32 Roquentin in Sartre's *Nausea*, hearing the jazz record again and again comes to value the form of artistic creation rather than the accumulation of historical 'facts'.

13: *Character*

1 Hewet in *The Voyage Out* asks 'can you imagine anything more hideous than one person's opinion of another person?' (p. 265).
2 *The Voyage Out*, p. 346.
3 *Jacob's Room*, p. 85.
4 Strachey, *Queen Victoria*, pp. 57–8.
5 *Night and Day*, p. 189.
6 *The Years*, p. 187.
7 *Orlando*, pp. 32–3.
8 Ibid., p. 76.
9 Ibid., p. 262.
10 *The Waves*, p. 196.
11 Quoted by David Daiches, *Virginia Woolf* (New Directions, 1963), p. 75.

12 *The Waves*, p. 55.
13 L. P. Smith 'First Catch Your Hare', *The Nation and The Athenaeum* (2 Feb. 1924), pp. 629–30.
14 Ibid.
15 *Essays*, IV, 211.
16 *Mrs Dalloway*, p. 11.
17 Ibid.
18 *The Waves*, pp. 125–6.
19 *The Waves*, p. 158.
20 Ibid., p. 142.
21 Wallace Stevens, *Collected Poems* (Faber, 1955), p. 82. (A version, perhaps, of Valéry's idea of the universe as the 'psittacus psittacorum'.)

14: *'To the Lighthouse'*

1 *To the Lighthouse*, pp. 29–30.
2 Ibid., pp. 52–3.
3 Ibid., p. 131.
4 *To the Lighthouse*, p. 100.
5 Ibid., pp. 101–2.
6 Ibid., p. 37.
7 Ibid., p. 40.
8 Ibid., p. 41.
9 Ibid., p. 58.
10 Ibid., p. 59.
11 Ibid., pp. 59–60.
12 Ibid., pp. 60–1.
13 Ibid., p. 76.
14 Ibid., p. 244.
15 Ibid., p. 43.
16 Ibid., p. 40.
17 Ibid., pp. 40–1.
18 Ibid., p. 78.
19 *To the Lighthouse*, p. 88.
20 Ibid., pp. 91–2.
21 Ibid., pp. 133–4.
22 Ibid., pp. 123–4.
23 Ibid., p. 78.
24 Ibid., p. 271.

25 Ibid., p. 320.
26 Ibid., p. 252.
27 Ibid., p. 259.
28 Ibid., pp. 177–8.
29 *Mrs Dalloway*, p. 90.
30 *To the Lighthouse*, pp. 202–3.
31 Ibid., p. 203.
32 Ibid., pp. 203–4.
33 Ibid., pp. 37–8.
34 Ibid., p. 39.
35 Ibid., p. 232.
36 Ibid., pp. 248–9.
37 Ibid., p. 305.
38 Ibid., pp. 296–7.
39 Ibid., pp. 43–4.
40 Ibid., p. 44.
41 Ibid., pp. 241–2.
42 Ibid., p. 26.
43 Ibid., p. 83.
44 *Vision and Design*, p. 52.
45 *To the Lighthouse*, pp. 84–5.
46 Ibid., p. 85.
47 Ibid.
48 Ibid., pp. 85–6.

14: 'To the Lighthouse'—continued

49 Ibid., p. 77.
50 Ibid., p. 42.
51 Ibid., pp. 40–1.
52 *Virginia Woolf*, pp. 87–8.
53 *To the Lighthouse*, p. 12.
54 Ibid., p. 207.
55 Ibid., p. 210.
56 Ibid., p. 52.
57 G. E. Moore, *Principia Ethica* (1903; Cambridge Univ. Press, 1959), p. 10.
58 *To the Lighthouse*, p. 51.
59 Ibid., pp. 11–12.
60 Ibid., p. 204.
61 Ibid., p. 204.
62 *Poetry and Prose*, p. 823.
63 *To the Lighthouse*, pp. 207–8.
64 Ibid., p. 101.
65 Ibid.
66 Ibid., p. 104.
67 Ibid., p. 275.
68 Ibid., p. 207.
69 Ibid., pp. 199–200. (Virginia Woolf gives the sense of yearning by denying the satisfaction of the 'accustomed curve' of the sentence. After 'but,. . .he stretched his arms out' we might have expected something like 'in vain', but the sentence halts abruptly and we are left with emptiness.)
70 Ibid., p. 198.
71 Ibid., pp. 63, 126.
72 Ibid., p. 267.
73 Ibid., p. 244.
74 Ibid.
75 Ibid., pp. 263–4.
76 Ibid., p. 206.
77 Ibid., pp. 99–100.
78 Ibid., p. 108.
79 Ibid., p. 280.
80 Ibid., p. 277.
81 Ibid., p. 86.
82 Ibid., pp. 303–4.
83 *Flemish Art*, pp. 33–4.
84 *To the Lighthouse*, p. 265.
85 Ibid., p. 119.
86 Ibid., pp. 204–5.
87 Ibid., p. 177.
88 Ibid., p. 150–1.
89 *Essays*, i, 70.
90 *To the Lighthouse*, p. 106.
91 Ibid., p. 306.
92 Ibid., p. 18.
93 Ibid., p. 24.
94 Ibid., p. 26.
95 Ibid., p. 34.
96 Ibid., pp. 319–20.

Bibliography

Alldritt, K. *The Visual Imagination of D. H. Lawrence*. Edward Arnold, 1971.

Arts Council, The. *Vision and Design. The Life, Work and Influence of Roger Fry (1866–1934)*. Catalogue of an exhibition held by The Arts Council and the University of Nottingham, 1966.

Barfield, O. *Poetic Diction, A Study in Meaning*. Faber and Gwyer, 1928.

Bell, Q. *Roger Fry*. Leeds University, 1964.

Blackstone, B. *Virginia Woolf, A Commentary*. Hogarth Press, 1949.

Blake, W. *Poetry and Prose of William Blake*, ed. G. Keynes (1927). 4th ed., 1939; Nonesuch, 1961.

Brower, R. *The Fields of Light* (1951). Oxford University Press, N.Y., 1962.

Brown, E. K. *Rhythm in the Novel* (1950). Toronto University Press, 1963.

Bury, J. B. *The Idea of Progress* (1920). Dover Books, N.Y., 1955.

Butler, S. *The Note-Books of Samuel Butler*, selections arranged and edited by H. F. Jones (1912). Jonathan Cape, 1921.
Selected Essays. Jonathan Cape, 1927.

Campos, C. *The View of France*. Oxford University Press, 1965.

Cassirer, E. *The Philosophy of Symbolic Forms*, trans. R. Manheim. 3 vols., Yale University Press, 1953, 1955, 1957.
The Logic of the Humanities, trans. C. S. Howe. Yale University Press, 1960.

Cervantes (Miguel de Cervantes Saavedra). *Don Quixote of La Mancha*, trans. W. Starkie. New American Library, N.Y., 1964.

Chekhov, A. *Plays*, trans. E. Fen. Penguin, 1959.

Conrad, J. *Typhoon and Other Stories* (1903). Penguin, 1965.
Within the Tides (1915). J. M. Dent, 1962.
Victory. (1915). Penguin, 1963.

Daiches, D. *Virginia Woolf*. New ed., New Directions, 1963.

Ehrenzweig, A. *The Hidden Order of Art* (1967). Paladin, 1970.

Eisenstein, S. M. *The Film Sense*, trans. J. Leyda (1943). Faber and
Faber, 1968.

Eliot, T. S. *Collected Poems 1909–1962*. Faber and Faber, 1963.

Fishman, S. *The Interpretation of Art*. University of California Press,
Berkeley and Los Angeles, 1963.

Forster, E. M. *Aspects of the Novel* (1927). Penguin, 1964.
Abinger Harvest (1936). Penguin, 1967.

Freud, S. *Beyond the Pleasure Principle* (1920), trans. J. Strachey.
Revised ed., Hogarth Press and the Institute of Psycho-Analysis,
1961.

Frisch, M. *A Wilderness of Mirrors*, trans. M. Bullock (1965).
Methuen, 1967.

Fry, R. *Giovanni Bellini*. Artists' Library no. 2; At the sign of the
Unicorn, 1899.
Vision and Design (1920). Revised ed., 1925; Chatto and Windus,
1928.
A Sampler of Castile. Leonard and Virginia Woolf, 1923.
Transformations. Chatto and Windus, 1926.
Cézanne, A Study of his Development. Hogarth Press, 1927.
Flemish Art. Chatto and Windus, 1927.
Henri Matisse. Z. Wemmer, 1930.
Characteristics of French Art. Chatto and Windus, 1932.
Last Lectures (1939). Beacon, 1962.
'The Arts of Painting and Sculpture', in *An Outline of Modern
Knowledge*, ed. W. Rose. Gollancz, 1931.
(ed.) *Discourses Delivered to the Students of the Royal Academy by Sir
Joshua Reynolds*. Seeley, 1905.
(trans.) C. Mauron, *The Nature of Beauty in Art and Literature*.
Leonard and Virginia Woolf, 1927.
(trans.) Stephane Mallarmé, *Poems*. Chatto and Windus, 1936.
'The Exhibition of French Primitives', I and II. *The Burlington
Magazine*, V (1904).
'Exhibition of Old Masters at the Grafton Galleries', I. *The Burling-
ton Magazine*, XX (1911–12).
'Modern French Art at the Mansard Gallery', I and II. *The Athen-
aeum*, (8 and 15 August 1919).
'Mr McColl and Drawing'. *The Burlington Magazine* XXXV (1919).
'The Baroque'. *The Burlington Magazine*, XXXIX (1921).
'Some Chinese Antiquities'. *The Burlington Magazine*, XLIII
(1923).
'*Horseman in a Wood* by Corot'. *The Burlington Magazine*, XLIV
(1924).

'Chinese Bronzes at Messrs. Yamanaka's'. *The Nation and The Athenaeum* (2 January 1926).

'The Courtauld Fund'. *The Nation and The Athenaeum* (30 January 1926).

'The French Gallery'. *The Nation and The Athenaeum* (6 March 1926).

'Sandro Botticelli'. *The Burlington Magazine*, XLVIII (1926).

'The Garden of Eden'. *The Nation and The Athenaeum* (30 June 1928).

'*La Parade*'. *The Burlington Magazine*, LV (1929). Partially reprinted in *Seurat*, ed. A. Blunt. Phaidon, 1965.

'De Gustibus'. *The New Statesman and Nation*. (21 January 1933).

(trans.) M. Denis, 'Cézanne', I and II. *The Burlington Magazine*, XVI (1909–10).

Gaunt, W. *The Aesthetic Adventure* (1945). Penguin, 1957.

Guiguet, J. *Virginia Woolf and Her Works*, trans. J. Stewart. Hogarth Press, 1965.

Hannay, H. *Roger Fry and other Essays*. Allen and Unwin, 1937.

Hart, C. *Structure and Motif in Finnegan's Wake*. Faber and Faber, 1962.

Harvey, J. *Character and the Novel*. Chatto and Windus, 1965.

Heller, J. *Catch 22* (1962). Corgi, 1968.

Hoffman, F. J. *Gertrude Stein*. University of Minnesota Press, 1961.

Holt, L. E. 'E. M. Forster and Samuel Butler'. *P.M.L.A.*, LXI (1946).

Hunter, I. M. L. *Memory*. Revised ed., Penguin, 1964.

Isaacs, J. *An Assessment of Twentieth Century Literature*. Secker and Warburg, 1951.

Johnstone, J. K. *The Bloomsbury Group*. Secker and Warburg, 1954.

Jones, D. *In Parenthesis* (1937). Faber and Faber, 1963.

Kierkegaard, S. *Repetition*, trans, with an introduction and notes by W. Lowrie (1941). Harper and Row, N.Y., 1964.

Kumar, S. *Bergson and the Stream of Consciousness Novel*. Blackie, 1962.

Langer, S. K. *Feeling and Form*. Routledge and Kegan Paul, 1953.

Lawrence, D. H. *Women in Love* (1921). Penguin, 1966.

The Virgin and the Gipsy (1930). Penguin, 1967.

Phoenix II, ed. W. Roberts and H. T. Moore, Heinemann, 1968.

Lodge, D. *Language of Fiction*. Routledge and Kegan Paul, 1966.

MacCarthy, D. 'Roger Fry as a Critic'. *The New Statesman and Nation* (15 September 1934).

MacColl, D. S. 'Mr Fry and Drawing'. *The Burlington Magazine*, XXXIV (1919).

Moore, G. E. *Principia Ethica* (1903). Cambridge University Press, 1959.

Murry, J. M. 'The Future of English Fiction'. *The Nation and The Athenaeum* (1 April 1922).

Myers, L. H. *The Near and the Far.* Collected ed., Jonathan Cape, 1940.

Priestley, J. B. *Three Time-plays.* Pan, 1947.

Proudfit, S. L. W. 'The Fact and the Vision: Virginia Woolf and Roger Fry's Post-Impressionist Aesthetic'. Unpublished Ph.D. thesis, University of Michigan, 1967.

Proust, M. *Remembrance of Things Past.* 12 vols.; 1–11 trans. C. K. Scott Moncrieff (1922–30), Chatto and Windus, 1966–8; vol. 12 trans. Stephen Hudson (1931), Chatto and Windus, 1968.

Richardson, D. *Pilgrimage.* (4 vols., collected edition, 1938). J. M. Dent, 1967.

Roberts, J. H. 'Vision and Design in Virginia Woolf'. *P.M.L.A.*, LXI (1946).

Schaefer, J. *The Three-Fold Nature of Reality in the Novels of Virginia Woolf.* Mouton, The Hague, 1965.

Shattuck, R. *The Banquet Years.* Revised ed., Jonathan Cape, 1969.

Smith, L. P. 'First Catch Your Hare'. *The Nation and The Athenaeum* (2 February 1924).

Sparks, H. G. 'Mr Sargent's *Gassed*' (a letter). *The Athenaeum* (12 September 1919).

Sprigge, E. *Gertrude Stein, Her Life and Work.* Hamish Hamilton, 1957.

Stephen, K. *The Misuse of Mind.* Kegan Paul, Trench, Trubner, 1922.

Stephen, L. *English Literature and Society in the Eighteenth Century.* Duckworth, 1904.

Stevens, W. *The Collected Poems of Wallace Stevens.* Faber and Faber, 1955.

Strachey, L. *Eminent Victorians* (1918). Chatto and Windus, 1948.
Queen Victoria (1921). Chatto and Windus, 1961.
Literary Essays (1948). Chatto and Windus, 1961.

Sturrock, J. *The French New Novel.* Oxford University Press, 1969.

Sutherland, D. *Getrude Stein, A Biography of Her Work.* Yale University Press, New Haven, 1951.

Troy, W. 'Virginia Woolf: The Novel of Sensibility' (1932). Reprinted in *Literary Opinion in America*, ed. M. D. Zabel. 3rd ed., revised, Harper and Row, N.Y., 1962.

Turnell, G. M. 'Mallarmé'. *Scrutiny*, v (March 1937).

Veblen, T. *The Theory of the Leisure Class* (1899). Allen and Unwin, 1970.

Waley, H. *The Revivial of Aesthetics.* Leonard and Virginia Woolf, 1926.

Waugh, E. *Brideshead Revisited* (1945). Revised ed., 1950; Penguin, 1962.

Wilson, A. *The Wild Garden, or Speaking of Writing*. Secker and
    Warburg, 1963.
Wilson, E. *To the Finland Station* (1940). Collins, 1960.
Wimsatt, W. K., Jr. *The Verbal Icon* (1954). Methuen, 1970.
Woolf, L. 'The Pageant of History'. *The Nation and The Athenaeum*
    (19 January, 1924). 'Words'. *The Nation and The Athenaeum*
    (26 July, 1924).
WOOLF, V. Where there has been more than one edition, the first of
    the two publication dates is that of the first edition (published by
    Hogarth Press unless stated to the contrary); the second that of
    the Hogarth Press Uniform Edition to which all references are
    made. B. J. Kirkpatrick's *A Bibliography of Virginia Woolf*
    (revised ed., Hart-Davis, 1967) was an invaluable guide in
    compiling this section of the bibliography.
The Voyage Out (Duckworth, 1915). 1929.
Night and Day (Duckworth, 1919). 1930.
Jacob's Room (1922). 1945.
Mrs Dalloway (1925). 1947.
To the Lighthouse (1927). 1930.
Orlando (Crosby Gaige, N.Y., 1928). 1933.
A Room of One's Own (1929). 1931.
The Waves (1931). 1943.
Flush (1933). 1933.
The Years (1937). 1940.
Three Guineas (1938). 1943.
Between the Acts (1941). 1953.
A Haunted House (1943 i.e. 1944). 1953 i.e. 1954.

Other Works
Monday or Tuesday. 1921.
Victorian Photographs of Famous Men and Fair Woman, introduction
    by V. W. and Roger Fry. 1926.
Roger Fry. 1940.
A Writer's Diary. 1953.
Letters of Virginia Woolf and Lytton Strachey. 1956.
Contemporary Writers. 1965.
Collected Essays. 4 vols.: I and II, 1966; III and IV, 1967.
Nurse Lugton's Golden Thimble. 1966.

Uncollected article
'The two Samuel Butlers'. *The Nation and The Athenaeum* (11 April,
    1925).

Index

Italicised figures denote main entries.

Anna Karenina, 122
antithesis, 4–5, 12, 23, 97, 177
Aspects of The Novel, 39
Austen, J., 85, 93, 204
autonomy, 23, 28, 43, *49–59*, 101, 115

Banquet Years, The, 118, 120, 121, 124
Barfield, O., 39–40
baroque, 22, 24–5, 50
Bell, C., 23, 116
Bell, Q., 19
Bellini, G., 50–1
Bennett, A., 9, 28, 29, 44, 166
Bergson, H., 101, 110–13, 118, 168
Beyond the Pleasure Principle, 104
Blackstone, B., 150
Blake, C. R., 101
Blake, W., 57–8, 97, 197, 202
Blanchard, M., 208
Bloomsbury, 4, 9, 39, 64, 128
Botticelli, S., 23–4
Braque, G., 208
Brideshead Revisited, 22–3
Brower, R., 149–51, 155
Brown, E. K., 98
Buried Day, The, 106
Bury, J. B., 158
Butler, S., vii, *3–13*, 23, 30, 38, 39, 40, 42, 49, 61, 97–9, 118, 131, 152, 189
Byron, 30, 66

Campos, C., 128
Cassirer, E., 38, 44, 46, 58, 73, 130
Cézanne, P., 19, 23, 28, 29, 34, 70–3, 77–9, 118–19
Character and the Novel, 166
Chekhov, A., 56
classic(al), 19, 20, 24–5, 50, 51, 71
Coleridge, S. T., 54–5

Collier, J., 27
colour, 70–84, 193–5
Composition as Explanation, 99
Conrad, J., *34–7*, 49, 106
convention, vii, 6, 7, 8, 9, 10, 12, 13, 30, 31–2, 49, 66, 167
Corot, C., 75
craftsmanship, 6, *60–9*, 64, 67, 68, 115, 119, 205
'Crystal Cabinet, The', 57–8, 97, 202
Cubism, 61, 207–8
Cymbeline, 155

Daiches, D., 193
Dante, 121
David Copperfield, 107
Defoe, D., 93–4, 180
déjà vu, vii, 106–7
Denis, M., 70–1
Dickens, C., 170
Don Juan, 30
Don Quixote, 63, 66, 166
Dostoevsky, F., 106
Dunne, J. W., 106–7

Ehrenzweig, A., 50
Eisenstein, S., 74
El Greco, 21
Eliot, T. S., 74, 129, 133–6, 155
Eminent Victorians, 65
evolution, 6, 12, 13, 68, 97–8, 114, 152

'Falk', 34
Fishman, S., 21–2, 23
Flaubert, G., 29
Flemish Art, 89, 202
Focillon, H., 118
Forster, E. M., 3, 5, 27, 39, 98, 103, 119, 120, 160

Four Quartets, 136
frame, 51, 55–6, 57, 195
French New Novel, The, vii
Freud, S., 53, 83, 104
Frisch, M., vii
Fry, R., vii, 6, *17–90*, 100, *113–21*,
    138, 149, 179, 191–2, 195, 202,
    205, 207–9, 210

Galsworthy, J., 9, 28, 29
Gassed, 27–8
Gaunt, W., 20
Giotto, 18
Gris, J., 208
Guiguet, J., 3, 67n.

Hamlet, 170
Hannay, H., 20
Hart, C., 100
Harvey, W. J., 166
Hegel, F., 121
Herrick, R., 76
Hidden Order of Art, The, 50
Hoffman, F. J., 99
Hogarth, W., 21
Holt, L. E., 3n.
'Hollow Men, The', 124, 129
Hughes, T., 20
Hunter, I. M. L., 107–8, 109

Idea of Progress, The, 158
impressionism, 4, 5, 22, 35, 37, 78, 79,
    80, 84, 116, 117, 118, 119, 179,
    181, 182, 184, 189, 195
Ingres, D., 21
In Parenthesis, 128–9
Isaacs, J., 49

Johnstone, J. K., 17n., 28, 124–5
Jones, D., 128–9
Joyce, J., 101, 156

Kant, E., 13
Kierkegaard, S., 58, 104–5
Kumar, S., 88, 110

Langar, S., 87, 109–10, 130
Language of Fiction, 99
Last Lectures, 62, 72, 114, 119, 206
Lawrence, D. H., 20, 53, 64, 92,
    101–4, 119
Lee, V., 88

Lewis, C. Day., 106
Lewis, W., 118
Lodge, D., 4n., 99
Lowrie, W., 104

MacCarthy, D., 4, 18, 22
MacColl, D. S., 115–17
MacNeice, L., 106
Making of Americans, The, 100
Mallarmé, S., vii, 52, 71, 83, 149, 151
Marcussis, L., 209
Matisse, H., 55, 61, 115, 119
Mauron, C., 43, 79, 83, 84, 149, 151
memory, 4, 10, 13, 97, 107–8, 112,
    161–5, 187–8
Memory, 107–8
Michelangelo, 117
mirror, 43, 47, 50–2, 55–9, 62, 87,
    101–2, 126, 163, 170, 196–7, 199
Misuse of Mind, The, 110–13
Molière, 67
Monet, C., 79, 80
Moore, G. E., 194
Murry, J. M., 54
Myers, L. H., 22n.

Near and the Far, The, 22n.
Note-Books (of Samuel Butler), *4–13*,
    38, 39, 49, 97, 131, 189

'Opifact', 54, 205

Passage to India, A, 119–20
Peacock, T. L., 93
Péguy, C., 100
Picasso, P., 21, 28, 115, 207–9
Pilgrimage, 101, 122–3, 131–2
Plato, 26, 126
Poetic Diction, 39–40
Pope, A., 77
post-Impressionism, vii, 22, 28, 37,
    77, 80, 184
Poussin, N., 19, 24
Priestley, J. B., 106
Principia Ethica, 194
Proudfitt, S. L. W., 17n.
Proust, M., 45, 92–3, 101, 163, 181

Queen Victoria, 167–8

Raphael, 19, 25, 117
Rembrandt, 18, 24–5, 78, 116

repetition, vii, 11, 12, 13, 18, 27, 31, 46, 54, 57, 58, 59, 62, 69, 72, 81, 84, 89, *97–173*, 177, 184–8
Repetition, 104, 165
representation, *17–25*, 50, 57, 71, 108, 115–16, 191
Revival of Aesthetics, The, 105–6
Reynolds, J., 62, 78, 117
Rhythm in the Novel, 98–9
Richards, I. A., 43
Richardson, D., 88, 99, 109, 113, 122–3, 131, 143
Robbe-Grillet, A., vii
Roberts, J. H., 17n.
Robinson Crusoe, 180
Rousseau, H., 118
Royal Academy, 25, 27, 54, 64, 171
Ruskin, J., 22

Sampler of Castile, A, 39, 63
Sargent, J. S., 27–8, 44
Satie, E., 120–1, 124
Schaefer, J. A., 17n., 133–4, 142
Scott, W., 93, 204
Seagull, The, 56
self-consciousness, 8, 19, 30, 49, 52, 54, 55, 58, 99, 142, 143
sensation, 6, 10, 11, 13, 38, 39, 41, 43, 45, 48, 63, 69, 73, 130, 132, 146, 151, 189–90, 193
Seurat, G., 87, 90, 120, 199
Shakespeare, W., 76–7
Shattuck, R., 118, 120–1, 124
Shaw, G. B., 3
Sickert, W., 74, 89
Significant Form, 23
Smith, L. P., 39, 170
space, 22–3, 67, 78, 79, *85–94*, *199–204*
Sprigge, E., 100
Stein, G., 99, 113
Stephen, K., 110–13
Stephen, L., 12
Sterne, L., 44–5, 87
Stevens, W., 173
Strachey, L., 4, 57–8, 65, 125, 166–8
stream of consciousness, 9, 41, 88, 99–101, 110
Strings are False, The, 106
Sturrock, J., vii
Sutherland, D., 100
synaesthesia, 48, 73

Teniers, D., 117
Tennyson, A., 12, 77
Time Plays, 106
Tintoretto, 117
Titian, 72, 117
Tolstoi, L., 122
Transformations, 43, 45, 47, 61, 89, 116
Troy, W., 85–6, 91
Turnell, M., 52

Ulysses, 39, 156

Valéry, P., 158
Van Gogh, V., 72–3, 81
Veblen, T., 210–11
Vico, G., 121
Victory, 34–7, 49
Vision and Design, 18, 26, 113, 191

Waley, H., 105, 114, 116
Waste Land, The, 127, 155
Water Lilies, 80
Waugh, E., 22
Way of All Flesh, The, 3–4, 5
Wells, H. G., 3, 9, 28
Whistler, J., 35
Whitman, W., 74
Wilderness of Mirrors, A, vii
Wilson, E., 121
Wimsatt, W. K., 38, 43, 51
Women in Love, 64, *101–4*, 119
Woolf, L., 110, 125, 159
WOOLF, VIRGINIA
 Between the Acts, 32, 49–59, 72, 73, 81, 90, 121, 123, 171, 185, 197
 Flush, 5, 45–8, 65–6, 73, 166
 Jacob's Room, 7–8, 31, 32, 88, 123, 124–7, 159, 167, 168, 179
 Mrs Dalloway, 5, 10–11, 13, *38–44*, 66–9, 90–1, 110, 128–9, 146, 149–57, 169, 186–7, 193, 196, 204
 Night and Day, 32–7, 49, 90, 125, 168
 Orlando, 5, 65, 71, 87, 159, 160–1, 162, 168
 Roger Fry, 26–7, 28, 29, 49–50, 113–14
 Three Guineas, 123, 185
 To the Lighthouse, 32, 37, 94, 99, *177–206*

Voyage Out, The, 29–32, 85–6, 167
Waves, The, 4, 5, 31, 32, 37, 52, 77,
    79–84, 90, 94, 124, *128–48*, 160,
    161, 169–70, 171–3
Writers Diary, A, 30, 33, 92

Years, The, 32, 33, 90, 107, 108,
    109, 110, 123, *158–65*, 168
Wordsworth, W., 53, 203

Zola, E., 98